THE FRAGMENTATION OF NEW ENGLAND

Recent Titles in
Contributions in American History
Series Editor: Jon L. Wakelyn

The Paradox of Professionalism: Reform and Public Service in Urban
America, 1900–1940
Don S. Kirschner

American Frontier and Western Issues: A Historiographical Review
Roger L. Nichols, editor

Continuity and Change in Electoral Politics, 1893–1928
Paul Kleppner

Arms at Rest: Peacemaking and Peacekeeping in American History
Joan R. Challinor and Robert L. Beisner, editors

Close Neighbors, Distant Friends: United States–Central American Relations
John E. Findling

American Urbanism: A Historiographical Review
Howard Gillette, Jr., and Zane L. Miller, editors

The South is Another Land: Essays on the Twentieth-Century South
Bruce L. Clayton and John A. Salmond, editors

A State Divided: Opposition in Pennsylvania to the American Revolution
Anne M. Ousterhout

The Collapse of the Middle Way: Senate Republicans and the Bipartisan
Foreign Policy, 1948–1952
David R. Kepley

Developing Dixie: Modernization in a Traditional Society
Winifred B. Moore, Jr., Joseph F. Tripp, and Lvon G. Tyler, Jr., editors

Shades of the Sunbelt: Essays on Ethnicity, Race, and the Urban South
Randall M. Miller and George E. Pozzetta, editors

Keepers of Our Past: Local Historical Writing in the United States, 1820s–1930s
David J. Russo

Voluntarism, Planning, and the State: The American Planning Experience,
1914–1946
Jerold E. Brown and Patrick D. Reagan, editors

THE FRAGMENTATION OF NEW ENGLAND

Comparative Perspectives on Economic, Political, and Social Divisions in the Eighteenth Century

BRUCE C. DANIELS

Contributions in American History, Number 131

GREENWOOD PRESS
New York • Westport, Connecticut • London

974.02
D18f

Library of Congress Cataloging-in-Publication Data

Daniels, Bruce Colin.
    The fragmentation of New England : comparative perspectives on
economic, political, and social divisions in the eighteenth century
/ Bruce C. Daniels.
        p.   cm. – (Contributions in American history, ISSN 0084–9219
; no. 131)
    Bibliography: p.
    Includes index.
    ISBN 0–313–26358–2 (lib. bdg. : alk. paper)
    1. New England–Economic conditions. 2. New England–Social
conditions. 3. Social classes–New England–History–18th century.
4. New England–Politics and government–Colonial period, ca.
1600–1775. 5. New England–Politics and government–1775–1865.
I. Title. II. Series.
HC107.A11D36   1988
974'.02–dc19   88–17775

British Library Cataloguing in Publication Data is available.

Library of Congress Catalog Card Number: 88–17775
ISBN: 0–313–26358–2
ISSN: 0084–9219

First published in 1988

Greenwood Press, Inc.
88 Post Road West, Westport, Connecticut 06881

Printed in the United States of America

The paper used in this book complies with the
Permanent Paper Standard issued by the National
Information Standards Organization (Z39.48–1984).

10 9 8 7 6 5 4 3 2 1

Copyright Acknowledgments

The chapters in this book are revisions of previously published essays by the author. We are grateful to the following sources for granting permission to reprint:

Chapter 1 was originally published as "Economic Development in Colonial and Revolutionary Connecticut: An Overview," *William and Mary Quarterly* 37: 3 (July 1980). Used by permission of *William and Mary Quarterly*.

Chapter 2 was originally published as "Long-Range Trends of Wealth Distribution in Eighteenth-Century New England," *Explorations in Economic History* (Winter 1973–74). Used by permission of Academic Press, Inc.

Chapter 3 was originally published as "Poor Relief, Local Finance, and Town Government in Eighteenth-Century Rhode Island," *Rhode Island History* (August 1981). Used by permission of the Rhode Island Historical Society.

Chapter 4 was originally published as "Connecticut's Villages Become Mature Towns: The Complexity of Local Institutions, 1676 to 1776," *William and Mary Quarterly* 34: 1 (January 1977). Used by permission of *William and Mary Quarterly*.

Chapter 5 was originally published as "Democracy and Oligarchy in Connecticut Towns: General Assembly Officeholding, 1701–1790," *Social Science Quarterly* 56: 3 (December 1975). Used by permission of the University of Texas Press.

Chapter 6 was originally published as "Patrician Leadership and the American Revolution: Four Case Studies," *Histoire Sociale* (November 1978). Used by permission of *Histoire Sociale*.

Chapter 7 was orignally published as "College Students and New England Society: A Qualitative Portrait of Yale Graduates in Colonial America," *Connecticut History* 23 (April 1982). Used by permission of *Connecticut History*.

Chapter 8 was originally published as "Emerging Urbanism and Increasing Social Stratification in the Era of the American Revolution," *The American Revolution: The Home Front* (1976). Used by permission of West Georgia College Studies in the Social Sciences.

Chapter 9 was originally published as "Samuel Adams' Bumpy Ride: Recent Views of the American Revolution in Massachusetts," *A Guide to the History of Massachusetts*, Martin Kaufman, John W. Ifkovic, and Joseph Carvalho III, Eds. (Reference Guides to State History and Research, Greenwood Press, Inc., 1988), pp. 45–68. Copyright ©1988 by Martin Kaufman, John W. Ifkovic, and Joseph Carvalho III. Reprinted with permission.

For Judith

Contents

III   SOCIAL DIVISIONS

IV   HISTORIOGRAPHICAL DIVISIONS

TABLES

Acknowledgments

An author of a book written over a 15 year span accumulates many debts. Few things give me greater pleasure than publicly thanking colleagues, friends, institutions, and family for their support.

Fred Cazel, Jr., of the University of Connecticut, read most of the chapters in this book and improved them immeasurably with suggestions for changes in style, organization, and argument. Albert E. Van Dusen, my Ph.D. advisor at the University of Connecticut, first introduced me to New England's primary research materials and has shared his knowledge of them with me ever since. Fifteen years of discussions in the hallway, over coffee, and at lunch with Donald Bailey, Daniel Stone, and Robert Young, all of the University of Winnipeg, have been the source of much intellectual profit and personal pleasure. Additionally, each of these three scholars rendered aid with specific chapters. Other Winnipeg colleagues and friends, Alan Artibise, Gail Bradbury, Hinton Bradbury, John Coté, Jim David, Dayle Everatt, Wendy Fraser, Evelyn Hinz, George Kaplan, Jack King, Kate Mac-Farlane, and John Teunissen, have not read any of the manuscript but have given me much professional and personal support.

The following historians read and offered suggestions on one or more of the chapters. Some of them did this so long ago that they may have forgotten. Several of them disagreed with me on specific points. I list their names not to suggest their approbation but rather to indicate that I have been the beneficiary of their advice. Richard D. Brown, Lois Green Carr, Christopher Collier, Edward Cook, Jr.,

Richard Ellis, John Ferling, Julian Gwyn, John Ifkovic, Sydney James, Glenn LaFantasie, Pauline Maier, Gloria Lund Main, Jackson Turner Main, Michael MacLean, Michael McGiffert, Russell Menard, Kent Newmyer, Gregory Nobles, William Pencak, David Roth, Darrett Rutman, Bruce Stark, Harry Stout, Louis Leonard Tucker, and Lynn Withey.

Several grants each from the Social Sciences and Humanities Research Council of Canada and the University of Winnipeg Research and Travel Committee have provided generous aid for research trips and manuscript preparation.

Most importantly, I wish to thank the people I love: my mother, Willa Daniels; my brother, Roger Daniels; and my sister and brother-in-law, Lea and Dan Riccio who are warm, supportive, kind people; my three daughters, Elizabeth, Abigail, and Nora Kate who are the greatest source of joy in my life; and the learned, witty, and beautiful person whose name graces this book's dedication page.

INTRODUCTION

Today's social historians are not the first scholars to argue that hidden underlying forces have a profound effect on visible surface behavior. Historians have long realized that to comprehend the meaning of any event requires the rooting of that event in multiple layers of causation. Edward Gibbon attacked the Church and Christianity for creating the intellectual circumstances that destroyed Roman civilization. Karl Marx and Friedrich Engels viewed the major events of the past as facets of the ceaseless struggle among historically developing social classes. To these historians and many others, discrete historical events were external manifestations of internal impulses buried deeply in society.

Thus, to argue that a bare narrative of events, by itself, is inadequate to explain any historical phenomenon is to affirm much of the wisdom of the past. Nevertheless, despite their awareness of milieu and context, most historians prior to the past two decades did try to tell a story as well as explain it. Narrative and analysis usually were woven together in the same fabric. Recent historians, however, differ from their predecessors in the character of their search for underlying causes. The search has become more widespread, explicit, and precise; and frequently no real narrative is included in the finished product.

Several factors account for this change. First, more historians today practice the craft than ever before. They carve out smaller areas of competence and explore their own niches more thoroughly. In one decade, hundreds of articles and dozens of books may be written on what would have been regarded in past centuries as a small topic. With this much attention, a narrative would become unduly repetitive. Probes into the underpinnings of society provide a more suitable method to absorb this creative historical energy. Second, although many scholars write about *an* underlying force, most believe that there are *many* underlying forces, all of which to some degree can be studied separately. This belief allows for a nearly limitless number of explorations into and interpretations of a given topic. Third, sophisticated methodological and theoretical tools are increasingly being used to impart precision or conceptual depth to historical work. As methods and theories that help understand the hidden social configurations in the present proliferate, the willingness and ability of historians to use them to study the past increase accordingly. In short, it seems fair to say that narrative history, although not eclipsed, has been relegated to a lesser role in the work of social historians who want to tell the story behind the story.

The following nine previously published essays on eighteenth-century New England society cannot claim to tell more than a slight part of the story behind the story of that century. I hope and believe, however, that they contribute in a modest way to an understanding of some of the currents that swirled about and encased politics, Imperial relations, the colonial wars, the Great Awakening, and the colonists' decision to declare themselves independent of England and to form a new nation. Aside from a broad temporal and geographical similarity, the chapters are not unified by substance. They treat subjects as diverse as economic growth, wealth distribution, poor relief, local government, officeholding, leadership, urban development, college students, and historiography. They are, however, tied together by a similar research technique and style of internal organization. To call this combination of technique and organization a "methodology" overstates its sophistication. I like to think of it simply as an "approach" to social history.

My approach originated in the late 1960s and early 1970s when as a graduate student and assistant professor I tried to identify something I could contribute to a world of scholarship much of which awed me with its erudition, comprehensiveness, and intellectuality. Social history commanded the interest of a majority of young scholars in these latter days of the student rebellion of the 1960s. In retrospect, I believe that the characteristics of my scholarly work derived from specific problems I could identify in the New Social History of this time and from a competence I felt to help solve some of them. Quite simply, I felt inadequate to add much to the worlds of political or intellectual history, but I thought some basic problems raised by the work of social historians could benefit from what I perceived to be my mundane talents to collect, organize, and analyze data systematically. I use the term mundane out of no sense of false modesty. My work has been relatively unsophisticated in its use of quantitative techniques. The problems are indeed basic and their existence posed serious problems for the legitimacy of social history. Their resolution was and is important.

Early American social historians, as do most historians, rely heavily on case studies. The beauty of the case study lies in its suitability as an historical laboratory to test oft-made generalizations and in its ability to provide large amounts of manageable data that can undergird new generalizations. Social scientists have long used a form of the case-study method; they draw samples as proxies for larger units of society and then generalize about the larger units by conducting tests of the samples. If the samples can be shown to be reliable representations of the larger units, then generalizations based on them should be reliable generalizations for the larger units. Social scientists, however, go to great lengths to "justify" their samples—that is, to establish their reliability as miniature replicas of the larger units. Alas, social historians often do not. Hence, historians have had difficulty convincing their readers, some of whom are predisposed to be hostile to the research methods of social science, that their data bases were sufficiently representative to sustain generalizations.

Indeed, most were not. Although a number of pioneer works appeared in the 1960s, a quartet of well written and provocative books published in 1970 launched the social history revolution in New England historiography: John Demos, *A Little Commonwealth: Family Life in Plymouth Colony* (New York); Philip J. Greven, Jr., *Four Generations: Population, Land, and Family in Colonial Andover, Massachusetts* (Ithaca, New York and London); Kenneth A. Lockridge, *A New England Town: The First Hundred Years* (New York); and Michael Zuckerman, *Peaceable Kingdoms: New England Towns in the Eighteenth Century* (Cambridge, Mass.). Most accounts of social and local historiography in New England begin with analyses of these four books. Hundreds of articles and dozens of monographs reaffirm, refute, or refine their hypotheses and conclusions.

Taken as individual books, each one of the four could easily be regarded as brilliant; taken together, they created a brilliance on the historiographical horizon that still has not diminished. Despite this luster, none of these four books, as their authors readily admit, is based on a community that could conceivably be considered a justifiable sample of a large segment of New England society. Greven's and Lockridge's works are each based on a single town, both of which are within twenty miles of Boston. Zuckerman recognized the difficulties of drawing conclusions from the experience of a single community and expanded his data base to lessen the problem. He included material from eight towns for parts of his work and from fifteen towns for other parts. Nevertheless, even the group of fifteen towns did not constitute a reliable sample for most of Massachusetts—the fifteen were all eastern and most were in Suffolk County, the area immediately surrounding Boston. Demos had the truest sample. He used probate records drawn from all the towns in Plymouth Colony. Plymouth, however, although the oldest, was the smallest and least representative of any of the New England colonies. As all four authors explicitly state, none of their conclusions could be extended with any degree of certitude beyond the immediate communities upon which they were based.

Earlier works which presaged this remarkable outburst of scholarship in 1970, such as distinguished books by Charles Grant, Sumner Chilton Powell, and Darrett Rutman, had also been based on single communities. And, to a substantial degree, this type of research continues to the present. Thus, when I was casting about to identify my niche in research, it seemed reasonable to me in 1970 and still does today to think that some intellectual profit could be reaped from an approach to social history that emphasized relatively large data bases and justifiable samples. These would sustain more secure generalizations and permit distinctions to be made among various types of communities, groups, classes, and so forth. The bulk of my work in my first decade as a scholar culminated in a book, *The Connecticut Town: Growth and Development, 1635–1790* (Middletown, Conn., 1979), in which I collected a large amount of data from thirty of Connecticut's towns and some data from all ninety-one of its colonial towns in order to attempt to sort out the typical from the atypical. The sample of thirty towns could not be created with the precision of a carefully weighted Gallup Poll; nevertheless, I tried to devise appropriate criteria for selection and to justify my sampling technique.

Although probably lacking the brilliance or flamboyance of some of the best-known social history, *The Connecticut Town* did attempt to inspire confidence in its conclusions by drawing them from a careful comparison of the experiences of many communities of varying types.

While working on *The Connecticut Town*, my sense of the importance of the comparative approach to social history increased and I used the technique in several other projects I was working on. In some cases this method proved easy and was made explicit in the published work. In others, it proved more difficult, less scientific in the traditional sense of social science, and was not explicitly discussed under a methodology section in the finished product. Essays on wealth distribution, officeholding, and college graduates, which appear in this volume as chapters 2, 5, and 7, fall in the first category. Essays on economic development, poor relief, local government, the personalities of major leaders, and urbanization, chapters 1, 3, 4, 6, and 8, fall into the second category. In all of this work, however, I tried to amass a significant number of cases to compare with one another in order to get a sense of general patterns and of regional, typological, and idiosyncratic variations. And, in all of this work, I tried to place my research in a larger context by comparing its conclusions with those of relevant case studies in and outside of New England. The final substantive chapter in this volume, on the historiography of the American Revolution in Massachusetts, also employs a comparative approach. By its nature, historiography is usually comparative, but I tried to be more explicit than many historians have been in devising categories of historical writing and in assessing the impact of work in each category.

Making comparisons within a large cross-section of society is one way of inspiring greater confidence in social history; identifying changes over time is another. Lengthening the vision of social historians is as important as widening it. To be sure, most social historians do take notice of linear change. But, often that notice lacks precision and sensitivity to nuance or changes of degree. Not uncommonly, scholars collect data for two different times and then fashion a theory of evolution or change based on a comparison of the two sets of data. This does not allow one to pinpoint with any precision when the change took place. Nor does it furnish any reliable proof that a meaningful change did occur. Many years or decades yield anomalous data. A host of variables—war, political turmoil, record-keeping, economic malaise—can skew data at any given moment.

I have tried in most of my work to be as attentive to change as is reasonably possible within the limits imposed by problems of data availability, collection, and analysis. In many of the chapters of this book, I have developed simple but relatively precise models for measuring changes in given phenomena at various intervals in the eighteenth century. In others, I have arranged the material in a chronological order and then attempted to identify the nature and time of changes. These methods seldom reveal dramatic, abrupt alterations in behavior. More commonly, however, I can identify trends of either a linear or cyclical nature. Long-range trends, of course, can collectively add up to dramatic shifts if they proceed consistently in one direction. By the same token, if data fluctuate in a cyclical manner, a long-range perspective will reveal places where historians have been mistaken about the quality or quantity of change. In either case, I believe that a longitudinal context created out of a series of data or qualitative assessments is essential to any serious attempt to chart the direction of change. Most of the chapters in this book follow their subjects from the beginning of the eighteenth century to or through the era of the American Revolution. I believe that the Revolution can be much more fully understood if it is placed in this long-range context instead of being situated primarily in the immediate surrounding years.

Before ending this self-examination, I wish to make a statement about my ideological orientation. It has become fashionable for scholars to state explicitly in prefaces that they are proponents of one or another ideological view of history. They may confess to a consensus, progressive, liberal, conservative, or Marxist perspective of the past. At the risk of sounding naive and with the knowledge that a value-free ideal is not attainable, I wish to state that I have always consciously tried to avoid subscribing in my historical work to any school of thought or mode of interpretation. I realize that eschewing an ideology is easier said than done. But, if there is a persistent bias in this book, I do not know what it is.

Finally, I wish to make clear my awareness that several other scholars have perceived and addressed the problems with which I have been grappling. Among New England historians, the work of Edward Cook, Jr., Darrett Rutman, and Jackson Turner Main comes to mind as distinguished examples of social history that utilize a comparative approach and carefully examine long-range trends. Outside of New England, a collection of colonial historians sometimes referred to as the "Chesapeake Group" has, in the last decade, produced a social history for that region that rests on an unusually secure foundation of evidence. I cannot claim that my approach is unique. I can claim that these essays show my long-standing commitment to this approach and to an effort to resist what many scholars have seen as the Balkanizing effects of the first wave of New England social history. I have never believed that case studies Balkanized knowledge any more than traditional monographs did. But, I do believe that it is a natural tendency for the first generation of practitioners of an historical methodology to raise unsettling questions and create much doubt, and for the next generation to try and answer some of these questions and resolve some of the doubts. The pioneers explore an unsettled frontier, the latter arrivals cultivate it. I am a late arrival. I applaud the originality of the pioneers, many of whom have stayed to cultivate also. And I offer the following essays as my contribution to the advances being made by social historians.

Of the nine essays that follow, five are on Connecticut, two are on all four of the New England colonies, and one is on each of the colonies of Rhode Island and Massachusetts. Although the analysis is thus weighted towards Connecticut, I do not feel presumptuous in putting New England in the book's title. The oldest of these essays was first published in 1973, the newest in 1988. Obviously, the colonial secondary literature has changed since some of them were written. A few changes have been made to take notice of developments in the historiography, but, by and large, the essays appear here as they were when first published. I do not believe that any have been rendered obsolete by other recent work, and to rewrite and re-research them to take account of all recent developments might have required another fifteen years. Like other authors of collections of previously published essays, I ask for indulgence in this matter. Short headnotes to each essay help integrate them into a smoother whole. Chapter 10, the afterword, identifies an overall theme arising out of the essays and assesses its implications for colonial scholarship.

ECONOMIC DIVISIONS

I

Economic Development in Colonial and Revolutionary Connecticut: An Overview

Specialized studies of the economy of colonial America have gradually created a picture of a sophisticated network of production, distribution, and consumption. Many of the internal dynamics of this complex system, however, remain dimly understood. Thus, despite recent advances, economic history presents a great challenge to colonial and Revolutionary historians.

The following chapter surveys what is known about the economy of colonial and Revolutionary Connecticut and speculates about the impact of economic growth and development on New England society. Unlike the other chapters in this book, this one ranges over the entire period from founding to 1790. It emphasizes the eighteenth century, however, and argues that Connecticut developed an increasingly specialized and commercial economy in the decades prior to the Revolution. A rapid rate of population increase, a declining availability of land, the bringing into production of less desirable land, the growth of the West Indian trade, and the building of an extensive land transportation system, contributed to a growing diversity in the way people made their living.

Colonial and Revolutionary New England has long commanded the interest of historians. In the present generation it has evoked some of the most vibrant work in American history. In interest paid to this area, economic history is no exception. An extensive secondary literature describes and analyzes commerce and shipping, wealth distribution, various crafts and industries, agriculture, and transportation. Few subjects have escaped monographic attention, but, surprisingly, admidst these scholarly riches no one has attempted a systematic analysis that would provide an overview of the economic development of the region or of any one colony in it.[1] We have many microscopic slides, but they have not been integrated into a full picture. This chapter does not pretend to be a complete synthesis but is, rather, a modest topical and chronological essay on the economic development of one colony, Connecticut, from its founding until the first federal census of 1790.

AGRICULTURE

The first task of pioneer farmers in a New England town was to ready the soil for cultivation. Frequently, along the coast and in the major river valleys, meadows totalling as much as 500 acres had been cleared and cultivated by the Indians before the white settlers arrived. Cutting and burning were the settlers' most common methods of clearing land; girdling was used less often because it was slow and hazardous. Clearing was hard work: one man working alone could clear three acres a month at most if he did not remove the tree stumps. Stumps at times were dragged out by teams of oxen but frequently were left for years, or even decades, and crops were planted around them. Connecticut farmers liked to "stub" all roots out of the land before planting it, but the difficulty of removing tree stumps usually precluded this.[2]

After land was cleared, Indian corn was invariably the first crop planted. It could produce a good yield without plowing, hoeing, or manuring, and the ashes from the cleared land furnished a good fertilizer; one man could plant as much as an acre a day. Moreover, corn yielded more per acre than any other crop, its yield was more uniform, and it ripened early. Yellow corn, commonly called "flint corn" because of the hard, abrasive quality of its kernels, was the standard variety. Within each hill of corn, seventeenth-century Connecticut farmers usually planted two squash or bean seeds. The squash would grow around the corn or the beans would climb its stalks. These crops were all a man could expect to reap within the first or second year of settlement. Indian corn was the staple of new towns and continued to be the main diet until nearly rivaled by wheat in the beginning of the eighteenth century. One man boasted (lamented?) that his wife had made an "Indian pudding" every day for forty years. After the first few years, most farmers also planted rye, wheat, and vegetables, as well as herb gardens. Leeks, melons, English gourds, radishes, cabbages, peas, and asparagus were commonly raised vegetables; mint, rosemary, and sage were the most common herbs. Root crops never became widespread in seventeenth-century Connecticut primarily because of tastes and demand; potatoes, carrots, and turnips were not appreciated as food.[3]

Connecticut farming in the seventeenth century can best be described as extensive and wasteful rather than intensive and careful. Farmers never manured; they rotated fields rather than crops. They usually let one-third of their cleared lands lie fallow each year, and when land no longer gave a good yield it was abandoned and new acreage was brought under cultivation. Indian corn depleted the soil, and crop yields declined noticeably after a few years of planting. As long as land was plentiful, clearing new was cheaper than fertilizing old. Not until the eighteenth century was crop rotation practiced, and not until after 1750 did it become widespread.[4]

Swine- and cattle-raising dominated animal husbandry during the first two decades of Connecticut's history. Little profit was seen in horse-breeding; plentiful wild fowl made turkeys, ducks, or chickens superfluous; and the prevalence of wolves made sheep-raising precarious. Colonists had much to learn about animal husbandry under new circumstances. At first they underestimated the severity of the climate and failed to provide shelter for their animals during the winter; the result was a heavy loss of stock. Another problem concerned the wild forage that was stored for winter feed. It had too high a proportion of roughage to nutrients, and, while it would bloat animals, it did not keep them in good health. As Captain John Smith warned the settlers of New England, the wild grasses "will deceive your cattle in winter." Although no precise figures are available for the average number of animals owned by Connecticut farmers in the first generation of colonists, it is clear from the few surviving tax lists and trade records that herds were small and that little surplus was generated for export or sale.[5]

For the remainder of the seventeenth century the pattern of the first two decades was modified in some ways but not changed in its essentials. Agriculture remained unspecialized by region or town, cultivation was the mode of production, and extensive methods predominated. The most significant modification involved the rising popularity of grains other than Indian corn. The production of wheat, first raised successfully in New England in the Connecticut River Valley, was temporarily halted in the 1660s by a disastrous blight called "the blast." A change from summer to winter wheat, however, ameliorated the problem, and wheat nearly overtook Indian corn in production. It probably would have done so—farmers preferred it for the table—but, unlike Indian corn, it could be raised only on soil of good quality. Moreover, Indian corn retained its priority as the first crop always grown on every type of soil. Farmers believed it killed weeds and prepared the ground for other crops. Rye, a strong competitor with wheat for good soil, was valued particularly for making beer, and oats also gained in popularity, although used only for animal feed.[6]

Table 1
Acreage Available per Family by Decade

1680	486	1740	208
1690	414	1750	166
1700	404	1760	131
1710	397	1770	106
1720	314	1780	93
1730	242	1790	81

Figures are computed by dividing the number of families in the colony into the total amount of land in settled towns. See Bruce C. Daniels, *The Connecticut Town: Growth and Development, 1635-1790* (Middletown, 1979), chap. 2, for the supporting methodology.

In the early eighteenth century three new trends developed: specialization occurred by region and town, commercial farming advanced, and meat and dairy production surpassed grain farming to become the dominant form of agriculture. Specialization occurred because settlement patterns and land shortages brought different types of land into use and farmers realized that different types of soils accommodated different crops. Commercial farming grew because specialization carried with it an inherent need to market crops. Conversely, the desire to market crops enhanced specialization. Meat and dairy production grew rapidly because much of the new land being settled was upland suited more to grazing than to cultivation and because of the high demand for animal products.[7]

The acreage available per family in Connecticut dropped steadily throughout the colonial and Revolutionary periods. Moreover, the new lands being settled in the eighteenth century, those of Windham and Litchfield counties in the landlocked northeastern and northwestern parts of the colony, were hilly uplands of thin soil, far different from the rich meadowlands of the river valleys where the seventeenth-century towns were located. This decline in the quality and availability of land necessitated changes in farming patterns.

In the Connecticut River Valley and in the coastal portions of Fairfield County farmers still raised much grain, but in the hilly, rocky regions of Litchfield, Windham, and Fairfield counties they specialized in cattle, as they did also in the stony coastal strip of New London County. As the quality of land decreased, the likelihood of its use for dairy and beef production increased. In the coastal portion of New Haven County farmers specialized in raising sheep. In the level areas of Hartford and Fairfield counties many farmers raised horses for export. Reputed to be the finest in the colonies, Connecticut's horses commanded high prices. By 1779, there were more than seventeen domestic animals per adult in the colony. The average farmer possessed ten cattle, sixteen sheep, six pigs, two horses, and a team of oxen. Domestic animals in 1779 totaled 166,552 cattle, 36,060 oxen, 42,583 horses, 272,217 sheep, and an unknown but large number of swine.[8]

Small pockets of specialization sometimes developed because of unusual conditions. Flax, discovered to be ideally suited to the soil of Fairfield County, became a specialty of that area. The prevalence of maple trees in the forests of Litchfield County enabled a few towns there to export maple sugar. Onions had a particular affinity for Wethersfield soil, and that town devoted a major part of its farming to producing them.[9]

At mid-eighteenth century, as specialization, commercialization, and grazing all became more important in Connecticut, criticisms were made of the extensive and wasteful methods of the colony's farmers. To some, a revolution in English farming techniques, which had begun in the late seventeenth century and was called the "new agriculture," had particular relevance to land-short Connecticut. Jared Eliot, a Killingsworth physician, minister, and farmer-turned-scientist, championed the new techniques in an influential series of six long essays published between 1748 and 1759. Eliot applied the new agriculture's empirical methodology to Connecticut; his two overriding concerns were the replenishment of worn-out land and the development of a staple crop for export that would command maximum return for the available land resources. Eliot declared that Connecticut farmers lagged significantly behind those of England in applying the new agricultural techniques. Scolding them, he gave "not an Account of what we do in our present Husbandry, but rather what we might do, to our Advantage."[10]

Although few Connecticut yeomen adopted Eliot's suggestions on manuring, crop rotation, and uses of red clover and lime, he was not alone in sensing the need for more productive practices. Newspaper editors and anonymous writers expressed criticism of Connecticut's farmers' methods, particularly their failure to use intensive techniques. But farming traditions yield slowly to change, and the farmers of the "land of steady habits" were more inclined to switch products than to adopt new ways. Not until the 1780s was the new agriculture thoroughly implemented; in that decade a wave of agricultural reform swept the colony. By that time, land shortage and soil exhaustion had become so acute that many young men were leaving the colony, and the questioning and millennial spirit engendered by the Revolution gave rise to a feeling that change was good. Foremost in publicizing the new methods in England, Arthur Young, the tireless editor of the journal *Annals of Agriculture*, made them well known to leading Americans as well. Jeremiah Wadsworth of Hartford, a gentleman farmer and scientist who experimented with new crops and methods, and a few of his close friends and associates founded the Connecticut Agricultural Society in 1785 to promote scientific farming. Under its influence, Connecticut agricultural practice was probably far better in 1790 than historians have previously thought. As in the rest of southern New England, husbandry was in the transition phase from extensive to intensive.[11]

The Revolution also heightened the propensity of Connecticut farmers to produce crops for export. The great demand engendered by the needs of the Continental army accustomed farmers to regard

Europe and Africa	Great Britain
.6	.8
1.1	3.2

lutionary Connecticut" (Ph.D.

rd overextension of credit

ution virtually halted the
pon which Connecticut's
new state prospered and
vities—the provisions busi-
—more than made up for
ecticut General Assembly
rgoing all exports of food
ary general, Joseph Trum-
e countryside to purchase
onnecticut's primacy as a
nent of Trumbull as com-
A symbiotic relationship
y and the demands of the
eeded Connecticut's pro-
necticut needed the army
ne a favorite activity for
th letters of marque from
seized over four hundred
wns, deprived of normal
cations, often survived as
teers. The use of printed
greatly during the Revo-
brokers and speculators

the export market as insatiable and made production of cash crops more attractive. Hosts of new merchants traveled the Connecticut countryside during the Revolutionary War, buying entire crops for cash. Farmers, frequently receiving specie for the first time in their lives and enjoying an exceptional prosperity, were reluctant to go back to old ways after the war. Though frequently heated in denouncing wartime profiteering merchants, farmers allowed themselves to become more dependent on the merchants' ability to market their produce—a dependence that continued into the early national period.[12]

TRADE

One of the best indexes for the growth of trade can be compiled from the number and tonnage of ships registered in Connecticut ports. These figures are available for irregular dates starting in 1730. The tonnage figures reveal a steady growth in the capacity of Connecticut shipping from 1,265 tons in 1730 to 17,500 tons in 1787. Not only did absolute tonnage increase, but tonnage relative to the population rose as well—from .018 tons per capita in 1730 to .077 in 1787, an advance of 428 percent. The two sharpest increases occurred in the aftermaths of the Seven Years' War and the Revolution. Hard data on ship arrivals and departures, and on the volume of trade, are not available for the long span but for a short one they corroborate the rapid growth in trade: in 1755–1756, 139 vessels arrived in Connecticut ports with 206 departing, while in 1768–1772 averages of 540 arrived and 579 cleared annually; the total value of goods in trade rose from £205,000 sterling in 1756 to £450,000 sterling in 1774.[13]

Connecticut's growth in the second, third, and fourth quarters of the eighteenth century contrasts somewhat to the declining per capita trade described for North America generally by James Shepherd and Gary Walton. However, Shepherd and Walton show that per capita trade to the West Indies increased, and since almost all of Connecticut's trade directly or indirectly involved the Caribbean, the colony's per capita growth is not surprising. Moreover, the price of foodstuffs, Connecticut's main export, increased nearly fivefold after 1740 relative to all other goods. This encouraged merchants and farmers to increase their exports. This growth was uneven. Trade did not increase between 1763 and 1767 when England and France restricted

access to Caribbean markets, decreased between 1768 [
when the imposition of the Townshend Acts occasion
English goods, was nearly eliminated by the British b
the Revolutionary War, and declined again at the en
owing to a glutted West Indian market and competit
states.[14]

Even during prosperous times, three problems rela
deviled the economy and revealed some basic weakne
necticut's colonial balance of trade had always been u
the new state started deeply in debt. Second, Conne
too heavily on merchants headquartered in Boston, R
New York City. Third, a lack of specie created diff
out the economic spectrum from importing merchan
their outside creditors to farmers hard pressed to
shopkeeper. These problems manifested themselves i
of debt suits and bankruptcies. Usually, the deb
Boston and New York City merchants and to a less
port and Providence creditors. For two reasons,
attempts, Connecticut's merchants never develop
direct trade with England and Europe. First, Co
staple commanding a high value in the transatlanti
the colony developed a sizable trade only long after
the neighboring colonies had established valuable
going patterns. The problem was clear; Connecticut
to cope with it but had little success in breakin
neighboring merchants.[15]

The expanding trade of Connecticut was conf
sively to other colonies and the West Indies. The s
1769 give a fair representation of its character
Revolution. Although the nonimportation agree
Connecticut merchants in protest of the Townshe
trade in general in 1769, the colony's trade rout
Approximately half the trade was with other An
percent with the West Indies, and only 2 percent
and 1 percent with the rest of Europe and witl
City and Boston were by far the dominant coasta
cut shipping. Between 1758 and 1767, 209 ships
harbor for New York, and 157 cleared for Bost
tant third with 35 clearances. The favorite We
the Revolution were Antigua, Barbados, Turks

Table 2
Origins and Destination of Ships in 1769 (by tons

	American Continent	West Indies
% From	55.3	43.2
%To	44.9	51.2

Source: Albert Van Dusen, "The Trade of Rev
diss., University of Pennsylvania, 1948), 146.

bickering over prices and a tendency towa
in a debt-ridden society.[19]

Military events of the American Revol
external coasting and West Indian trade
economy was based, yet most parts of the
mercantile enterprise grew. Three new acti
ness, privateering, and financial speculatio
the loss of normal external trade. The Conn
responded to the Lexington alarm by emba
from the colony and appointing a commiss
bull, and nine commissaries who scoured th
provisions for the military. Indicative of C
supplier for soldiers was the later appointr
missary general of the Continental army.
obtained between the Connecticut econom
war. The state and national governments
visions to keep armies in the field, and Co
market for its produce. Privateering beca
merchants; about 380 Connecticut ships w
the assembly preyed on enemy shipping an
prizes. Prominent merchants in coastal to
trading activities because of their exposed l
businessmen by owning or outfitting priva
money in commercial transactions increase
lution, and this development gave rise to

who traded widely in French notes, Continental notes, soldiers' bounties, and Connecticut state bills.[20]

Thoughtful Connecticut merchants must have wondered what would happen to the new state's economy with the end of the war and its artificial demands. They could not have been certain of economic survival apart from the British economic empire. As they would find, trade, to a remarkable degree, followed the old patterns to the West Indies and neighboring states, and swiftly increased in volume about 50 percent over its prewar levels. There were limits to this heady expansion, however; the trend peaked in 1785 and then declined slightly for the last three years of the decade. Even with this slight downswing (which proved to be temporary), Connecticut in 1790 emerged from the Revolutionary experience with a larger trade than before and a greater need to maintain that trade—the fortunes of farmer and merchant alike were tied to it.[21]

CRAFTS AND MANUFACTURING

Milling was the most common industrial activity in colonial and Revolutionary Connecticut. Gristmills were essential to every community, and sawmills almost so. Before laying out highways or building a meetinghouse, a new town would arrange construction of a gristmill, usually through a combination of public and private enterprise. An applicant to the town meeting might be given a monopoly on the process, a specified amount of labor from townspeople, land on a stream, and even a lump sum of money in return for grinding grain at a stipulated price. In those rare cases where no one applied for grinding privileges, the town elected a committee to construct a mill and hire a miller. Frequently, a town would elect a committee to work with the miller for the best interests of the community.[22]

The concern each town showed for gristmills and the ubiquity of their construction testify to their vital role. In twenty-one towns for which the dates of the first mills can be determined, on average the mill began operation within the first two years of settlement and frequently preceded incorporation. Reasons for this urgency are apparent. Until a mill was constructed, the townspeople had to use the laborious hand mortar and pestle process or cart grain to the mills of a nearby town, a job made difficult by the size of Connecticut towns. Not content with one gristmill, most towns constructed several as population grew and dispersed from the center. Sawmills were not needed as urgently as gristmills and were not so frequently a subject of public business at a town meeting. Nevertheless, most towns wanted and got sawmills; in eight towns for which the date of the first sawmill can be determined, the mill began operating within a decade of settlement. Most towns had more than one within two or three decades of their founding. The towns of Middlesex County (and there is no reason to believe they were atypical) averaged a total of seven gristmills and sawmills in the late eighteenth century.[23]

In addition to mills to produce flour and lumber, towns required artisans to provide other products and services. Few artisans plied their crafts full-time in Connecticut towns during the period under view; most also farmed. The first artisans of most towns moved to the community to farm but had other skills to offer as well. If a town needed a skill that no resident could provide, it might conduct a systematic search to secure the needed craftsman. In 1651, New London, for example, sought to attract a blacksmith by offering a house, shop, transportation to the town, half a ton of iron, 20 to 30 pounds of steel, home lot, meadow, uplands, and a proprietorship. When a local man in Guilford volunteered to be a blacksmith but explained that he could not afford the equipment, the town supplied what it called the "town smith's tools." Tax lists make clear that the number of artisans in a community was in reasonably constant ratio to the population. On the eve of the Revolution about 25 percent of the adult white men practiced a trade—a slight increase over the proportion in the first half of the eighteenth century. The practice of having several part-time rather than full-time artisans made good economic sense: the towns were so large and the population so widely dispersed that the area was too great for a single full-time man to service. Consequently it was more convenient to have a part-time man in each neighborhood. Types of artisans varied widely in prosperity and status: shipbuilders, tanners, millers, and smiths, for example, were more prosperous and stood higher than carpenters, shoemakers, and tailors.[24]

Until the middle of the eighteenth century, shipbuilding was the colony's only major manufacturing activity that went beyond serving local needs. By the fourth quarter of the seventeenth century, shipyards existed in several towns along the coast and the Connecticut River. Groton alone had three in operation in 1700. At some point in its colonial history, every town located on navigable water engaged in shipbuilding, although the output of most was modest. In the 1760s and 1770s, shipbuilding became a major industrial activity, producing an average of fifty ships a year. The best-educated guess would place the number of ships constructed at five to ten per annum during the late seventeenth and early eighteenth centuries. As trade grew after 1730, so did the construction of ships. In the late colonial period, when the industry peaked, an average shipyard employed five to ten workers. The largest in New London had about twenty-five, which made it the biggest industrial unit in the colony. The yards generally constructed small ships of 25 to 35 tons, although occasionally the size could be greater; the New London shipyard built one of 700 tons in 1725.[25]

The most important industry in colonial Connecticut can best be termed "agricultural manufacturing." The processing of farm produce into goods better suited for storage and transportation became widespread with the growth of the export trade in foodstuffs. As with artisanal activity, however, few devoted their full-time attention to agricultural manufacturing. Usually it was a part-time activity of the farmer who produced the raw materials. Most of the processing was done by the family unit, though large merchants occasionally employed two or three men for that work. Merchants usually bought goods for export after they had been processed. Meatpacking, the most important of the processing industries, was carefully regulated by the colony government, which specified standards for quality and size, and required each town to elect inspectors to stamp the finished product and attest to its "goodness or badness."[26]

Large quantities of other products were manufactured. Cider replaced beer as the drink of New England in the eighteenth century, when every town operated a cider mill in the late summer and early fall. Perry, a drink made from pears, ran second in popularity. Some local taverns brewed their own beer, and a few exported it, although it was more common to export malt to the larger breweries of New York and Pennsylvania. Cheese production boomed in the mid-eighteenth century—in some years over 150,000 pounds were exported. Much potash and lye were produced by farmers from Connecticut's hardwood forests. Wood products often were a new town's first manufactured exports because they were a natural result of the process of clearing land. Tinsmithing, introduced into Connecticut about 1750, was limited almost exclusively to Hartford County, where the first tinsmith, Edward Pattison, set up shop. This industry grew quickly. Housewives preferred tin to pewter because it could be more easily handled and cleaned. Pattison trained several tinsmiths each year, and by the time of the Revolution most of the towns of Hartford County had at least one.[27]

The iron industry, too, was concentrated in one area, northwestern Litchfield County, where rich deposits of ore were discovered in the eighteenth century. As early as 1658, when John Winthrop, Jr., built a blast furnace at New Haven, the colony had produced some iron, but the New Haven furnace, like subsequent ventures at Stonington, Woodstock, Voluntown, Hebron, Stafford, and Killingworth, was unprosperous and short-lived. The Salisbury Iron Industry, as the mines, forges, and furnaces in Litchfield County were collectively known, did better. The first mine opened at "ore hill" in 1732, and the first forge began turning out iron in 1734. Mines and forges were started in Sharon and Kent, and in Salisbury, too—all before the area was settled by farmers and divided into towns. The high quality of the ore ensured the success of the local iron industry by giving it an advantage its predecessors elsewhere had lacked, and the industry grew to employ as many as 75 men on the eve of the Revolution. The Salisbury Iron Industry's importance should be viewed in perspective: despite its success, it provided Connecticut with but a small fraction of the ironware the colony needed. During the Revolution, however, it was an important source of cannon, cannonballs, grapeshot, and other military hardware.[28]

Silversmithing, which began in Connecticut between 1700 and 1710, grew slowly at first but flourished in the period 1750–1790. Before 1700, the little silver in the colony was imported from Boston. When, early in the eighteenth century, demand for silver spoons and church plate developed, a few silversmiths were encouraged to settle in the colony, but it was not until mid-century that amassment of wealth was sufficient to support a large number of producers. Only 13 silversmiths can be identified in Connecticut before 1750, but 125 set up shops between 1750 and 1790. These were concentrated in the five largest urban centers: Norwich had 19, New Haven 18, Hartford 15, and Middletown and New London 11 each, although 37 towns at some time included an active silversmith among their artisans.[29] A number of smiths farmed or operated stores or taverns. Most, however, worked in areas allied to silversmithing and, like shipbuilders and people employed in the iron industry, frequently had no connection with farming. They often were engravers, jewelers, watchmakers, blacksmiths, gunsmiths, or workers in copper, brass, and pewter.

Crafts and manufacturing were always an important component of Connecticut's economy. All evidence indicates that this economic segment intensified at mid-eighteenth century as exports soared, population grew, and land supplies dwindled. Shipbuilding and the processing of agricultural goods expanded significantly, a successful iron industry developed, and artisans increased in number—some changing from part-time to full-time craftsmen. Although the General Assembly downplayed this growth of manufacturing in its reports to the Board of Trade, because it did not want to risk antagonizing England, the colony government fully recognized the nature of the growth and took steps to encourage it by granting bounties, loans, and monopolies to new manufacturers.[30]

The Revolution intensified manufacturing activity and the government's efforts to encourage it. The first such impetus to industry arose from the embargoes on English imports in the 1760s, which heightened the demand for American manufactures. The stoppage of all commerce with England during the war perpetuated the high demand, and the special need for military equipment required new industries that needed government assistance in the initial stages of development. Two areas emerged as manufacturing centers during the war: Norwich and the east society of Hartford, which was to become East Hartford in 1783. Before the Revolution, Norwich was the colony's preeminent manufacturing town. Under the leadership of Christopher Leffingwell, an innovative entrepreneur, its manufacturing expanded massively in the years of the nonimportation agreements. Mostly owned or organized by Leffingwell, a paper mill, a chocolate factory, a felt-manufacturing plant, several fulling mills, a combmaking mill, a nail factory, a bookbindery, and a clock factory started operations between 1767 and 1774. Leffingwell's success encouraged emulation, and several other Norwich businessmen began manufacturing on "Leffingwell's Row" after the war broke out. The wealthy Pitkin family owned several cloth mills on the east side of Hartford before the war and, with the colony's assistance, turned their organizing talents and wealth to the manufacture of gunpowder, paper, and iron, all needed to prosecute a war. Immediately after the war, the Pitkins built mills to produce glass and snuff. The east society of Hartford also had a large manufacturing plant for finished iron products such as anchors, screws, and iron rods, and several paper mills in addition to that of the Pitkins. Strong industries that predated the Revolution increased their activities during it: The Salisbury

Iron Industry more than doubled its production during the Revolution, as did Connecticut's shipbuilders. Manufacturing grew only slightly in the 1780s, but the significant fact is that the gains made during the Revolution were not lost when manufactured goods could again be imported from England.[31]

TRANSPORTATION

Transportation conducive to commercial activity was almost entirely lacking throughout the seventeenth century in most areas of the colony. Few intertown roads were built, and most intratown ones were bridle paths to facilitate travel to the village center from outlying areas and the conveyance of goods on horseback. In the coastal towns, particularly, little attention was paid to roadmaking until the eighteenth century; mere paths connected the interior areas to the shoreline. These paths were almost always former Indian trails improved slowly by the white settlers; roads were expensive to construct and most new towns had other priorities—mills and a meetinghouse. Most of the seventeenth-century towns were sited on navigable waterways. Despite the fact that internal town transportation was rudimentary, they were thus well connected to the outside world. Ferries were of more vital concern than roads to the early inhabitants. People could pick their way along the Indian trails well enough without substantially improving them, but crossing the many rivers was far more difficult. Nine ferries across major rivers, created and regulated by the colony, were in operation by 1700, providing service on demand. Most towns built small bridges or supplied part-time ferry service across the smaller rivers when occasions such as religious services or town meetings required it. The primary purpose of both colony and town ferries, however, was to move people and small amounts of goods short distances; they were little flatboats, rafts, or canoes.[32]

Most towns in the first half of the eighteenth century slowly but steadily improved their transportation systems. Bridle paths were upgraded to highways, and intertown roads received more attention. In northeastern Connecticut, the only region isolated from navigable waterways until the settlement of Litchfield County, the General Assembly took the initiative and constructed two "cartways" connecting parts of Windham County with Rhode Island. Some exceptional advances were made in building bridges. One built in Norwich over the Shetucket River in 1728 was over 250 feet long, a marvel for its time. Another crossed the Housatonic River at New Milford in 1737, and Hartford spanned the Farmington River in 1742 with "the Great Bridge," as contemporaries called it. Yet despite these improvements, until 1750 Connecticut's transportation system was still designed mainly for local purposes.[33]

This changed abruptly at mid-century. The trend from a subsistence to a commercial economy placed new demands upon the transportation network, and the colony responded with an outburst of intertown road construction in the 1750s. Hartford was connected by highways to Boston, Windham County, and Albany; Middletown was linked by cartway to Saybrook; two roads connected Connecticut with the Hudson River Valley; and Norwich became the hub for a network of highways in eastern Connecticut. By the end of the decade, the transportation of the colony had been transformed from a system to facilitate local travel to one that enabled large amounts of goods to be moved. Virtually every town was connected by cartway to a seaport or riverport. Ferries also proliferated. In 1769 there were eight across the Connecticut River in Hartford County and seven operating in what is modern Middlesex County (more than the number of bridges and ferries across the river today). This rapid increase in road building and ferry service was not only directly related to economic specialization and commercialization but was also a means of coping with the land shortage. Improving transportation, as agricultural engineers know, enhances the value and efficiency of land; many modern societies combat critical land/man ratios by developing sophisticated transportation networks. Connecticut's road-building program lessened the economic disadvantage experienced by Windham and Litchfield counties' farmers and made the declining supply of land in the colony more capable of supporting the population.[34]

The new roads were not designed for comfort, as complaints by travelers from Europe and other colonies indicated, but they effectively crisscrossed the colony and functioned well in moving goods between farm and market. Never paved with good gravel, they often meandered from a straight course to touch isolated pockets of settlement. The goal of the colony was to build many roads quickly and to give every farmer access to them rather than to build a few highways of superior quality. While resulting in some inconveniences and loss of time, this type of cheap and serpentine construction is, according to modern transportation specialists, economically advantageous in a society with limited resources: in the 1950s and 1960s Mexico constructed a road grid on similar principles. Connecticut's roads had a well-justified reputation for discomfort, but their extent and distribution after the 1750s substantiates the judgment of a recent geographer that they constituted a good system of transportation.[35]

GENERAL TRENDS

Connecticut's economy between 1635 and 1790 consistently changed from greater to less homogeneity and self-sufficiency, and from greater to less production for local markets. An increasingly diverse array of goods and services was produced for more distant markets. Yet we must keep in mind that Connecticut's economy, even in the founding years, depended on trade and was not without diversity, and that in the Revolutionary years Connecticut's citizens still consumed much more than they exported and achieved significant production in only a few types of goods.[36] It is the relative weighting of these phenomena that is important. In this weighting Connecticut was passing from an internal to an external economy. Although the change should not be overstated, its effects were powerful enough to transform the way people traveled, farmed, made their livings, organized their society, and viewed the political and trading world.

As is shown by William Sachs and Marc Egnal, these changes were common to the colonies in general.[37] In Connecticut they were conditioned by three factors related to land and to pressures of population on the land. First, the practices of seventeenth-century farmers were wasteful, relying on extensive cultivation of large amounts of land without regard for land care. This rapidly exhausted the soil and created a need for more land. Second, the towns settled after the 1680s were increasingly located on rough, hilly upland, unsuited to cultivation. Third, the growth of population reduced the availability of land in the settled towns. These three factors generated the first major crisis in the colony's economy—a land shortage. One cannot date this crisis precisely but the land/man ratio decreased most sharply between 1710 and 1730 (see Table 1). The problem became urgent by 1750, when all of Connecticut's lands were settled, and could only get worse unless the economy was restructured or the population reduced.

This land crisis was not unique to Connecticut; the other southern New England colonies also experienced it. As a historian of Massachusetts has recently pointed out, there were three possible responses to the crisis that might have ameliorated its effects: (1) better or different farming methods could have increased productivity or used land more efficiently; (2) crops could have been made more marketable by developing transportation networks, urban markets, and external markets; and (3) nonfarming occupations could have been developed to engage the increased population.[38] Connecticut's inhabitants tried all three tactics in fighting the battle against land shortage and in doing so drastically changed the colony's economy. As the foregoing topical analysis indicates, the mid-eighteenth century, when the last of Connecticut's lands were settled, brought the greatest changes.

Agriculture changed in response to the demands of the Atlantic economy and to the need to utilize worn-out and hilly lands. Animal products commanded more value in the export market than grain, and Connecticut farmers shifted their basic orientation from cultivation to grazing. Intertown transportation systems were developed that connected all Connecticut's interior towns to depots on the rivers or coast. Towns became more differentiated in size and function as some emerged as major mercantile centers and others as secondary centers of collection and distribution. Large-scale merchants appeared and developed contacts with much of the Atlantic world. A larger proportion of the population engaged in manufacturing. In particular, a sizable business developed in processing foodstuffs for market.[39] Finally, when all else failed, after 1760, people left the colony/state in search of land elsewhere. No longer available in Connecticut, unsettled lands in northern New York and in New Hampshire and Vermont provided a safety valve. For more than twenty years Connecticut tried to enlarge its land supply by taking advantage of the sea-to-sea clause in its charter. The Susquehannah Company, formed to settle towns beyond Connecticut's western boundaries, though ultimately unsuccessful, briefly maintained a town in the Wyoming Valley of Pennsylvania. There is no way to ascertain how many people left Connecticut, but when one subtracts the population figure in the census of 1790 from the number that would have been obtained had normal growth rates continued, it appears that the exodus between 1760 and 1790 may have totaled as high as sixty thousand.[40]

The metamorphosis of Connecticut's economy did not indicate good health. During the Revolutionary period, land continued to decline sharply in availability, so that still greater efficiencies of production and more commercialization were needed to stave off depression. The price of land was becoming prohibitive; by the Revolution, it averaged £2 to £3 per acre. A normal rent in 1760 was one-third of the crop produced, an extremely high sum by previous standards. With the massive increase in trade came a widening gap between imports and exports. Connecticut never had enjoyed a favorable balance of trade, and even as its commerce grew, its residents became increasingly indebted.[41] Moreover, trade, so essential to the economy at mid-eighteenth century, made Connecticut precariously dependent on the vagaries of the world market and external events. As the pre-Revolutionary years revealed, events beyond the colony's control could tilt the economy into decline.

During the Revolutionary period, 1763 to 1790, the economy was buffeted by British imperial policy, economic boycotts, wartime depredations by the enemy, high demand for Connecticut's products by the Revolutionary military forces, and the exigencies of constructing a new nation and economy. Under these conditions of artificial restraints and stimuli, the economy performed unevenly.

Trade declined drastically in 1764 and 1767 after the passage of the Sugar and Townshend acts. The need for wartime provisions inflated demand for all manner of produce and kept the economy in high gear during the Revolutionary War, and the reopening of trade after the war picked up the slack from the end of provisioning. But in 1785 trade leveled off, and in 1787 it declined due to mercantile restrictions by the European powers, a shortage of specie, and a glutted West Indian market. Nor was the impact of these forces felt evenly by all segments of society and all geographical sections. Commercial farmers and merchants suffered from trade problems and artisans profited from them; the seaboard languished during the Revolution and the interior thrived. By 1790, however, the economy of the new state appeared to be on an even keel—but it was a more complex and highly developed economy than before the Revolution.[42]

This growth in sophistication and size, dating from founding years, was conditioned primarily by market, geographical, and political circumstances. Yet the government of Connecticut played a significant role in the economy. It set prices and wages for various goods and services in the seventeenth century and, though abandoning this practice in the early eighteenth century, continued to guard against excessive charges by insisting on the principle of a "just price." The General Assembly instituted many of the improvements in transportation and encouraged new industries through bounties and monopolies. It also passed several brief embargoes on the export of foods when supplies dwindled, and it enacted several laws, usually discriminatory duties, that gave citizens of Connecticut a competitive advantage in the colony's trade. Additionally, the colony government moved to ensure the reputation of Connecticut's exports by requiring town governments to elect such officers as sealers of leather to ensure that exported goods conformed to high standards of quality.[43]

Government had an important effect on the money supply. Beginning in 1709, it emitted currency that greatly expanded the money supply. During King George's War the amount emitted totaled nearly £80,000. Connecticut's currency, like that of its neighbors, suffered from a lack of proper controls, and the several issues depreciated greatly. The first issue, called Old Tenor after a second one was emitted, eventually depreciated until it was exchanged at a rate of £7.6 for £1 Lawful Money after 1755. Thus the colony's currency policy was a mixed blessing. It encouraged economic development by partially remedying the shortage of money, but it created much havoc by complicating business accounting and the relationship between creditor and debtor. Not surprisingly, currency policy became a matter of public debate, with established merchants who were creditors favoring a reduction in emissions and aspiring merchants and farmers who were debtors favoring an increase.[44]

CONCLUSION

One might speculate about the social effects of the growth and change in the economic system. The specialization and commercialization of the economy occurred as an unchoreographed response by thousands of individuals to the economic conditions of their world. As such, these developments may have had some unintended and unforeseen consequences for society. Economic growth results in a rationalization of the economic system, but it also tends to atomize primary social arrangements. As Emile Durkheim and Max Weber noted a half-century ago, as an area becomes more economically developed and specialized, it usually becomes more productive of individualism. Durkheim's and Weber's theories have been verified by Robert Redfield's empirical study of the Yucatan peninsula. As Redfield shows, when areas become tied together by networks of production and distribution, they become more integrated economically but less so socially. The economic rationalization of villages produces social disorganization, secularism, and individualism. With the development of markets outside the neighborhood comes a loss of social groups.[45] Connecticut's experience seems consistent with these observations. The burgeoning economic system fostered rivalry and weakened neighborly cooperation. As Connecticut's political and social historians have shown, conflicts between regions, controversies between village residents and outlying farmers, rising numbers of civil suits, and struggles between farmers and merchants for control of the General Assembly all characterized the colony and new state in the second half of the eighteenth century. Undoubtedly, social, political, and religious factors played vital roles in creating these tensions, but the theoretical and empirical evidence suggests that the changing nature of the economy played as important a role in replacing a spirit of community with one of individual aspiration.

Two

LONG-RANGE TRENDS OF WEALTH DISTRIBUTION IN EIGHTEENTH-CENTURY NEW ENGLAND

The distribution of wealth among the population was not a topic of much interest to colonial historians prior to the mid-1960s. Since then, however, trying to sort out who owned what has absorbed the energies of several dozen early American scholars. Probate inventories and tax lists provide the best sources for studying wealth distribution. By necessity, they require quantitative analyses. While rich in detail, both probate and tax records present some difficult methodological problems to anyone trying to use them. Consequently, although the literature on wealth distribution grows rapidly, as of yet no conclusions command widespread agreement. As this book was going to press, a symposium devoted to wealth distribution in the colonies was published by the *William and Mary Quarterly*, 3d Ser., XLV (1988), 116-170. The sophistication of the methodology and substantive arguments show how much we have learned about the subject in the last decade. The disagreement among the participants shows how much more we still have to learn.

Much of the work in wealth distribution suffers from a static quality: a scholar stops the clock and analyzes the relationships among economic classes at that moment. Similarly, much of it suffers from a restricted geographical base: one town or county provides the data base for broad generalizations. The following chapter tries to deal with both of these problems by developing time series to measure changes in wealth distribution in several different types of New England communities.

Since the publication of Jackson Turner Main's *The Social Structure of Revolutionary America*, a great deal of attention has been focused on the distribution of wealth in the American colonies. Main and others, such as Alice Hanson Jones, have overturned the long-held assumption that great inequalities of wealth did not occur in the United States until industrialization in the nineteenth century.[1] While the inequality in 1776 was not as great as in 1860, Main believes that the top 10 percent of colonial wealth holders owned at least 50 percent of society's wealth.[2] Jones found that in 1774 the top 10 percent among people who left probate records owned 40.4 percent of New England's wealth. When she upwardly adjusted this figure to compensate for people who did not leave probate records it, too, approached 50 percent.

While both Main's and Jones's figures are sometimes questioned, an unequally skewed distribution of wealth and a heavy concentration of wealth in the top parts of society in the 1700s are inescapable facts. The questions now become: When did this heavy concentration begin? What were the trends in wealth distribution prior to the 1770s? The only time study to deal even partially with these questions is James Henretta's "Economic Development and Social Structure in Colonial Boston."[3] Henretta examined two Boston tax lists at specific points in time, 1687 and 1771, and found that in 1687 the top 10 percent of the taxpayers owned 42 percent of Boston's wealth, while by 1771 they owned 57 percent. These conclusions, however, are based only on two tax lists, apply only to a mercantile center, and do not supply any data on the long period in between the two dates. Probate records, when systematically sampled and drawn from the entire eighteenth century up to 1776, can provide more information on the trend towards wealth concentration.

Main's work in the probate records of the Revolutionary years has established a hypothesis concerning trends of wealth distribution. While Main did not examine different periods of time, he did examine areas that were in differing stages of development. Generally, Main found that as the economic system of a northern area became more complex, wealth became more concentrated in the upper elements. He discussed four distinctly different types of settlements—the frontier areas, the subsistence farming areas, the commercial farming areas, and the urban areas. Main found that with each succeeding degree of economic complexity, the distribution of wealth became more top-heavy. He theorized that possibly there were stages through which communities progressed.[4] Of course, Main's thesis remains a tentative hypothesis because he has not actually followed the same areas through changing periods of growth. That task—the following of differing New England areas through their stages of growth in the period 1700-1776 and analyzing what the changing trends were in wealth distribution—is the object of this essay.

For purposes of analysis, the pre-Revolutionary eighteenth century was divided into three twenty-year periods, 1700-1720, 1720-1740, 1740-1760, and one sixteen-year period, 1760-1776. Seven different types of population areas in New England were analyzed for distribution of wealth in these time periods. Fifty random inventories were arranged in a distribution for each of the seven geographic areas in each of the four time periods. Fifty was selected as the smallest number (except for early Worcester County in which forty was used) that would accurately reflect the population areas being examined. A difference of means test applied to two samples of fifty estates drawn from the same geographical area and same time period revealed only a slight deviation in samples of fifty. In all, 1250 inventories of estates comprised the entire sample (it would have been 1400 had not some of the frontier areas been omitted for the period 1700-1720 due to lack of inventories). Wealth estimates for different percentages of the population were calculated from the samples by averaging the top 30 percent (71st percentile through the 100th), the middle 40 percent (31st percentile through the 70th) and the lowest 30 percent (1st percentile through the 30th). The accuracy of the method was tested by comparing the averages of the top 30 percent of separate samples taken from the same area and the same time. This was done in Boston and Portsmouth and the margin of error did not exceed 2 percent in either case.

There are two questions historians may raise about the accuracy of the figures used in this article. Are the probate inventories an accurate representation of the population as a whole? Did inflation distort the figures? Jones found that only 32.7 percent of adult white males had their estates inventoried in the year 1774.[5] Kenneth Lockridge estimated that 40 percent of adult white males did.[6] Thus, we can assume that approximately 60 percent to 68 percent of these men did not leave probate inventories. Probably, a large percentage of the unprobated men fell in the lower half of the population. Certainly, not all did. Many men who appear wealthy from all the qualitative evidence available left no probate records and many poor people with just a hand tool and the clothes on their backs had these items carefully inventoried. It is an untenable proposition to assume that as many as 68 percent of the adult white males had no goods worth inventorying. The majority of the unprobated people, however, would probably fall in the middle or lower ranges of society and this certainly reduces the accuracy of the absolute figures. The percentage of wealth figures cited in this article for the top 30 percent of the probated men are undoubtedly lower than the actual figures should be for all of the men. For absolute figures, Jones has made several adjustments that make her figures more reliable. However, this article is interested in relative relationships in differing time periods. The relative relationships of the figures are not distorted by the absence of the nonprobated men. While the absolute accuracy may be questioned, the relative relationship is unaffected if the probating process stayed the same throughout the seventy-six year period, and there is no evidence that it did not. Similarly, while inflation may distort the absolute figures it does not seriously distort the relative figures. The shorter time periods should help reduce inflationary effects and inflation should operate equally on all estates, both high and low. However, in Connecticut and Massachusetts when inflation was most rampant in the 1740–1760 period an equalizing chart was used (see Table 3). Inflation was even more rampant in this period in New Hampshire and an equalizing formula was also applied, but available knowledge does not enable it to be as precise as the formula for Connecticut and Massachusetts. Prior to the 1740 inflation was not as serious and in the 1760s when Old and New Tenor local currency

Table 3
Adjustment for Inflation in Connecticut and Massachusetts[7]

ESTATES IN YEARS	MULTIPLY ESTATE BY
1740–1744	1.46
1745–1746	1.39
1747	1.36
1748	1.25
1749–1750	1.15

was replaced with the accounting unit of lawful money it once again ceases to be as serious a problem for the historian.

The samples were drawn at random by using the first three cases in the one year, followed by the first two cases of the next year. Only the estates of adult white males were used. No factor was used to counteract the age bias caused by the fact that the sample estates were the estates of people at their death who were generally older than the population mean. However, the age bias does not affect the validity of the present conclusions, since this study is interested in relative relationships over a period of time and the age bias should remain constant over this period of time.

Boston, the first urban area studied, needs little introduction to American historians. It was the largest port and mercantile center in New England and grew from a population of 6,700 in 1700 to over 16,000 by 1775.[8] The samples show that during this period of Boston's rapid growth, the wealth distribution was remarkably constant. The great inequality of wealth that characterized Boston in 1776 was present in the same ratios in the period 1700-1720 and continued along approximately the same line in the succeeding periods, 1720-1740 and 1740-1760. A graph showing the wealth owned by the top 30 percent of Boston society between 1700-1776 would be a relatively straight line. Among people who left probate records, the top 30 percent in Boston owned 84.25 percent of the wealth in 1700-1720, 82.45 percent in 1720-1740, 87.94 percent in 1740-1760, and 85.30 percent in 1760-1776. The slight differences in these distributions over the seventy-six year period can be attributed to the margin of error in the sampling technique. When adjusted slightly upward to compensate for the probability that the people who did not leave probate records may have had a slight tendency to fall in the lower half of the population, the percentage of wealth the top 30 percent of Boston owned probably was between 85 percent and 88 percent. The important point for the present analysis, regardless of the accuracy of the absolute figures, is the remarkable stability of Boston's wealth distribution in the eighteenth century. The top 30 percent of Boston's probated males changed their percentage of the total wealth by less than 1 percent over this seventy-six year period. The percentage of wealth owned by the middle 40 percent of society, the 30th to the 70th percentile, changed only from 14.04 percent in 1700-1720 to 13.94 percent in 1760-1776. The concentration of wealth in the 1770s, noted by historians, had started in

Boston by 1700–1720 and simply remained constant during the eighteenth century.

Suffolk County, with Boston and some atypical towns excluded, was the second area in Massachusetts examined. Suffolk County was settled in the 1630s during the first Puritan migration and most of the county was characterized as a commercial farming area in the eighteenth century. It was one of the oldest and most stable farming areas in Massachusetts. An average prototype town sampled in Suffolk County would progress from approximately 1,200 people in 1700 to 3,000 in 1776 if its original boundaries were not altered by the creation of new towns.

Suffolk County's wealth distribution did not show the same stability as Boston's, during the same time period. Suffolk County did not change its patterns of wealth distribution dramatically, but it did show a steady increase in the percentage of wealth owned by the top 30 percent of society. The top 30 percent of Suffolk County owned far less of society's wealth than the same class did in Boston, but between 1740 and 1776 the upper elements of society in Suffolk County did show a steady increase in the percentage of the county's wealth which they owned. The top 30 percent among probated people owned 62.52 percent of the total wealth in 1700–1720, 59.8 percent in 1720–1740, 67.5 percent in 1740–1760, and 68.05 percent in 1760–1776. The percentage of wealth owned by the middle 40 percent of the county declined from 29.28 percent in 1700–1720 to 25.87 percent in 1760–1776. The percentage of wealth owned by the lowest 30 percent of society steadily declined from a high of 8.20 percent in 1700–1720 to a low of 6.08 percent in 1760–1776. The distribution of wealth in eighteenth-century Suffolk County was much less concentrated than in Boston, and changes over the century were not dramatic. But the county did experience a slight but steady increase in the relative wealth of the top 30 percent.

Worcester County in Massachusetts, a newly settled frontier county prior to 1740, which was moving into an economy of subsistence farming after 1740, showed a different pattern than either Suffolk County or Boston. Most of the towns of Worcester County progressed from small villages of two or three hundred settlers in the formative stages to still relatively small towns of between 1,500 and 2,000 people by 1776. Between 1700 and 1720 the county was being settled and did not leave enough probate records for sampling. From 1720 onward, however, the samples show a society in a state of flux going constantly towards a greater inequality of wealth distribution. The period 1720–1740 showed the least concentration of wealth in the upper parts of society of any of the areas sampled in Massachusetts in any of the time periods. The top 30 percent among men who left probate records owned 57.23 percent of the total wealth, while the middle 40 percent owned 34.14 percent and the lowest 30 percent owned 8.62 percent. As the eighteenth century progressed in Worcester, and presumably as the frontier condition of the area gave way to more settled conditions, the top 30 percent steadily gained more relative wealth at the expense of the middle 40 percent and the lowest 30 percent. By 1760–1776 the top 30 percent among the probated people owned 68.60 percent of the wealth which equaled the concentration of the top 30 percent of Suffolk County. The lowest 30 percent of society steadily declined from 8.6 percent in 1720–1740 to 4.07 percent in 1740–1760 to 3.89 percent in 1760–1776. Worcester County progressed from a relatively unconcentrated distribution of wealth in 1720 to a concentration in 1776 that approximated the oldest settled county in the colony.

Table 4
Top 30 Percent of Estates, 71st Percentile Through 100th in Massachusetts

	1700–1720	1720–1740	1740–1760	1760–1776
Boston	84.25	82.45	87.94	85.30
Suffolk County	62.52	58.01	67.57	68.05
Worcester County	–	60.24	64.42	68.60

In Connecticut, three types of communities that differed from the three types which were studied in Massachusetts were selected for analysis. Hartford, the first area selected, was one of the three founding towns of Connecticut in the 1630s. By 1700, it had already taken on the outline of an urban center with a population of around 3,000, which made it considerably smaller than Boston. By 1774, the year nearest 1776 in which a comprehensive census was taken, Hartford was the fourth largest urban area in Connecticut, with a population of 5,031.[9] Carl Bridenbaugh classified it as one of the secondary urban areas that was secondary only when compared to the five major cities in the colonies.[10] The second area examined in Connecticut comprised the three towns of Danbury, Waterbury, and Windham. These three towns were geographically separated but all three were founded in the last quarter of the seventeenth century and all three progressed from the frontier stage prior to 1720 to a subsistence stage after 1720. The three towns were similar in size in 1774 with populations that ranged from 2,700 to 3,400 and were relatively typical middle-size communities by Connecticut standards at that date. The Litchfield County towns of Canaan, Kent, Salisbury, and Sharon, all of which were founded from 1739 through 1741 and which had populations in 1774 that ranged from 1,550 to 1,900, were the third type of area that was examined. During the period 1760 to 1776, these four towns were evolving from frontier to subsistence farming economies.

Hartford, in the period 1700 to 1776, showed a strong stability in its pattern of wealth distribution. The top 30 percent of wealthholders owned 74.03 percent of the total wealth in 1700-1720, 73.02 percent in 1720-1740, 77.27 percent in 1740-1760, and 73.94 percent in 1760-1776. The total change between 1700 and 1776 was substantially less than 1 percent, a remarkably small change considering the length of time. Neither the middle 40 percent of wealthholders nor the lowest 30 percent changed significantly during the time period. The middle 40 percent owned 22.98 percent of the wealth in 1700-1720 and 23.13 percent of the wealth in 1760-1776, while the lowest 30 percent went from 2.99 percent of the wealth in 1700-1720 to 2.93 percent in 1760-1776. Obviously, over the intervening 76 years, Hartford economic classes had not changed their relative share of the distribution of the wealth. The only exception to the pattern of great stability is the high figure of 77.27 percent that the top 30 percent owned in 1740-1760. This might at first suggest statistical error but when it is remembered that Boston also showed a higher percentage in the top 30 percent during the same period it may well be that urban areas experienced a slight dislocation in wealth distribution patterns in this period. Even with this slight deviation, however, the salient feature of the 1700-1776 period in Hartford is the uniformity and stability of the distribution of wealth.

There was, however, little stability evident in the pattern of wealth distribution shown by the three towns of Danbury, Waterbury, and Windham that were founded in the late seventeenth century and had grown to middle size by the time of the Revolution. The top 30 percent of the wealth-holders in these towns owned 50.12 percent of the total wealth in 1700–1720, 63.95 percent in 1720–1740, 69.05 percent in 1740–1760, and 69.07 percent in 1760–1776. The top 30 percent had increased their share of the wealth from around one-half in the frontier stage to well over two-thirds in the mature subsistence stage. The towns evolved in this period of time from a wealth-holding structure that was remarkably egalitarian to one that was far more concentrated in the upper elements. The gains made by the top 30 percent were achieved at the expense of the middle 40 percent who declined from 38.25 percent of the wealth in 1700–1720 to 26.44 percent in 1760–1776 and also at the particular expense of the lowest 30 percent who declined from 11.63 percent of the wealth in 1700–1720 to 4.45 percent in 1760–1776. The trend in these towns is unmistakable: the top 30 percent was growing relatively wealthier and the rest of society was growing relatively poorer. The towns were in a constant process of increasing the concentration of wealth in the upper elements.

In the four Litchfield County towns sampled, the same trend towards concentration of wealth is shown. The top 30 percent in these towns owned 60.83 percent of the total wealth in 1740–1760, the first 20 years of the town's existence, and this figure was increased to 67.50 percent in 1760–1776. This increase was made at the expense of the middle 40 percent which declined from 35.34 percent of the total wealth in 1740–1760 to 28.69 percent in 1760–1776. The lowest 30 percent of the population had a low figure of 3.83 percent in 1740–1760 which stayed approximately the same, 3.81 percent, in 1760–1776.

Table 5
Top 30 Percent of Estates, 71st Percentile Through 100th in Connecticut

	1700–1720	1720–1740	1740–1760	1760–1776
Hartford	74.03	73.02	77.27	73.94
Middle Towns	50.12	63.95	69.05	69.07
Small Towns	–	–	60.83	67.50

The last area sampled in New England was Portsmouth, the mercantile center of southern New Hampshire. Portsmouth was founded early in New England's history, in the 1720s, and was known as Strawberry Bank until it was incorporated in 1653. However, it is a unique urban center. In 1700, Portsmouth could hardly be called a mercantile center, even though it was over a half-century old, but by 1775 it had a population of 4,590, comparable to Hartford, and was designated along with Hartford, by Bridenbaugh, as one of the leading secondary cities in the colonies.[11] Portsmouth, quite unlike Boston and Hartford, developed into a major urban center not prior to the period 1700-1776 but during it. Portsmouth, also unlike Hartford and Boston, did not show a pattern of stability in wealth distribution in the eighteenth century. The pattern was one of a steady increase in the concentration of wealth in the top 30 percent between 1700 and 1760 and a leveling off at a high level in 1760-1776. The top 30 percent owned 65.5 percent of the wealth in 1700-1720, 75.3 percent in 1720-1740, 79.7 percent in 1740-1760, and 79.1 percent in 1760-1776. The steady increase in the complexity of Portsmouth's economic life, which was a function of its emergence as an urban area between 1700 and 1760, was accompanied by a steady increase in the percentage of wealth owned by the top 30 percent. The middle 40 percent and the lowest 30 percent of society both shared the loss of relative wealth; the middle 40 percent declined from 29.2 percent in 1700-1720 to 17.1 percent in 1760-1776, while the lowest 30 percent declined from 5.3 percent in 1700-1720 to 3.8 percent in 1760-1776.

Table 6
Top 30 Percent of Estates, 71st Percentile Through 100th in Portsmouth

	1700–1720	1720–1740	1740–1760	1760–1776
PORTSMOUTH	65.5	75.3	79.7	79.1

The absolute accuracy of all the figures in this chapter can be challenged for various reasons. Historians differ over what percentage of New Englanders left probate records and they also differ over whether or not probated men were broadly representative of all classes. The basic bias of looking at society from the standpoint of its oldest people is obvious. However, if we accept the assumption that the probating policy was generally the same throughout Massachusetts, Connecticut, and New Hampshire, and if we accept the assumption that it did not change significantly in the period 1700–1776, it is then possible to draw some conclusions concerning the relative trends in the distribution of wealth in differing time periods and differing types of communities.

The tendency Jackson Turner Main found in Revolutionary America for communities to increase the concentration of wealth in the upper elements of society as they became more economically complex is essentially accurate for the entire eighteenth century. Every area studied that was undergoing economic changes showed a constant tendency to increase the amount of relative wealth owned by the top 30 percent of society and decrease the relative amount of wealth owned by the middle 40 percent and bottom 30 percent. Communities increased the concentration of wealth the most in the second twenty-year period of their existence, presumably when most of them moved from the frontier to the subsistence stage. Major changes toward a higher concentration in wealth distribution occurred in the second twenty-year history of most new areas, and lesser, but steady, increases occurred in subsequent years. Perhaps the one qualification that should be added to the Main thesis concerns the distinction he made between commercial farm areas and the normal economy in New England, subsistence farm areas. Subsistence farm areas, like the ones examined in Connecticut and Worcester County, Massachusetts, after the first forty years of development, showed precisely the same degree of concentration of wealth in the top 30 percent of the wealth-holders as did Suffolk County, the commercial farm area. The difference between distribution of wealth in the subsistence farm areas and the commercial farm areas was not to be found in the top 30 percent of record, but in the middle 40 percent and lowest 30 percent. The lowest 30 percent in all of the nonfrontier subsistence economies owned a significantly lower percentage of the wealth than the comparable lowest 30 percent in the commercial farm area. There were more relatively poor people in the subsistence farm economies than in Suffolk County. This phenomenon, however, may be irrespective of the nature of Suffolk County's economy and may reflect the fact that Suffolk County was settled in a different era than any of the subsistence areas.

Areas that had taken on all the characteristics of urban economies by 1700 clearly had achieved a high degree of concentration of wealth by that time and continued on at the same level through 1776. Neither Boston nor Hartford, both of which clearly were mercantile centers in 1700, showed any significant change in its pattern of wealth distribution between 1700 and 1776. Both cities were stabilized at a level of concentration of wealth throughout the period that exceeded the level of any other nonurban area. Portsmouth was in a not clearly demarcated transition stage from a middle-sized town to an urban center. Correspondingly, it was in a state of flux moving toward a greater concentration of wealth as the community became more clearly a city and less clearly a town.

Generally, the assumptions that historians have widely held concerning economic classes in different communities are accurate. Cities did have the greatest inequality in wealth distribution of any areas. There were more relatively wealthy and more relatively poor in Boston, Hartford, and Portsmouth than in any other type of community. Boston, as might be expected, showed more inequality than both secondary cities and had both a higher percentage of wealth owned by the top parts of society and a lesser percentage of wealth owned by the lowest classes. Also, the much vaunted egalitarian frontier economy does have some validity in eighteenth-century New England. Communities in frontier conditions at any time between 1700 and 1760 did have fewer inequalities in their distribution of wealth than nonfrontier areas. However, the relative equality of the frontier wealth pattern lasted less than a generation, and by the third twenty-year period of a community's existence, its concentration of wealth was about the same as any nonurban area. The four nonurban areas studied, all of which were founded at different times, had remarkably similar patterns of wealth distribution by 1760–1776. The percentages of wealth concentration in the top 30 percent of society in all nonurban areas tended to be approximately the same after the area had passed through a forty-year growing period.

The increase in the maldistribution of wealth, thus seems to be primarily a function of the advance of urbanism and the decline of the frontier. Within this Turnerian framework, a fair degree of stability characterized local wealth-holding structures once communities moved from their early stages to more established, mature patterns of economic activity. Nevertheless, because the frontier *was* receding and because new urban units *were* emerging, there was a trend in many eighteenth-century New England communities toward a greater inequality of wealth distribution. This trend developed at the same time that the New England economy was diversifying. Hence, measured by one standard—that of choice and opportunity—economic life in New England became more democratic over the course of the eighteenth century. The young men of 1770 had more choice about how to make a living than the young men of 1700 did. Measured by another standard—that of condition and result—economic life in southern New England became less democratic over the course of the eighteenth century. The city and the well-established farming towns, both of which were increasing in number, had greater gaps between the top and bottom of society than did the frontier towns which were on the decrease.

Three

Poor Relief, Local Finance, and Town Government in Eighteenth-Century Rhode Island

Surprisingly, the recent expansion in social and economic history has not produced a large body of work on poverty in colonial America. The elite fascinate historians; the poor usually appear in the secondary literature as members of crowds, soldiers, or statistics in analyses of voting and wealth distribution. Several significant exceptions to this pattern of scholarly neglect must be made, but the living conditions of those at the bottom of New England society remain to be described.

This historical myopia stems in large part from the perception that relatively few colonial New Englanders lived and died in poverty. Until the second quarter of the eighteenth century, the poor tended to be a small percentage of the population who had experienced some unexpected catastrophe: illness or injury, death of parents, or widowhood. Local communities had sufficient economic resources and the political will to provide care at a reasonable level for these unfortunates. Poor relief occasioned little debate or contention in most towns in the seventeenth or early eighteenth centuries.

After 1730, however, the number of people living in poverty increased until they and their care became major social problems. The administration and financing of poor relief absorbed much of the energy of local government, drained town treasuries, and plunged communities into bitter disputes. A combination of economic factors caused the problem: rapid population growth, an increased dependence on commerce and shipping, wars, and the declining availability of good land. The debate over the care of the poor created deep divisions in New England at mid-century and on the eve of the

Revolution. The following chapter discusses poor relief and the financial and political difficulties it caused in Rhode Island, the New
England colony in which the problem became the most severe and
divisive.

Local governments in the United States today are beleaguered
with financial problems. Education, police and fire protection, highway and sanitation maintenance, and welfare programs, along with
many other lesser but collectively significant costs, place a strain on
communities—almost all of which derive the bulk of their revenue
from a property tax. Recent attempts to lessen the strain range from
cutting services and streamlining administration to seeking funds
from federal and state levels to borrowing heavily and mortgaging
future generations. Taxpayers frequently blame their local officials,
and tax revolts by disgruntled local inhabitants have become com-
monplace as people simply refuse to endure what they regard as
oppressive levies.

Every generation tends to think its problems are unique, and indeed to a certain extent they are, but a similar financial crisis on the
local level developed in the middle of the eighteenth century in Rhode
Island. The response of colonial Rhode Island taxpayers bears many
similarities to responses today. During the colonial period, however,
the costs of local government were relatively small. Rising welfare
costs accounted primarily for local financial problems. Like today's
local governments, Rhode Island's colonial towns tried to cut the
cost of welfare and administer it more efficiently. While they did not
seek funds directly from the colony, they tried to reduce the colony's
taxes and tried to borrow money to pay immediate bills. Local taxpayers frequently refused to pay their taxes and at times allowed
their local officials to take the blame.

The two major and closely related problems facing town government in eighteenth-century Rhode Island were the administering of
poor relief and local finance. Surprisingly, little has been written
recently about local practice in either area. Most of the new community studies concentrate on power relationships, family patterns, and
social structures; they ignore, or mention only in passing, welfare and
finance. If we are to penetrate the lives and minds of colonists, we
must know more about the issues that absorbed their attention.[1]

As with all aspects of local government, the ultimate power over
poor relief lay with the town meeting, although as early as 1647 the

money. It not only secured enough money to end colony taxes on the towns for more than four decades, but had enough left over to remit some excess money to the towns. In the words of Rhode Island's most distinguished historian, Sydney V. James, the colony went on a "tax holiday." Towns, relieved of paying colony taxes, only occasionally levied local taxes, and these were invariably small. At the same time that poor relief costs began rising sharply, however, the colony's finances were strained by the exigencies of fighting major wars in the 1740s and 1750s. Moreover, the British Parliament ended the tax holiday by passing legislation that compelled the colony to retire its currency emissions within two years of their issuance.[9]

The impact of rising local and colony-level costs began to be felt at mid-century. Finances had played a remarkably small role in town government between 1700 and the late 1740s, but thereafter every town began to complain about rising costs. Finances, in fact, became the most discussed matter of local government. Portsmouth, for example, had been so flush in the 1730s that its town meeting voted to give every resident in town twenty shillings out of money it had received from the colony and prefaced the vote by declaring that there was "more money in the town treasury than to defray the town's charges." After experiencing surpluses as high as fifty-one pounds in 1744, Portsmouth's financial situation began to deteriorate. In 1750 the treasurer complained to the town meeting that he "hath not received one penny . . . for the rent of any highway." In the following two decades, Portsmouth was forced to raise taxes to the point where nonpayment became a serious problem and the names of delinquents were recorded in the town records. Still, Portsmouth remained solvent and was one of the most fortunate towns. Warwick, which once had surpluses, experienced large deficits and made numerous references in the late 1740s and the 1750s to the town treasury being exhausted." By 1765 the town audit recorded a deficit of £3,434 Old Tenor, a huge sum for a town. East Greenwich's first indication of financial problems occurred in 1748 when auditors reported to the meeting that "there is no money in the treasury and the town is greatly in debt." There was no doubt in anyone's minds as to the primary reason for the indebtedness. As the town meeting recorded before passing a tax in 1754: "The town treasury of said town is very much exhausted . . . and many persons make considerable demands upon the treasurer for the supporting of the poor of said town." Nor were these cases unusual. In towns as

General Assembly ordered each town to elect an overseer of the poor to assist in "maintaining the impotent."[2] In the seventeenth century, relief was such a minor problem that the town meeting usually handled all cases itself. The overseer had little discretionary powers and merely implemented the meeting's orders. The normal method was for the town meeting to authorize payment to some willing person who would in turn provide care for the person needing assistance. Recipients of care incurred no debts for the aid extended them and were not required to work in return for their support. If, however, a person needing aid was completely healthy—not a very common condition among recipients—or if he or she were underage, an indenture was sometimes arranged. By and large, those few needing care in the seventeenth century were the elderly and infirm who were cared for out of a sense of community duty, or orphans who were placed in a relative's or neighbor's home. Even in this period when cases were few, and involved people that everyone knew, the meetings exhibited some penuriousness. In 1649 Portsmouth handled its first case of relief and voted that "old John Mott shall be provided for of meat, drink and lodging and washing by George Parker at his home," for which Parker would be paid five shillings per week, "so far as the treasury will go." Warwick's town meeting authorized money to pay for medical care for a disabled resident, but made the payments to the physician conditional upon a successful cure. Providence saved money by ordering the sale of the estate of John Jones to help pay for his "comfortable existence."[3] Despite these examples of towns attempting to hold down welfare costs, no evidence exists to show that a significant number of people were denied relief. The townspeople, assembled together as a community, authorized and administered the care, and the poor were kept in reasonable circumstances in the homes of neighbors and friends.

Toward the end of the seventeenth century and in the early eighteenth century, as relief costs increased, the towns began to transfer the decision-making to the town council, a body composed of six men who acted as the town's chief executive officers, and to the overseers of the poor, who were called upon to exercise more judgment in everyday cases. The overseers usually arranged the details of finding someone to care for an indigent person and also agreed upon the financial compensation given for providing the care. The council, however, had to make the final authorization of funds for each relief case, which they usually did on the recommendation of the overseers.

The council also decided some difficult cases itself, and in a couple of towns the councilmen were also elected as overseers of the poor and served in dual capacities.

Unfortunately, records of the overseers do not survive. We only know of their actions through the records of the councils. Town council records reveal, however, that the councils, working in conjunction with the overseers, were inclined to tighten up on relief expenses and in some cases took precautions to ward off relief charges before they appeared. Providence's council ordered a man to post bond to guarantee that a bastard child being raised in his home was not "likely to become chargeable" to the town. At the same meeting it ordered a woman and baby out of town because it appeared they might at some future time require town support. When the Providence council was informed that Thomas Cooper had posted notice of his marriage to a woman outside of town, it ordered that the marriage be prevented because Cooper "a person infamous [might] depart leaving the said woman . . . as charge to the town." Portsmouth's town council ordered two men to place a man in a home "to diet as cheap as they can." The councilmen maintained this man at a low enough level that it required their special authorization to buy him a shirt. The Portsmouth council also refused to support the children of a couple who claimed they could not "subsist" without aid. The couple was cared for, but the children were found out as apprentices. A Warwick woman, presumably well-advised of the council's hopes for saving money, volunteered to surrender her estate in her petition to the council for relief. In response to an inquiry by Providence in 1682, the General Assembly passed the first of what would be many laws authorizing the town councils to regulate admission to their towns to head off potential poor relief charges. The councils were allowed to require a bond from any person seeking to move to town or they could reject any prospective inhabitant. If a person refused to post bond or refused to leave the town, the council could apply to a justice of the peace for a warrant and fine the person five pounds or administer a whipping not to exceed 20 stripes. This legislation was repeated and broadened to eliminate loopholes in 1727.[4]

Despite the severity of a law authorizing the laying on of twenty stripes, and despite the town councils' decided attempts to avoid any extra expenses, relief did not cause great problems for Rhode Island towns until the 1730s. It then became a pressing concern and grew more pressing every decade of the colonial period. The increasing

need for poor relief resulted primarily from economic forc beyond anyone's direct control. First, Rhode Island, a colonies, experienced a high rate of population growth, a favorable ratio of land to man began to decline. Th density of population have never been precisely tabulat Island's towns, but in Connecticut and New Hampshir density became critically high in the second quarter of t century.[5] Rhode Island, a small colony with no fro settlements, had a rapidly growing population that n between 1730 and 1748, growing from 17,935 to 34 ony, like its Puritan neighbors, was severely affected b land. Second, Rhode Island's small area and the prox every one of its towns to the ocean made it more de going commerce than most other northern colonies. nity for a vast amount of ocean trade was a mixed positive side it absorbed much of the excess populati a stimulant to the economy. On the negative side it pool of workers who were injured or killed, leaving lies, and it subjected many of the workers to the Atlantic economy that swung erratically betwee depression. Third, all of the northern colonies exper the distribution of wealth in the eighteenth cent historians' knowledge of these changes is far from that as the frontier receded, the upper elements creasing their percentage of society's wealth. A g the distribution of wealth characterized New Eng especially in communities with much merchant a of Rhode Island's towns.[7] Finally, the colonial and 1750s diverted many men into the military juries and much loss of life, leaving many famili or permanently without able-bodied men to prov four phenomena coalesced to create grave econo northern colonies. In Rhode Island these probl financial crisis that brought about changes in welfare.

Although towns scrimped here and there early eighteenth century, they were relatively actually paid less in taxes than they had in th In the first decade of the eighteenth century, developed a system of financing its expenses

diverse in social structure, population, location, and age, as Cranston, Newport, New Shoreham, Providence, Scituate, South Kingston, Tiverton, and Westerly, similar problems surfaced at this time, and finances became the central focus of the town meeting.[10]

Financial problems wrought a change in attitudes toward poor relief that were reflected in the "warning out" system, whereby towns refused to accept responsibility for maintaining certain people and ordered them out of town. Rhode Island law specified that a person's native town assumed responsibility for that person's welfare unless he or she gained a "legal settlement" elsewhere. A legal settlement was defined as being admitted in full faith to a town and could only be granted by the town council. Most town councils were loath to grant that status if there were any chance that a person might ever become "chargeable" to the town. A newcomer was usually asked, as the Warwick town council phrased it to a recent arrival, "by what means he doth dwell in our town?" An unsatisfactory answer was grounds for immediate expulsion or for being told that one could only stay in town without the status of legal inhabitant. The Rhode Island General Assembly strengthened the hand of the town councils with a 1748 law that reaffirmed the principle that all people must be admitted to a legal settlement. More important, it provided a mechanism for the town councils to implement the principle. Because (as the preamble to the law stated) of "great controversies between towns in the removal of their poor," persons coming to a town and desiring to settle there had to give, within a month of their arrival, written notice to the town council of the place of their birth, their last legal residence, and the number of persons in their family.[11] This would prevent anyone from entering a town unnoticed and later making claims upon the town for support.

In the towns where warning-out writs can be quantified, the number increased substantially in the middle of the eighteenth century. Portsmouth averaged between one and two warning-out writs per year between 1700 and 1727, but after issuing nine of them in 1728 the town averaged more than six warning-out writs in subsequent years until it reached a peak in 1774, when it issued them to nineteen families and sixteen single persons. Of course, since the population of the towns was also increasing, the ratio of writs to population may not have increased, but the absolute numbers being issued caused administrative difficulties and took much time. In an effort to overcome these difficulties, Providence in 1758 printed blank warrants that the clerk of the town council could sign in advance and authorized the town sergeant to "insert the names of any transient persons he may hear of."[12]

Towns lacked compassion by refusing to accept any responsibility for persons to whom they were not legally obligated. In spite of the obvious hardships involved, Providence ordered a man "who is *non-compos mentis*" to return to Salisbury, Pennsylvania. Pregnant women were frequently ordered to leave if it appeared they would become chargeable after the birth of their children. Most people had to travel to nearby places in Rhode Island or Massachusetts, but distance was no barrier and an occasional traveler was sent back to the southern colonies or the West Indies. If departure would clearly hazard a person's life, the council would delay it, but no longer than necessary. A man in Warwick, "in a very poor condition with a sore arm and also attended with a fever," had his removal to Maryland reluctantly postponed by the council but only "until his arm be cured." One month later the expulsion writ was issued. Colony law required anyone entertaining a stranger to report to the town council or be liable for a fine of five pounds Current Money. Even if a local resident was voluntarily supporting a visitor in great distress from another town, the council might act to head off charges. South Kingston required one of its respected citizens to post bond for a woman with a "bastard child . . . and lying in sickness" to guarantee she would be cared for. Otherwise she would be warned out. Mere longevity in town did not supercede the legal requirement of obtaining a settlement. One woman lived in Providence from the age of ten to nineteen with her father who worked for a Providence freeholder. But because her father had never obtained a legal settlement in Providence, she was sent back to Newport, her place of birth, when she became pregnant out of wedlock, even though she had not been there for over nine years. Similarly, another woman, "with child and likely to become chargeable to this town if not timely removed," was sent from Providence to Newport although she had not lived in Newport for fourteen years. Most people did have a home town that was required to support them, but some transients never succeeded in persuading a town to accept responsibility for them, and became footloose wanderers—the "strolling poor."[13]

In many such cases the town to which a person was dispatched was reluctant to accept him. Towns frequently bickered over questions of responsibility for individuals. Portsmouth and Newport, the two towns on Aquidneck Island, experienced endemic strife over who was responsible for whom and appointed a joint committee about once every three years to recommend settlements. In one case that could not be settled by committee, the two towns asked a third town to be a referee and to decide who should support the two families in question. Providence sent a pregnant woman back to Attleborough, Massachusetts, which refused to accept her and returned her to Providence, which, conceiving that this was "directly contrary to law," refused to accept her back. In another dispute over a pregnant woman, when neither Providence nor Rehoboth, Massachusetts, would assume responsibility for her, Rehoboth suggested third-party arbitration. Providence refused and referred the matter to the courts, which was the formal legal recourse if towns could not agree. Arbitration was employed only occasionally because findings did not have the force of law and could be ignored. Another woman, whose case was disputed by Providence and Rehoboth, told a sad tale of being moved by towns five times in the preceding ten years. Neither town was moved to compassion by her story. Towns could go to great lengths to avoid accepting a person on the relief rolls. The town council of Portsmouth asked the town meeting for guidance when North Kingston refused to accept a man who had been warned out, and the town meeting appointed a committee to collect evidence to prove in court the justice of its case.[14]

Although defiance of warning-out orders was not uncommon, the town councils meant the writs to be enforced and did not take defiance lightly. If a person was warned out and returned without the council's permission, the council could not directly punish the person but could apply to the court for a judgment (which was usually issued) to whip or fine him. Nor was the whipping symbolic. Usually it was "ten stripes upon the naked back," but a woman returning to Portsmouth was whipped fifteen stripes and two women in Providence were whipped fifteen and twenty stripes respectively. In these two Providence cases the whippings were to be repeated each time the women returned.[15]

Warning out was the most prevalent means, but not the only one, employed by town councils to avoid charges. The "binding out" of poor children as apprentices was widely practiced and colony legislation in 1742 strengthened the town councils' powers to do so. Ten months later, the assembly extended these powers to include the binding out of persons "non compos mentis" as workmen. In 1753 it further extended this to "idle or indigent persons or disorderly persons" and included allowing the person bound out to be sent to sea. Town councils did not hesitate to implement this legislation. Warwick, for example, bound out children as young as seven or eight to serve as servants or apprentices until they were twenty-one. One bastard named Freelove Sweet (probably with no irony intended) was bound out at the age of four to serve until she attained the age of eighteen. Providence directed its council to bind out dependent children "with all convenient speed." Much evidence suggests that towns also saved money by giving differential care to indigent persons of differing social status. Providence, for one example, contracted for the "drink, washing, lodging, and attendance as may be necessary for a Negro man," and in another example South Kingston voted funds necessary to support a woman of "quality." The degree of difference can never be known with certitude but seems to have been substantial; the Providence town council voted fourteen shillings per week for the care of a white man and at the same meeting authorized eight shillings per week for a black. Towns also forced financially able residents to support their relatives instead of keeping them at the taxpayers' expense. When one man, "being old, impotent and . . . chargeable to this town," was not maintained by his children, the Providence town council applied for a writ from the court "to oblige his relations to support him." If supporting one's relatives worked an unacceptable hardship on a person, however, the council would be lenient. When an old farmer complained to the Warwick town council that he could not afford to completely support his two sisters who "were very often *non compos mentis*, at which times they were very troublesome," the council voted to give "from time to time . . . such relief out of ye town treasury." The Portsmouth town council, in two instances, did not force widows to support completely their aged relatives and dispersed funds to assist them. A final method of preventing what the towns regarded as unnecessary expenses was to proscribe certain people from being served at taverns, hoping to avoid the possibility of a future relief bill. In a typical town council proscription order, South Kingston forbid local taverns from serving a woman, "who is very excessive and extravagant in drinking . . . and spends what she labors for at the tavern . . . which reduces her to so low a degree that she is likely to become chargeable to this town." The phrase used to indicate this restriction was that a person was "posted."[16]

Despite all the best efforts of the town councils to avoid or mini-
mize poor relief responsibilities, costs still rose and caused severe
financial problems. In response to the seemingly unalterable fact that
some poor people had to be fed, lodged, and clothed, many towns
employed a workhouse system, widely used in England, but which
did not appear in Rhode Island until the 1720s. As might be expected, Newport, by far the largest town in the colony, and the one
with the most pressing relief problems, built the first workhouse. It
was ordered to be constructed in 1723 and was apparently finished
shortly thereafter. No others were built until Providence, the second
largest town, did so sometime in the early 1750s, when its financial
problems had become clearly manifest. Small towns sometimes
grouped together to construct a workhouse. Warwick built one in
1763 with aid of a lottery authorized by the colony and with support from several other towns who would have recourse to it. In the
same year, Portsmouth and Middletown began negotiations on a
jointly administered workhouse. Even a town as small as Tiverton,
after earlier defeating a proposal to build a workhouse, authorized
the construction of one.[17]

The theory behind the workhouse movement was twofold. First,
costs would be reduced by grouping the indigent together in a com-
mune closely supervised by appointed or elected officials. Second, as
the name of the institution suggests, people there would be compelled to work and produce something of value to be sold, and the
town would recapture some of its expended monies. Towns may
have initially regarded the workhouse a panacea for their problems.
Providence ordered "every person maintained by the town" to be
put into one. Warwick authorized its town council "to put any person in the house as a tenant as they shall time to time see fit for the
interests of the town." Everyone knew, of course, that a workhouse
could never be entirely self-supporting and that some tax money was
still needed to maintain a minimum standard of survival for the poor.
Money was given to the overseers of the workhouse on a sliding scale,
whereby residents received support according to their needs. It is difficult to say precisely what kind of food, shelter, clothes, and so
forth, the poor received, but it is clear that the standard was near an
absolute minimum. The workhouse keeper of Warwick was given an
average of three shillings per week per person by a town council that
authorized an equal three shilling payment to each town councilman
for his dinner on the night of council meetings. The council could

save money on some people such as a "suckling child" who needed only six pence a week.[18]

Other fragments of surviving evidence indicate that the workhouses did not solve the financial crisis to everyone's satisfaction and that life in a workhouse was far from a happy experience. Newport, with the most experience in running a workhouse, appointed a committee in 1760 to examine how it was functioning and the "reasons for such an expense arising to the town, and to consider some proper method to endeavor to lessen said charges." The committee recommended, among other things, that the workhouse "be immediately cleared" of anyone who could probably make his own living and that all residents in the workhouse should be "kept to such work or labor" that more profit could be made. In other words, the workhouse-keeper was advised to either throw people out or work them harder. The regulations for the workhouse already gave the keeper nearly complete control over the lives of the residents and authorized him to administer fairly severe punishment such as being "confined in ye manner as ye master shall think fit." Adding to the indignity of being in the workhouse, the Newport town meeting required all residents "maintained by the town or receive of the town's charity" to wear distinguishing badges on their clothes. During the Revolutionary period, when Warwick was feeling an acute financial pinch, a special town meeting held to deal with relief voted that "whereas it is bad policy and injurious to any community for persons ... to be supported in idleness ... all persons whatsoever ... in the workhouse shall be kept at *constant labor* [italics added]." Warwick ordered a troublesome resident to be kept confined in iron chains. Providence invited the heavy-handed use of arbitrary power when it paid its workhouse-keeper by authorizing him to make "some profit from the labor of the poor." As far as can be determined, and the evidence is indeed lacking for a positive statement, most people put in the workhouse were not given specific terms but were kept there until they became self-sufficient or totally incapable of any work, or until they died.[19]

Notwithstanding all of these attempts to hold down costs by cutting aid to many and by putting the bulk of the poor in workhouses, the taxpayers of each town still remained unhappy and frequently denied the towns the money they needed to pay their bills. Every town whose records have been examined voted down proposed taxes at least once, and most voted down proposed taxes several times. Nonpayment of taxes became a chronic problem. Most nonpayment was a thinly disguised attempt by the towns to avoid paying what they thought were unfairly apportioned colony taxes, although some nonpayment was outright defiance of the town government. The towns, of course, proceeded legally against people who did not pay local taxes and usually were ultimately successful. But the process was costly, fractious, and time-consuming, and a significant minority of marginal residents evaded taxes by moving before the legal proceedings were completed. In attempts by towns to lessen colony taxes, the apportionment of them became a matter of partisan activity between factions vying for control of the colony government. Both the Ward and the Hopkins factions, when in power, rewarded and punished towns that supported or opposed them by changing the method of apportionment to favor some towns over others. As a last resort to procure funds, many of the towns attempted to borrow money or "hire" it, as they said, to pay their debts. Sometimes this was temporarily successful; more often no new creditors could be found.[20]

At times the towns' financial problems took on the air of tragicomedies as local officials walked a thin line between the demands of their constituents and their creditors. The two officers who bore the greatest responsibility for financial matters, the treasurer and tax collector, frequently found themselves the subjects of suits. Occasionally one of them sued the other, both sometimes lost much personal wealth in the performance of their duties, and a few of each were jailed. Both officers received fees for their jobs, usually calculated as a percentage of the money they dispensed or collected, and both were personally liable for public debts—the treasurer for bills the town could not pay, and the tax collector for taxes he could not collect. Both positions involved much work, power, and risk, and both had the potential for profit or ruin. In Westerly, the town treasurer had his property seized and advertised for sale at public action. Although the town meeting finally authorized a tax to pay the debts and prevent the sale of the treasurer's lands, it doubted if it could be "collected timely" enough to do him any good. Four years later, a Westerly treasurer, sued for money by creditors, in turn sued the tax collector. The tax collector filed a countersuit against the treasurer, claiming that he had not been paid his fees for the taxes he had collected. The suit was filed from jail where the tax collector had been placed because he owed the town money for taxes he was obligated to collect. In Newport a treasurer promised a town meeting to "do his utmost" to "hire" money sufficient to pay the town bills. Undoubtedly he was earnest in that pledge because, when his utmost proved unsuccessful, he was placed in the county jail. The town graciously voted to support him in jail in a "handsome and generous" manner. Gratified by their support, the treasurer "who was eventually released" continued to serve in office and found himself back in jail four years later. His fellow officer, the tax collector, had similar problems. The town voted not to give him his commission because he did not collect all of the tax money, even though the terms of his service had specified that he was not responsible for delinquent taxes. The tax collector then refused to collect any more taxes and found himself briefly in jail. When he was released, he was relieved of his office. Not surprisingly, there was "no person appearing who was willing to collect rates" to replace him. George Babcock, the treasurer of South Kingston, probably held the record for the number of times committed to jail. He was jailed three times, with one term that was to last at least six months. A little sobered by his first short term in jail, Babcock had specified upon re-election that if "he be obliged to go to jail," the town had to pay his board. When Babcock finally had enough and refused to serve any longer as treasurer, his successor was instructed by the town meeting to apply the "first money he shall receive of this town . . . for the payment of the town debt for which George Babcock the late treasurer stands committed to jail."[21]

It is difficult to obtain hard data on town finances and relief costs, but a rare record of expenses for the three years, 1763, 1764, and 1765, survives for one town, Scituate, and shows the relative weighting of town expenditures. Poor relief and its attendant costs comprised 55 percent of expenditures, payments to the tax collectors for collecting both colony and town tax comprised 30 percent, and all other expenses totaled only 15 percent. Thus, relief and tax collection absorbed 85 percent of the town's local revenue, an amount that by almost any standard would be regarded as extraordinary.[22]

In the final analysis, one would have to conclude that Rhode Island towns were not very successful in solving either of their two major problems, welfare or finance. Under the pressures of mounting demand and rebellious taxpayers, Rhode Island towns diminished the compassion showed to unfortunates and moved the administration of poor relief away from a system based on neighborly care and concern toward a system based on asylums to isolate the poor and reduce the costs of caring for them. Despite this, the economic problems of the mid-eighteenth century and three successive wars created enough need for relief that the towns faced continuing financial crises. Their response to these crises was extremely haphazard, with greatly fluctuating tax rates, frequent insolvency, chronic tax delinquency, a high level of contention, and a total inability to bring order and stability to the towns' finances. The problems did not lay with town leaders such as the councilmen, overseers of the poor, treasurers, and tax collectors; they all did their best to act responsibly and in accordance with the wishes of the townspeople. It lay instead with the residents of towns who dominated town meetings and passed votes that hamstrung town officers. And it also lay with these same residents who defied tax collectors.

It might appear easy to indict colonial Rhode Island as a heartless and selfish society for not caring enough to pay for the maintenance of its poor. But this indictment would probably be grossly unfair to Rhode Islanders. The early modern world was based on a much harsher view of the realities of life than in twentieth-century America. For example, Rhode Island's criminal code, which would seem near barbaric to our present sensibilities, was no more severe (and probably less so) than the criminal codes of Puritan Connecticut and Massachusetts. We do not fully know how Rhode Island's welfare system compared to the rest of New England, but trends identified in Massachusetts of attempts to deal with the increasing problem of transiency seem to parallel changes that occurred in Rhode Island.[23] And, after all, if welfare was a subject of great debate in Rhode Island, it does show that society accepted some responsibility for the care of its poor; probably no one died directly from lack of food or protection from the elements. One can find examples in America today of much callous thought about the plight of the poor, even in the midst of our welfare society.

The haphazard nature of local finance must also be placed in its social context. Rhode Island, more than any other colony and in marked contrast to the rest of New England, was nurtured on a tradition of individualism. This could easily be translated into an unwillingness to pay taxes. While we may praise it for the political and social independence it gave Rhode Islanders, we must be willing to recognize other aspects that may be regarded as less desirable today. People carving out their own way in an acquisitive world did not want to sacrifice financially for the good of others. In this sense, as in the change in the system of poor relief, the Rhode Island towns' behavior foreshadowed the nineteenth century. The nineteenth century was a world of competitive individuals striving for self-assertion, who wanted to keep the money they made. Individuals who could not compete either perished or were isolated in institutions. Eighteenth-century Rhode Island towns, in dealing with their two major problems, welfare and finance, moved very close to that world.

POLITICAL DIVISIONS

CONNECTICUT'S VILLAGES BECOME MATURE TOWNS: THE COMPLEXITY OF LOCAL INSTITUTIONS, 1676 TO 1776

The New England town plays a central role in accounts of the rise of American democracy. The *structure* of town government, however, remains little studied despite its fame. Most community studies of the past two decades concentrate on the personnel of the town and pay scant attention to the institutional milieu in which this personnel functioned. The political genius and beauty of town government in the eyes of its admirers derived from its structural simplicity—a simplicity so self-evident that detailed study seemed superfluous.

During the founding years of the New England colonies, this picture of simplicity corresponded to a semblance of reality. In the late seventeenth and throughout the eighteenth century, however, growth in the number of local officers and governing bodies and in the diversity of local practice turned the traditional view of town government into an anachronism. At times confusing to contemporaries, eighteenth-century town government equals and probably surpasses the complexity of government in today's New England towns.

Many of the institutions and positions created after the founding years embodied tensions within the towns and between the towns and the colony governments. Rival groups and impulses used various parts of the complex local structures as outlets for their views and as instruments for political action. The following chapter on the growth of local government in Connecticut argues that the proliferation of institutions reflected divisions within the towns but also helped mitigate some of the more harmful effects of those divisions.

According to the folk cultural view of American history, the town meeting was the only major governing body in the communities of colonial New England and was an eminently democratic institution. The men met, exchanged ideas, decided policy, and elected committees and officers. What could be more democratic? Professional historians, of course, have long pointed out the inadequacy of this view, specifically in its failure to deal with restrictions on voting, family dominance, the politics of deference, oligarchical officeholding, economic power, and other factors that influenced the meeting and its officers. While sophisticated in their perception of the complexity of the problem of town meeting democracy, however, these same historians are not as sophisticated about the character of town government.[1] The debate goes on at length about the nature of local power elites and social structures, but seldom are the institutions of local government described even briefly, let alone in their full complexity. Consequently, those who have not done research in local New England history have been entitled to assume that the town meeting was a simple governing body and the only significant one beneath the county level. Those working in the field know that local institutions were complex and included other significant bodies besides the town meeting, but they have not communicated this knowledge in any comprehensive fashion, probably because they themselves are not fully aware of how the various local units meshed and worked together.[2] It is the intent of this chapter to correct that deficiency with regard to one colony, Connecticut, over the hundred-year span before the American Revolution.

Town government in Connecticut was simple at the inception of the colony but steadily grew in complexity through the colonial period. At first, the town meeting with its officers was the only local governing body. The proprietors, who were the owners of the common land, and the society, which was the governing body of the church parish, were not distinctly separated from the town meeting. Generally, all adult white men were proprietors, and each town was coterminous with a parish. Hence, the town meeting performed duties which would later be administered by two separately functioning bodies—the proprietors and the society. The freeman, voters in colony-level elections, who would eventually constitute a fourth local self-governing body, had a collective existence apart from the town meeting, but their membership was controlled entirely by the central government, and they were therefore more an extension of the colony government than a local institution. The original form of local government was thus simple, and it was unified in the town meeting.

Beginning as early as the last quarter of the seventeenth century, this unity was broken in the older towns as the other three corporate bodies—proprietors, freemen, and ecclesiastical society—emerged as separate governing units. The differentiation of institutions was not planned by either the central government or the towns; rather, it resulted haphazardly from the growth of population within each town and from the increase in the number of towns.

PROPRIETORS

Nowhere was the unplanned character of institutional differentiation more apparent than in the roles the proprietors played in the towns that had been founded during the colony's first thirty-five years. Unlike the Massachusetts General Court, which organized and regulated town proprietors in the 1670s and 1680s, the General Court of Connecticut did not pass legislation dealing with the proprietors until 1723.[3] The proprietors' role in local government developed indigenously before that date. The proprietors began to separate from the town meetings because, as the towns grew in population, many inhabitants who were qualified to vote at a town meeting were not proprietors. The first recorded proprietors' meeting took place in Hartford in 1665.[4] There was, however, such confusion over who was and who was not a proprietor that the town finally declared that all inhabitants who paid town rates would be considered legal proprietors.[5] Hartford thus resolved its difficulty by making the membership of the town identical with that of the proprietors.

The proprietors' evolution in Middletown was more typical of the older towns. The first mention of them as a separate group appears in 1686, about thirty-five years after the town was settled. At that time the town meeting substituted the phrase, "the proprietors grant," for the usual "the town grants" in a land distribution. In 1696, the qualifying phrase, "the town meeting also a meeting of the proprietors," shows that, although one meeting acted for both, a need was felt to legitimize its functions by giving it both titles. In 1715 a Middletown town meeting listed the names of 176 men who were proprietors, a number half of the total of the eligible town meeting voters. Two years later a town meeting divided the proprietors into four geographic groups and gave each some authority in settling land problems, although major questions regarding land divisions were to be decided by all four groups together.[6] Even though divided, the proprietors still did not meet separately from the town meeting; each fourth would be polled during a town meeting for a proprietary decision relating to its section. Between 1717 and 1733 the town members would shift hats and deal with proprietary matters at the same meeting, prefacing the action by "the proprietors vote" or "the town votes," according to the nature of the business. In 1733 the town meeting ceased to act on proprietors' business, and thereafter separate proprietors' meetings were held and separate records maintained. Middletown still had a sizable parcel of undivided land, and the new proprietors met frequently in the 1730s to dispose of it. In 1734, for example, they met six times, while the town meeting met only twice. They elected a three-man proprietors' committee and a clerk in 1733. The next year, they expanded the committee to five men and elected a moderator. By 1740 the proprietors had disposed of almost all of Middletown's undivided lands, and in the 1740s they held only five meetings, all of which were one-item meetings either to deal with a specific problem or to elect an officer to replace one who had died. After 1750 the proprietors' meeting ceased to be a force in Middletown, although it continued in legal existence until 1822, when it dissolved itself.[7]

Norwich's and Farmington's proprietors evolved into separate bodies later than Middletown's. In Norwich, although the town meeting performed proprietary functions, not until 1717 did it feel the need to legitimize them by using the phrase, "the proprietors and inhabitants." In 1718 Norwich, like Middletown, divided its proprietors into four groups: East Side, West Side, Crotch of River, and Southwest.[8] However, Norwich's town meeting continued to perform proprietary functions until 1733, when the proprietors began to meet separately and to maintain their own records. Farmington started to separate its proprietors in 1727, when the town meeting appointed a committee to find out "who are ye proprietors of commons."[9] In 1733 this had apparently been ascertained, and the proprietors started meeting separately and keeping separate records. By 1736 the separate identities of the two groups were so clearly established that the town meeting records mention negotiations with the proprietors.[10] The Farmington proprietors, like those of Middletown, had a flurry of activity in the 1730s, meeting forty-two times from 1733 through 1739. By 1739 all but an inconsequential fraction of the lands had been distributed, and the proprietors did not meet again until 1746 and not thereafter until 1759. They dissolved themselves in 1786, when Bristol and Berlin were split off from Farmington.

The General Assembly gave little direction to the proprietors, though it was almost certainly responsible for the sudden and complete separation of town and proprietors everywhere in 1733. The assembly in 1723 had ordered the proprietors of each town to meet, but most towns ignored the order. In 1732 the assembly repeated this order and the towns, probably perceiving that the statute was meant to be enforced, all obeyed. The 1732 act also repeated and expanded a statute of 1727 that gave the proprietors the power to "make Rates to defray the necessary Charges" arising from their new responsibilities.[11] Most proprietors elected a clerk, a treasurer, a surveyor, and a proprietors' committee of three to seven members.[12] These elections, unlike those of the towns, were not annual; rather, the officers served either until they died or, though more rarely, until someone expressed dissatisfaction with their performance and asked for a new election.

A fundamental difference existed between the town proprietors of the seventeenth century and those of the eighteenth. In general, early seventeenth-century proprietors were residents who received their land free from the General Court, while those of the late seventeenth and early eighteenth centuries were speculators who bought the land from the assembly and frequently did not reside in the new towns.[13] The Narragansett War in 1675 divides the two periods. During the war a large tract of land east of the Connecticut River came into the possession of a small but influential number of speculators, who persuaded the assembly that the planting of towns would furnish an investment opportunity for private citizens as well as income for the colony.[14] In one example of proprietary speculation, 105,793 acres, obtained from Massachusetts after a border dispute, were sold in 1716 at auction by the assembly to William Pitkin, representing a group of investors.[15] These men surveyed the town site, built roads for it, and then resold the land to settlers for a profit.[16] In 1737, however, the assembly required every town proprietor to build a house on his land and fence at least six acres within two years, and these stipulations usually prevented absentee proprietors from owning land in a town after that period.[17]

There were two other major differences between the proprietors of early seventeenth-century towns and those of towns founded after

1675. The later communities differentiated town meetings and proprietary meetings from the outset. In addition, beginning with Lebanon in the 1690s, the later towns were settled in nonnucleated fashion, with most of the land parceled out early.[18] Seventeenth-century proprietors had divided their lands more slowly; some of them husbanded it over a hundred-year period. Among the younger towns, however, Kent divided 32,000 of its 50,000 acres within the first two years of its existence, and in Lebanon the proprietors distributed virtually all of the land by 1730.[19] When they divided the land, they let their powers go as well, so that in most of the eighteenth-century towns, proprietors were operationally defunct after twenty or thirty years, even though they were still important in older towns like Farmington, Norwich, and Middletown in the 1730s when these towns were almost one hundred years old. But even in the old towns most proprietors, carried along by the speculative mania of the 1730s, gave away their powers through land divisions.

FREEMEN

Because freemanship involved less complex duties and obligations, and required a less formal structure, than the proprietary, the development of the freemen as an organized body proceeded more uniformly. Connecticut, unlike Massachusetts, never required freemen to be church members but did require them to possess property of a certain value. The qualification was high at first—£30 in personal property—but was lowered to £10 estate in land in 1675.[20]

The early system, whereby prospective freemen had to travel to Hartford and be personally admitted by the General Court, was always burdensome for the individual seeking freemanship, and it became onerous for the court as the population of Connecticut grew. In 1678 the court met this problem by instructing the town selectmen to certify that each person applying to the court for freemanship met the property requirement and was of "honest, peaceable, and civil conversation."[21] Since the deputies would admit the applicant if they were satisfied with the selectmen's recommendation, control of the admission of freemen was thus shifted in practice to the town, although in theory it remained with the central government.[22] The laws regarding freemanship did not change until 1729, when the formal power of admission was transferred to the freemen of each town, owing to the administrative difficulty of central control.[23] In actuality, after this date the freemen usually delegated the admitting power to the selectmen, even though the selectmen were officers not of the freemen but of the town, which included the inhabitants as well. The selectmen met a few hours in advance of the freemen's meeting, examined oral applications for freemanship, and admitted those whom they found satisfactory. The assembly specified that the town clerk must record in writing the names of all new freemen.[24]

Until recently, historians commonly estimated that as few as 10 percent of the eligible adult white males were actually freemen.[25] It appears, however, that with the transfer of control over freemanship from the colony to the locality, the number of freemen increased. After 1729 in Farmington, Norwich, Lebanon, Kent, East Haddam, and East Guilford, 52, 47, 54, 51, 64, and 79 percent, respectively, of those eligible were admitted as freemen.[26] The cluster of the first four towns—differing in age, size, and location—at about 50 percent suggests that this was perhaps an average, even though East Haddam and East Guilford show that the percentage could go much higher. In all of these towns, however, at least 70 percent of the population could have qualified economically for freemanship, and admission after 1729 seemed almost effortless.[27] The actual figures were much lower undoubtedly because many men who lived a long distance from the meetinghouse did not normally attend meetings. The farther away a man lived, the less likely he was to be a freeman.[28] Connecticut towns were large geographically, and it was not unusual for an "outliving man" to have to walk ten or so miles over poor roads to attend a meeting—a formidable undertaking even in good weather.[29] Substantiating the thesis that many men did not think freemanship worth a tiring walk is the fact that admissions were always much higher in years of turmoil and controversy, when political interest might be aroused. From 1761 through 1765 Farmington admitted only twenty-six men, but forty in 1766, the year of the Stamp Act election.[30] Many of the qualified men who were not freemen were young men in their twenties who almost certainly would seek admission when political events touched them closely.

The freemen met twice a year—in the first week of April and of September. At each session they elected two deputies to the assembly. To emphasize that the freemen's meeting was legally distinct from the town meeting, the town meeting of Middletown addressed a petition to the Middletown freemen asking their deputies to act also as agents for the town. Similarly, Sharon's town meeting authorized the freemen's deputies to argue a case for Sharon at the next assembly.[31] In both instances, the deputies were not representatives of the town government specifically but of the freemen alone, and a special deputation of powers was required for them to act for the town.

At the September meeting each freeman could vote for up to twenty men as nominees collectively for governor, deputy governor, and assistants. The constable of each town tallied the votes and forwarded them to the colony secretary, who announced at the October session of the assembly the names of the top twenty vote-getters for the entire colony. At the April freemen's meeting each freeman could vote for one of these nominees as governor, one as deputy governor, and twelve as assistants. The results were announced at the May session of the assembly.[32] Many towns took advantage of the gathering of the freemen in April to hold a town meeting on "freemen's day," but to emphasize the separate character of the two meetings, the freemen's meeting was held in the morning and the town meeting in the afternoon.

SOCIETIES

Society government came into existence only when a town was divided into two or more parishes; in towns that had only one church the town meeting administered the parish. Societies increased markedly in the eighteenth century as parishes divided. In 1708, the year of the Saybrook Platform, there were forty-three parishes in thirty-three towns, but between 1708 and 1740, eighty-six new parishes were created while only thirty new towns were founded. Since the population of the colony increased 400 percent during that same period, the average number of inhabitants per parish rose from 380 to 760. By 1760, 187 parishes existed in seventy-one towns, and the population probably averaged 1,000 per parish. Only very small or very new towns had but one parish and therefore no society government, whereas large towns usually had five or six by the end of the colonial period.[33]

Until the 1720s societies were allowed to develop unstructured by central authority; thereafter, their functions were outlined by the assembly. Society voters had to be either freemen or full communicants of the church. A man might be a town voter but not a society voter. Societies were empowered by the assembly in 1728 to levy rates, choose officers, erect meetinghouses, hire ministers, and regulate society schools.[34] Law followed custom, for the societies were already performing all these functions. Beyond these broad delegations of powers, there were no specific instructions. The assembly, for instance, did not stipulate what officers should be elected or what particular duties they should have. In practice, most of the societies set up positions similar to some of those of the first towns. Once established, society government grew little, unlike the rapidly expanding government of the town meeting. Most societies elected a three-member governing board called the society committee, a clerk, a treasurer, two raters, and perhaps a three- or five-man school committee.[35] Although as early as the 1640s some town meetings chose a moderator, it was society government that regularized this practice.

Only the assembly could create a new society. It usually did so for one of two reasons. First, when one part of a town was geographically distant from the town center, and when that distant part acquired enough inhabitants to make a society viable, it might seek society status in order to bring neighborhood government and church services closer to home. Second, a society might become split in a dispute over doctrinal matters, the location of the meetinghouse, or the hiring of a new minister. If the split became irreconcilable, the minority might petition the assembly for separate society status.[36] Dissidents who sought a new society were usually opposed by the parent one, for old societies were reluctant to lose any sizable part of their tax base. In these cases the assembly would almost always appoint an ad hoc arbitration committee of three or four assistants and deputies. The location of a new meetinghouse was a common cause of dissension—even a distance of one or two miles could provoke bitter strife. Lebanon societies built eight meetinghouses in the eighteenth century; assembly arbitration was requested for six of them. Selecting a minister also caused frequent quarrels. Societies and candidates usually agreed that a majority vote for a new minister was not sufficient grounds for calling him to "settle among us." Unanimity was always striven for.[37]

Religious and political questions were closely intertwined in the functions of a society, since the issues the society dealt with—building a meetinghouse, hiring and paying a minister, running schools, and enforcing proper social conduct—while essentially political, were separated from religion only with difficulty. The distinction the colonists drew, however, was that the minister and church elders alone, as distinct from the society meeting, handled matters concerning doctrine, the covenant, and church membership and discipline. Ultimately, of course, the minister and elders could be replaced by action of a society meeting.[38]

Congregational localism assured the society a large measure of autonomy, although it was always subject to interference from the town and the assembly.[39] When societies did ask for arbitration or had it forced upon them from above, they might reject the result and defy the assembly as the Amity Society of New Haven did when it rejected the assembly's choice of a site for a new meetinghouse on the grounds that the assembly was prejudiced. The efforts of the assembly were of limited value in solving local problems unless the society cooperated. Guilford did not ask for arbitration of a controversy concerning the selection of a minister, and when the assembly appointed a committee, the society indignantly refused to acquiesce on the grounds that the assembly had no jurisdiction. The religious controversies of the 1740s not only shook the colony and splintered many societies but intensified societal autonomy. There is strong evidence, for instance, that the famous General Assembly law of 1742 that banned itinerant preachers was disobeyed in mass by the societies. The eighteenth-century movement in Connecticut toward a more pluralistic view of religion made central control of society affairs more difficult. One student of the subject believes that the victor in the religious disputes was "neither the New Lights nor the Old Lights but the local congregation, whose power was secured." Decisions from above were usually made only at the request of a society, and they were viewed "as merely advisory opinions" which could be accepted or rejected.[40]

TOWN MEETING

The town meeting in the mature towns elected officers, appointed committees, and ratified decisions made by the town officers. Usually it was not an active part of the decision-making process, but in almost every town at some point in the eighteenth century a controversy propelled the town meeting into action as the forum not only for airing the controversy but also for settling it. It was normal for a town to hold one, two, or three perfunctory meetings a year for a twenty-year period, then suddenly hold as many as eight significant meetings in a single year, and then return to its previous composure. Most new towns held frequent meetings, often as many as ten or twelve a year, but once the difficult task of setting up a town was accomplished, the meetings declined to three or fewer in normal years. Although the meeting usually chose not to involve itself in decision-making beyond electing officers, its frequent flurries of activity during controversies left no doubt where internal power ultimately lay.[41]

In most towns the only important meeting in a normal year was the one held in December to elect town officers. It often lasted two days and occasionally part of a third. If other meetings were held, they were often one-item meetings of short duration. Many towns held their second meeting on freemen's day in April to choose officers to replace any who had resigned, left town, or died. A third meeting was occasionally held, perhaps to appoint a special committee or to ratify some especially important decision by the selectmen. It was not rare for a town to hold only the December meeting; many towns went four or five consecutive years with only one meeting a year.

The temper of the town meeting depended on whether it was held under normal circumstances or had become politicized by local controversy. Under normal circumstances, lack of attendance was often a problem. The Hartford annual meeting of 1769 adjourned for a week after merely selecting a moderator who then declared attendance too low to conduct any further elections. Waterbury, plagued by poor turnouts at town meetings during the 1740s and frequently forced to adjourn for that reason, tried to solve its problem by starting the meeting at 10 a.m. instead of 9 a.m. In Sharon, where inhabitants frequently refused to attend meetings on cold winter days, meetings were postponed "considering the extremity of the weather and the fewness of the people," and "on account of the great coldness of the season." When the Norwich meeting of August 1715 voted on a previously unannounced issue, twenty-five votes constituted a majority. The attendance must have been less than fifty in a town that had at least 2,500 inhabitants. In a petition to the next meeting thirty-two men complained that the calling for this vote was a "surprise" and stated that while they normally did not attend meetings, they would have done so had they known the vote was to be taken.[42]

Meetings ranged from small quiet affairs with little debate to highly charged sessions almost impossible to control. In 1729, apparently in response to rowdy meetings, the assembly passed a law forbidding tumults and riotous behavior at them.[43] After one such meeting in Middletown the town voted that no one should "interrupt the meeting by disorderly speaking." In a 1709 election meeting in Farmington, a committee was named to "keep the youth in order during the meeting." Most communities recorded votes with the succinct expression, "the town votes," but occasionally they would preface this with "after much deliberation" or "after great discourse," indicating a more than usually heated debate. Middletown recorded tallies "by unanimous vote" often for periods as long as ten years and then would distinguish a rare vote as "by majority vote." During the 1720s and 1750s Ridgefield usually recorded votes as unanimous—"yea universally" one clerk wrote—but during the 1730s and 1740s the town had a long series of votes which were "by major vote," indication that town consensus, while desired, could break down for protracted periods. Voting on issues was frequently oral, but towns could go to great lengths to protect the anonymity of voters on sensitive questions. Norwich, in a secret ballot which was tailored so that even illiterates could vote, specified that marks on a ballot meant that a minister should be let go while a blank ballot meant that he should be kept.[44]

The election of town officers was the main business of the annual meeting after the founding years. Election procedures were never codified either by the General Assembly or by any town in its written records. From indirect and occasional evidence in the records we can surmise that procedures varied both from town to town and within towns. In 1712 Middletown proposed that the three selectmen be chosen "by nomination and then voting upon nomination." This was defeated, and instead the town voted by "papers." Five years later, Middletown chose officers by "nomination and by lifting the hand." The moderator instructed the meeting to "shout to nominate." Still a third method in Middletown was used for the election of selectmen in 1720. The voters queued up and each gave a name orally to the clerk, who declared a man elected when he had a majority of the meeting. Other towns employed this oral system, but if someone requested it the vote would be by "proxies" (written ballots). Although discussion of voting procedures was only occasionally recorded, and discussion of qualifications of candidates was never recorded, elections must have involved some debate. Election meetings lasted from nine or ten in the morning to four in the afternoon, and usually took at least two days.[45]

An election system known to have been utilized by several towns may have been widespread and could explain how the meeting handled the election of large numbers of officers. In 1765 the Farmington moderator told the selectmen "to bring in their nominations of town officers to the meeting *as usual*" (italics mine). The selectmen must have prepared a slate of officers in advance. The meeting could add or subtract nominations, but the consistency of Farmington's officeholding patterns supports the view that a small group of men constantly controlled them. The Newtown meeting voted that the "selectmen shall nominate the selectmen" for the following year, Ridgefield "disapproved of the nominations published," and Norwalk "brought in nominations"—all suggesting that a small group of men, usually the selectmen, nominated officeholders in advance. As further evidence supporting this hypothesis, elections were smooth and seldom contested after the fact. In five of seven towns examined— Fairfield, Hartford, Kent, Lebanon, and Middletown—there were no controverted elections during the eighteenth century. The other two towns in the sample, Farmington and Norwich, each had but one.[46]

In the founding years, when the town meeting was the sole local governing body, it elected at its annual meeting three or five selectmen who were the key executive officers, two constables who enforced the law, a clerk who kept the records, two ratemakers who assessed property for tax purposes, two surveyors of highways who maintained fences, and two or three packers and sealers who inspected local produce and certified its salable quality. These offices, though created by the General Assembly, were responses to practical local problems, and many towns elected an additional officer or two to answer other local needs.[47]

The three major officers of the early towns were the selectmen, the constables, and the clerk. The selectmen had both judicial and executive functions. They served as judges in the lowest courts in the colony, with jurisdiction over petty criminal and civil cases, provided that neither the suit nor the fine exceeded forty shillings. In a Puritan colony, where men and women were concerned with their neighbors' morals, the selectmen, along with the constables, had the obligation of ensuring that each person's conduct conformed to social expectations. The constable supervised the "watch" and provided for the town's security, collected the colony tax, and arrested those who broke colony or town laws. The clerk, while not often involved in major decision-making, was of crucial importance. He was ordered by

the assembly to "keep an entry of all grants, deeds of sale or mort-
gages of lands, and all marriages, births, deaths, and other writings
brought to you and deliver copies when required." To the joy of
historians, most clerks performed their duties well.[48]

As the towns grew in size and complexity, the kinds and numbers
of officers needed to administer their affairs increased correspondingly. Much of the increase resulted from additions to the numbers
of such officers as fenceviewers and surveyors of highways, required
by expansion of settlement to the outer geographic limits of the
towns. In addition, several new offices were created. Their functions
were outlined by town practice and by the assembly.

The position of grandjuryman offers an interesting example of the
evolution of a local office. In 1666 the General Court created four
counties—Fairfield, Hartford, New Haven, and New London—each of
which was a judicial unit presided over by a county court. In 1667
the General Court ordered each county court to appoint a "grand
jury of twelve able men at least" from among the towns. These grandjurymen were to meet once a year with their county court and
"make presentments of the breachers of any law."[49] They could also
at any time make a presentment of a breach of law to a local justice
of the peace, a magistrate appointed by the colony government. Most
towns had at least one justice, who assumed the local judicial duties
exercised earlier by the selectmen; large towns sometimes had two or
more. Over the next forty-five years the General Court added to the
grandjuryman's duties, making him a social constable in each town.
Grandjurymen were required to assist the selectmen and constables
in maintaining order and assuring high standards of moral conduct.
At sessions between 1667 and 1712, the assembly frequently en-
joined the selectmen, constables, and grandjurymen to watch out for
unacceptable social or moral behavior.[50] These injunctions were
issued in Connecticut at the same time that Massachusetts took similar action. This is, of course, the period in which historians have seen
the falling away of many people from strict Puritan codes of behavior. In 1679 Massachusetts created the local office of tithingman for
each town to help combat this moral decay.[51] Grandjurymen were
the Connecticut General Court's answer to the same problem. But
unlike the Massachusetts tithingman, who was elected by the town
meeting, the Connecticut grandjuryman was appointed by the county
court. In 1712, however, the assembly ordered all towns to elect at
least two grandjurymen a year, and at the December 1712 annual

meetings all the towns complied. Grandjurymen were thus incorporated into the operating structure of every town.[52]

Similarly, the office of tithingman, borrowed from Massachusetts, was created by the General Assembly in 1721 to combat moral laxity. Hartford began electing tithingmen in that year, and many towns did the same in 1722 and 1723. From then on, the assembly always included tithingmen when it issued annual pronouncements about social control to town officers. It instructed the tithingmen to "carefully inspect the behavior of all persons on the Sabbath or Lord's Day" and to make "due presentment of any prophanation." By 1732 all the towns were electing tithingmen, who assumed the same constabulary functions that grandjurymen had originally performed. Neither the tithingmen nor the grandjurymen were given additional duties until 1761, when they were instructed by the assembly to meet with the constables once a year in June to discuss provisions for the effective enforcement of local morality.[53] This was a last and anachronistic institutional attempt to preserve the old moral facade of the Puritan village.

The town offices of lister and rater, although originally created by the assembly, developed their functions in response to local needs, and in a variety of ways. In the early seventeenth century the towns were ordered to elect ratemakers who assessed all townspeople's wealth for tax purposes. Originally, the selectmen, not the ratemakers, set the tax rates. Between 1675 and 1700, however, ratemakers took over that function in most towns. In some they kept the name of ratemakers, and in others they were newly designated as "listers and raters" or "list makers and rate makers." Between 1700 and 1720 some towns began to elect separate "listers" and "raters," while others still kept the functions combined. These changes took place without any interference by the General Assembly. Although the assembly did finally decree in 1724 that each town must elect between four and nine listers,[54] the towns still took eclectic approaches to the creation of financial officers. A few towns elected financial auditors, such as the inspectors of Hartford and the auditors of Middletown, to whom the listers and raters were directed to report.[55]

The offices of moderator and treasurer were both shaped more by local needs than by enactments of the General Assembly. In the early years of the seventeenth century a selectman performed the functions of each position. Gradually, with no prodding by the legislature, the towns began to elect treasurers. Hartford chose its first treasurer in

1706, and by 1749, when Fairfield elected its first, the practice had become general. The moderator's office evolved similarly. In the founding years most towns did not designate a moderator, although Windsor did so as early as 1642. Instead, one of the selectmen usually presided over the meeting. Between 1680 and 1720, however, virtually every town began electing moderators, who might or might not be selectmen. Practice varied because the central government never prescribed rules concerning moderators. For instance, while in most towns the moderator was elected for a single meeting, Fairfield named its moderator to serve for a number of meetings in a year. Theoretically, the moderator was not presiding over two meetings but over two parts of an adjourned meeting. However, the two sessions were often months apart and may have considered totally different business. Middletown elected its first moderator in 1708, stopped electing the officer in 1712, and started again in 1720. Derby elected one man to serve continually as moderator during the town's pleasure.[56]

As grandjurymen, tithingmen, raters and listers, moderators, and treasurers were added to the roster of town officers, the number grew to sometimes staggering proportions, further increased by the addition of branders, key keepers, rate collectors, and sealers. Not only were new officers added, but each multiple office had its numbers expanded. Towns averaged fifty to sixty officers in 1725, sixty to seventy in 1750, and seventy-five to ninety in 1776. Two separate phenomena were probably at work in this expansion: larger towns required larger administrations, and increased population produced more aspirants for office. Farmington, in what must have been an attempt to involve as many men as possible in town government, elected 206 in 1776. These included, in addition to the clerk and the treasurer, seven selectmen, twenty-two grandjurymen, twenty-two listers, ten constables, twenty-five tithingmen, fifty surveyors of highways, seven leather sealers, seven weight sealers, nine measure sealers, sixteen fenceviewers, eight key keepers, seven branders, nine collectors for rates, one packer, and four ratemakers.[57] It should be noted, however, that Farmington had the largest square mileage of any Connecticut town, and with 6,069 inhabitants it was the third most populous town in the 1774 census.

It was clearly growth that caused the proliferation of local deliberative bodies and their offices. The proprietors came into existence as a separate group as a town's population grew to include many nonproprietors. The societies were constituted because the growth of both population and divergent religious opinions created a need to divide parishes. The method of admitting new freemen was decentralized because the increase in size and number of towns precluded a central admission policy. It was necessary to have many town meeting officers—grandjurymen, tithingmen, listers, raters, moderators, and treasurers—because the growth in population and the diffusion from a nucleated center to outlying farmsteads made it impossible for the selectmen personally to perform all of these functions. Other town officers, such as surveyors of highways and fenceviewers, became much more numerous because expansion to the outer edges of the towns placed new demands upon the services the towns provided.

As local government grew, the selectmen exercised increased authority. The assembly passed more and more general enabling acts delegating greater discretionary powers to the selectmen. As noted above, in 1690 the selectmen were given supervisory power over all other town officers and were told "to take cognizance of such as do neglect the duties of surveyor, hayward, fenceviewer," and so forth. In 1703 the assembly passed an act providing the selectmen with broad military power "to order what houses shall be fortified and what they do order shall be done forthwith." In 1708 they were delegated the extremely important power to levy a tax whenever the town's finances required it. An act of 1719 gave the selectmen virtually carte blanche power over the administration of local welfare. An unusual grant of authority in 1715 permitted them to reduce or eliminate an individual's colony rate if, in their judgment, it constituted a hardship. Acts of the assembly passed in 1775 and 1776 enhanced the ability of the selectmen to deal with the problems of civil strife. They could issue warrants against suspected loyalists and confiscate the estate of anyone deemed a partisan of Britain. All persons who traveled between towns had to carry letters from their selectmen. Charles Grant's study of Kent led him to conclude that much of the local war effort in that town was directed by the selectmen. This was the case throughout the new state and is, of course, hardly surprising. In most emergencies or crisis situations, people rely on executive power rather than group deliberation. Selectmen could provide quicker decisions than town meetings could.[58]

The authority of the selectmen was expanded not only by enabling acts from above but also by delegations from the town meeting. When Hartford elected new officers in 1706, the meeting directed them to report to the selectmen. In Farmington in 1708 the meeting gave the selectmen total control of town finances in a sweeping delegation of power and later empowered them to act as the town's agents in such external matters as relations with the assembly or with other towns. The Norwalk meeting in 1702 and again in 1704 put its weight behind the selectmen in all their decisions between meetings. As we have seen, in several towns, perhaps in most, the selectmen nominated all town officers, and in some they prepared an agenda for the town meeting. In Norwich, in the 1740s and 1750s, the many problems for which the town usually named ad hoc committees were turned over to the selectmen, and the number of such committees steadily declined.[59] Selectmen, although officers only of the town meeting, became involved in the affairs of the proprietors, the freemen, and the societies. They were the institutional factor that integrated all of the complex local structures and made them work. The assembly in 1713 gave the selectmen the right to judge land disputes; they had practical control over the admission of freemen, and they frequently stepped into society affairs when societies became embroiled in controversies.[60] Although the three other local deliberative bodies were clearly differentiated from the town meeting, the selectmen nevertheless exercise influence over them and kept them *a part of* town government, not *apart from* it.

Other factors also served to integrate the elements of local government. Since the selectmen were the creatures of the town meeting and the meeting became a vital forum during controversies, it could also bind the structure together. Moreover, many persons were members of all four different organizations in a single town, and solutions to problems must often have been hammered out by the same men in four different forums. In most towns many large families were knit together in kinship networks that provided great cohesion. Nor should the widespread practice of multiple officeholding be overlooked. Frequently, a single individual held proprietary, society, and town offices simultaneously, and the freemen's deputies invariably held other local offices as well.[61] Leadership was indivisible, and leaders were expected to serve the public good in all the bodies of local government. All of these factors helped the selectmen to ensure that the meetings and offices that proliferated to meet the needs of rapidly growing towns did not result in fragmented local governments that might well have frustrated efforts to meet those needs.

CONCLUSION

The effects of the differentiation of local government on the townspeople and on town politics are not the concern of this inquiry. It may be, however, that institutional differentiation militated against other trends in the society of eighteenth-century Connecticut. From recent quantitative and demographic work on New England, a picture is emerging of increasing social stratification, leading to the supposition that townspeople were becoming progressively alienated. Town populations grew; land became critically scarce; wealthy families grew in prestige and power, while younger sons of other families were forced to leave town to seek their future; and major officeholding patterns became more oligarchical.[62] All of these factors are indicative of a stratifying society with declining opportunities for most people. The ideological and political trends of the eighteenth century, however, led men to have higher expectations of participation in public life.[63] While demographic factors weighed heavily against increased involvement in decision-making, institutional differentiation probably worked in the opposite direction. The expansion in the number of officers elected in each town, the growth of neighborhood government in the form of societies, and the increased openness of freemanship all meant more opportunities for involvement in public affairs. It is true that the transfer of powers over land from the town meeting to the proprietors resulted in a narrowing of the political arena, since the proprietors were a smaller, more select group. This, however, ceased to be a factor in all but the newest towns after the 1740s when the common lands were all divided. Hence, the only institutional factor contributing to the closing of the polity in the late colonial towns was the low level of activity of the town meeting and the corresponding enhancement of the functions and authority of the selectmen. Yet it should be remembered that despite the important increase in the selectmen's executive powers, the relationship between them and the town meeting was much the same as that between the seventeenth-century minister and congregation described by Samuel Stone: "a speaking *Aristocracy* in the face of a silent *Democracy*."[64] And, although content in normal times to allow the selectmen to be the speaking aristocracy, the "silent democracy" made its voice heard whenever an issue politicized it. When this potential involvement is added to the growth in local offices, neighborhood governments, and freemanship, one must conclude that the institutional arrangements of local government on the eve of the Revolution were as much in agreement with the growth of participatory ideology as they were with the contrary demographic trends.

Five

Democracy and Oligarchy in Connecticut Towns: General Assembly Officeholding, 1701 to 1790

Since the early twentieth century when the work of the progressive generation challenged whig notions of colonial democracy, historians have been transfixed by the relationship between power and class. A vigorous reassertion of the whig view in the post World War II period gave new life to the debate. The basic issues addressed by the debaters revolve around the question: did a small, upper-class, interconnected elite dominate colonial government? The answer is crucial to an understanding of the Revolution.

No answer, however, will ever be as simple as the question. As historians probe the relationship between power and class they find it a matter of intense complexity. Differing regions, levels of government, and types of communities have distinctive political patterns none of which permit short, simple descriptions. The research of the present generation of social historians has resolved no basic issues, but it has refined them considerably.

Much of the recent work analyzes officeholding patterns quantitatively in order to test generalizations arrived at by traditional historical methodologies. To argue that propositions can be "proven" or "disproven" by quantitative testing overstates its power. Nevertheless, some generalizations are amenable to some degree of empirical verification. The following chapter evaluates some long-standing beliefs about elitism in Connecticut through an analysis of officeholding patterns in the General Assembly between 1700 and 1790.

No one knows where and when the phrase "Land of steady habits" was first applied to colonial Connecticut, but Connecticut's first comprehensive historian, Benjamin Trumbull, writing in the late eighteenth century, commented that the colony's "sobriety ... peaceableness, good order . . . and respectability" could all serve as lessons in how man should live.[1] The deans of colonial history in the first half of the twentieth century echoed this sentiment and believed that it was reflected in the officeholding patterns of the colony, where "almost invariably the incumbent officeholders were renominated and normally ... reelected." The evidence usually cited for this propensity to "continue in office those who were already there" was the long terms of the governor, the deputy governor, and most importantly the assistants' council which was composed of 12 men elected at large in the colony, who served as the governor's closest advisers and the upper house of the legislature.[2] Working from this evidence, really scant when one considers the number of other major officeholders elected in the colony, historians long assumed a similar pattern permeated the entire officeholding structure of the colony.[3]

In 1955, Robert Brown's monumental study of Massachusetts challenged similar assumptions about that colony, and implicitly questioned the oligarchic nature of colonial Connecticut as well.[4] Other historians, goaded into responding to and empirically testing a fresh viewpoint, then reexamined the elections of Connecticut's assistants and found that institutional election gimmicks may well have been the reasons for the fabled steadiness.[5] Coupled with this doubt about the steady, oligarchic nature of Connecticut officeholding, a series of political, intellectual, social, and economic studies of the colony depicted an unsteady climate that would not appear conducive to the continual reelection of incumbents.[6]

Amidst these intellectual currents, historians in the 1960s and 1970s began reexamining officeholding in colonial Connecticut. Most of these new studies take the form of case studies of one or a few towns.[7] This method, while valuable and revealing, has severe limits, as the historians practicing it well know and are themselves careful to acknowledge. Generalizing about Connecticut society or New England society from the evidence of a few towns cannot be done in more than a suggestive manner, particularly when historians now realize that there were different types of towns with differing social, economic, and political structures and norms.[8]

Besides the problem of providing one answer or example for many types of towns, additional difficulties surround recent work. Most studies treat the pre-Revolutionary eighteenth century as a static period in terms of structure without dealing with the probability that it was changing within this period.[9] If historians do look for change, they look for it in the immediate Revolutionary period to see if the Revolution "democratized" or merely continued the old structure.[10] Researchers compare the 1760s, 1770s, and 1780s but ignore the long-range perspective of comparing the 1780s with earlier eighteenth-century society. Also underemphasized is the evidence that the balance between oligarchic and democratic patterns differs among even different major policy-making offices. What was true for the deputies to the General Assembly may not be true for town select-men, and what was true for selectmen may not be true for town meeting moderators or town clerks.

Hence when one probes beneath the well-worn outlines of the debate touched off by Brown and uses officeholding as the evidence for the probe, there emerges a labyrinth of complicated problems that require sophisticated methodologies. The present inquiry analyzes the officeholding patterns of one type of Connecticut officeholder—the deputy to the General Assembly, who was the most important officeholder elected entirely by the towns—for the period 1701–1790 in all of the Connecticut towns that elected deputies for a period long enough to enable effective analysis.

METHODOLOGY

This chapter will examine first the overall pattern of deputy office-holding in the aggregate between 1701 and 1780, then the changes that occurred in the overall pattern between 1701 and 1790, and finally differences in the patterns between towns of differing locale, age, size, and function.[11] Section one will attempt to deal with the old chestnut of oligarchic versus democratic patterns; section two will examine whether the degree of oligarchy increased, decreased, or fluctuated as the eighteenth century progressed; and section three will discuss how Connecticut town variables affected the degree of oligarchy.

The overall pattern presents the most difficulty because historians do not agree what constitutes an oligarchic or democratic system. To one historian, averages of six terms per officeholder and turnover rates of 50 percent may be indicative of a closed restrictive system, while another may feel this reveals an open system of opportunity for most. This chapter does not pretend to have a definition of oligarchy that everyone will accept, but it will describe statistically the dimensions of the overall pattern of officeholding and then label these dimensions "the degree of oligarchy." If one prefers, the term "the degree of democracy" could be substituted without a sacrifice in meaning. It does appear to this author that the opportunity for deputy officeholding was quite restricted, but that is a subjective value judgment and all officeholding systems are somewhat restrictive. While the vast majority of colonial Connecticut men could never reasonably hope to serve in the General Assembly, neither can the vast majority of modern Americans reasonably hope to serve in a modern state legislature. The latter two parts present more objective conclusions because they are comparing relative degrees of oligarchy (or democracy) over time and between types of towns. For example town type A was more oligarchic than town Type B for deputy officeholding and time Y was more oligarchic than time Z.

Among historians no consensus of the best measuring models for officeholding analyses will probably ever exist, but the following measures will be used because they readily lend themselves to the data presented here and to the intellectual questions raised by it.

(A) Turnover Rates: A turnover rate is the percentage of office-holders not reelected in any given election. Hence, a turnover rate of 100 percent would mean that no incumbent deputies were reelected and one of 0 percent would mean that all were reelected. Turnover rates will be graphed yearly, compared by decades, and compared by historically significant periods such as those surrounding the Revolutionary War.

(B) Average Terms Per Officeholder: Average terms will be measured for the overall period 1701–1780, for four twenty-year periods between these dates, and for the ten years preceding and the ten years succeeding independence.

(C) Dominance Factors: In each town the largest number of terms served by one individual, and the percentage of all terms served by the leading five individuals, and by one family, three families, and five families between 1701 and 1780 will be measured.[12]

At the outset, a word of caution on my use of language may eliminate a potential source of confusion. When I use the terms "significantly higher" and "significantly lower" to describe changes in percentages, I am using them in a subjective manner reflecting my judgments as an historian and not reflecting any mathematical or statistical test. No statistical tests exist that could make these judgments. They are a measure of one's sense of normal rates of change.

OVERALL PATTERNS

Each town in Connecticut could elect two deputies to the General Assembly twice a year in April and September on "freeman's day." While almost all of the well-established towns did this and hence had a total of four representatives' terms per year, some of the newer or poorer towns would occasionally send only one deputy in order to cut expenses. Also, in their first ten years of existence some towns would send no deputy at all, or send them sporadically. Thus, while there were eighty-four towns in the new state of 1780, only sixty-one of them had consistently elected deputies to the assembly by 1760 and are included in the data used to obtain the overall average, overall turnover, and average of most terms served by each town's leading deputy officeholder. Because individual and family dominance is being measured as a percentage of the entire eighty-year period, only the thirty-four towns that were electing deputies by 1700 are included in these later figures. Neither the sixty-one towns nor the thirty-four towns are a sample; they are the entire universe of Connecticut towns capable of being measured without distortion.

The overall figures derived from this analysis for the entire period persuade this author that even without a precise, objective definition, a general consensus will emerge behind an oligarchic picture of a few men serving most of the terms, with these few men often coming from the same families. The average number of terms per officeholder, 7.3, includes a range of averages as high as 10.3 in Hartford and as low as 4.3 in Norwalk. Similarly, the average of the most number of terms served by the leading deputy in each town, forty-one, included tenures as long as the seventy-three terms and sixty-nine terms served by Jonathan Hoyt of Stamford and John Fowler of Milford, but in no town did the figure go lower than the seventeen terms served by Suffield's leading officeholder, William King. The average turnover rate, a moderate 44 percent, reveals that, for deputies serving multiple terms, the pattern was to have their terms be interrupted rather than consecutive. Some men, like Isaac Dickerman of New Haven, did serve fifty-three consecutive terms, but more often the pattern for men serving more than four or five years was not a consecutive one. Thus, while a small oligarchy may have dominated the deputation from each town, some newness was injected in each assembly by the practice of rotation among the few.

When one looks at the dominance of a few individuals and families over the eighty-year period, the figures also seem exceptionally high. For each town five men held nearly one-half of all deputies' terms for the eighty years, while one family held nearly one-fourth, three families nearly one-half, and five families nearly two-thirds. What to call the patterns these figures represent may be open to question, but I suggest: family-dominated oligarchy.[13]

Massachusetts, which elected deputies annually as compared with Connecticut's semiannual elections, had an almost identical turnover rate of 43 percent, compared to Connecticut's 44 percent.[14] Of course since Connecticut was turning over its 44 percent twice as often as Massachusetts, one could conclude that the Connecticut Assembly was less oligarchic and always had more fresh blood in it. However, a limited sample of six towns in Massachusetts between 1700 and 1780 reveals that the longest serving deputies from each of these towns averaged approximately the same years in the Massachusetts Assembly, twenty, as the longest serving deputies from Connecticut towns did in the Connecticut Assembly (forty-one terms divided by two, or 20.5 years). This would suggest that facing elections twice as often as their Massachusetts counterparts did not stop Connecticut men from amassing as many years of service in the assembly. In a sample of fifteen years drawn from the 1730s, 1760s, and 1780s, Rhode Island, with annual elections like those in Massachusetts, had a significantly higher turnover rate, 53 percent, than either of the old Puritan colonies, and hence can be called less oligarchic.

CHANGES IN THE OVERALL PATTERN

Decadal averages of turnover rates reveal that the rates fluctuated between 1701 and 1790 but declined slightly until independence. The high turnover rates of 47, 49, 47, and 48 percent occur respectively in 1701–1710, 1711–1720, 1721–1730, and 1781–1790. When the turnover rates for the entire assembly are graphed by the year, rather than by the decade, the periods of fluctuation become more precise. The rates were highest between 1702 and 1712, declined in 1713 and maintained this level through 1743, declined more in 1744 and then shot up sharply in the years 1754 through 1759, declined to the lowest rate for a period from 1760 through 1773, shot up sharply again from 1774 until 1784, and then declined from 1784 to 1790 to approximately the same rate as in the period 1713 through 1743. The low point of the turnover rates occurred from the end of 1743 through the elections of 1773 with the exception of the years 1754 through 1759.

Historians of Connecticut know that the 30-year period stretching from the beginning of the Great Awakening debates to the eve of the Revolution was the most controversial era in Connecticut's history and involved the General Assembly in more heated and rancorous debates than ever before.[15] The Great Awakening and the pre-Revolutionary struggles blended together as the issues of politics and religion blended together and the colony had its stormiest and unsteadiest years. Yet these stormy years clearly correspond with the lowest turnover in membership that Connecticut's Assembly knew in the eighteenth century. The exceptional six-year period 1754–1759 when there was the highest turnover rate since 1712 has to be explained, but if one looks at the three highest turnover periods of the century—those six years, 1702–1712, and 1774–1782—all three periods were during the actual military prosecution of a war.[16] Queen Anne's War, the Seven Years War, and the Revolutionary War all accompanied unusual discontinuity and a high turnover, while fiery debates over religion and society accompanied unusual continuity and low turnover. Substantiating this conclusion, the three periods, 1766–1774, the years of the pre-Revolutionary debates; 1775–1782, the military years of the Revolution; and 1783–1790, the first seven years after the hostilities ceased, have turnover rates of 37.3 percent, 50.9 percent, and 41.6 percent respectively. The election of 1766, acknowledged by contemporary Connecticut citizens and by historians as the most heated election in the colony's history, had the fifth lowest turnover rate of the 90 years.

The high turnover rates during years of military involvement accord well with expectations because so many of the men who normally sat in the assembly were militia officers. However, what can explain the seeming paradox that during the time the colony was involved in its bitterest internal strife, which from all qualitative evidence politicized it beyond any other experience, and resulted in elections fought viciously in the taverns, public meetinghouses, and pamphlet press, the assembly elections reflect the greatest continuity of the century? One might plausibly suggest that the freemen of each town considered the debates in the assembly of such importance that they wanted the accumulated wisdom of the incumbent deputies. Another, equally plausible explanation is that when men were fighting desperately to unseat incumbents, the incumbents were fighting as desperately and more successfully to stay in office. The rising intensity of political controversy did not result in sweeping candidates out of office but resulted instead in harder fought elections in which an increasing proportion of incumbents won. The extreme continuity in time of internal stress may also show both a conscious and subconscious attempt to maintain the harmony of community that was so prized in Connecticut by relying on established and respected leaders.[17] Another possibility was that towns became internally divided between two recognizable factions with one having a clear majority that mitigated against open elections where personalities could be issues. Regardless of reason, the decline of turnover rates cannot be denied. The politicization of the colony during these heated years did not result in bringing a large percentage of new blood into the assembly.

Given the exceptionally low turnover rates of the pre-Revolutionary years, it would be misleading to analyze changes made by the Revolution in leadership patterns of society solely by examining the years before and after independence.[18] If one did examine the ten years immediately preceding independence and the ten years immediately after, one would have to draw the conclusion that the Revolution democratized the assembly considerably. Nor would just the turnover rate suggest this. Of sixty-two towns consistently sending deputies to the assembly, thirty-eight had significantly lower average numbers of terms per deputy in the ten years after independence than before, twenty had no change, and only four had a higher average after independence than before. A historian basing his view on the immediate Revolutionary struggles would be excited by the overwhelming proof of democratizing change; however, when placed in the larger perspective, it is clear that the change is only indicative of the extremely oligarchic nature of the assembly accompanying the Great Awakening debates, and the discontinuity accompanying the exigencies of fighting a war. Assembly officeholding patterns after 1783 were remarkably consistent with century-long trends, and showed no lasting changes wrought by the Revolutionary experience. Comparing averages of terms per deputy for all towns for the four twenty-year blocks between 1700 and 1780 confirms the picture of oligarchic rates that fluctuated greatly. The high averages are 6.4 and

5.9 terms per deputy in 1721-40 and 1741-1760 and the low rates are precisely the same—5.5 terms per deputy—in 1701-1720 and 1761-1780. The same average tenure at the beginning and end of the eighty years again argues that while heated debates and military exigencies caused fluctuations in the officeholding patterns of the assembly during the eighty years, the assembly's overall officeholding pattern was similar in 1790 to what it was in 1700. The closeness of the turnover rates of 47 percent in 1701-1710 and 48 percent in 1781-90 reinforces this conclusion. The entire period 1721-40 which was untouched by war, had the highest terms-per-deputy averages and hence might be called the most oligarchic period between 1700 and 1790. However, one would assume that this was the normal noncrisis rate for the assembly and that, had either extreme politicization or military emergency occurred during this time, it would have affected the assembly in the same way as at other times.

VARIATIONS AMONG TYPES OF TOWNS

The crucial variables for analyzing the relationship of town typologies to officeholding patterns are the geographic location, age, size, and in one instance, economic function of Connecticut's many communities.

Historians have long realized that the Connecticut River separated the colony into two politically hostile camps during the eighteenth century. While scholars often refer to the disputants of eighteenth-century Connecticut by the nineteenth century terminology of "radicals" and "conservatives," the participants often used the phrases "eastern men" and "western men." The many towns that bordered the river itself were caught between the two parties, and, though no contemporary referred to their residents as "river men," they were neither East nor West and cannot accurately be placed in either category. In this text the river towns will form a third distinct geographic unit to be compared along with the towns in the East and the West.

It is becoming increasingly apparent to demographic historians how important the age of a colonial town was to its pattern of social stratification, which of course was in turn crucial to officeholding patterns.[19] Nothing clearly demarcates early Connecticut towns from later ones and perhaps many dates would suffice, but 1675 is the one chosen here. Between 1636 and 1675, the twenty-four towns founded comprise the first generation of towns and will be designated "old towns" in this study. Many of the first settlers of the towns in the 1630s and 1640s were still alive in 1675. Historians now sometimes describe colonial towns by the number of generations they have produced, and the old towns of New England usually had leaders from the fourth generation in power during the Revolutionary years. This was true for towns founded up to 1675 but not for many founded after that. Eleven new towns founded between 1675 and 1700 form an easily identifiable group which will be called "late seventeenth-century towns." In the eighteenth century, towns were created at irregular intervals; they will be designated "new towns" and will be measured whenever the data make it possible, although this generally precludes towns founded after 1735.

Connecticut towns, large in population by New England standards because of the General Assembly's unwillingness to allow outlying parts of existing towns to become new towns as they did in Massachusetts, can conveniently be divided into three sizes: large, medium, and small.[20] Drawing the dividing lines may be somewhat arbitrary but few colonial contemporaries would quarrel with the assertion that the 13 towns with populations of over 4,000 in the census of 1774 clearly stand out as the largest and most important group of towns in the colony. The remaining 21 towns founded in the seventeenth century range from Lebanon's 3,960 to Durham's 1,076 in the same census. Splitting the difference is not always the best measure for determining relative size, but generally the towns under 2,500 were the towns that seldom played a leading role in colonial affairs and seem to have been considered small places. Few, if any, assistants to the governor, for example, came from towns under 2,500. Hence, they will be designated as small, while those between 2,500 and 4,000 will be designated as medium. Of the towns founded after 1700, none were above 4,000 and only two were above 2,500. Almost all eighteenth-century towns that consistently elected deputies had populations between 1,000 and 2,500.

Generally towns of the same size had common economic functions. Thus towns under 2,500 were usually farming communities with little other economic activity, and towns between 2,500 and 4,000 were primarily engaged in agriculture but also had a significant trading and mercantile role. The towns over 4,000, however, would have to be divided between those like Farmington, which were like the medium towns and primarily engaged in agriculture along with some significant mercantile activity, and the five large towns, Hartford,

Middletown, New Haven, New London, and Norwich, which had the clear outlines of urban centers. Of course, in a basically agrarian society, even these five mercantile centers contained their segment of farmers. Nevertheless, their economy clearly made them a type of town distinct from the other large towns, and they will have to be analyzed in yet a fourth separate category. They will be designated "urban" towns as distinct from the other towns with over 4,000 persons, which will be designated simply "large" towns.

Between 1701 and 1780, towns that were settled early, had western or river locations, or had small populations showed a propensity toward the highest family dominance of officeholding, while towns that were settled later, had an eastern location, or had large urban populations all showed the lowest family dominance. Medium or large towns did not differ in family dominance and fell at a midway point between the small and the urban towns. The five leading families held 69.4 percent of all deputy offices in the small towns, 66.4 percent and 65.5 percent in the medium and large, and 60 percent in the urban ones. The same ratios prevailed for three-family and one-family dominance. The highest dominance of five families, 87 percent in the small town of Glastonbury, contrasts sharply with the lowest dominance, 48 percent in the urban center, New London. The western and river towns with five-family dominance figures of 68.7 percent and 68.4 percent rank significantly higher than the 58.1 percent of the eastern towns. At first old towns and late seventeenth-century towns seem to have equal five-family dominance percentages of 65.8 percent, but this figure is distorted because all of the urban towns with their low percentages were old towns. When only small towns were compared, the old towns had a significantly higher rate, 73.8 percent, than the 66.0 percent of the late seventeenth-century towns. When large towns were similarly removed from the groupings, the West had a higher five-family dominance figure, 70.0 percent, than the East's 58.7 percent. Measuring the dominance of the five leading individuals, the geographic and age factors acted in the same way as in family dominance but the size factor did not. Small towns still had the highest dominance figures, but large towns had the lowest individual dominance instead of the urban towns.

All of the foregoing accords well with our present knowledge of the social structure of colonial New England. It should surprise few to learn that the more socially stratified old towns assigned more importance to family connections in officeholding than newer ones.

Nor should it surprise Connecticut historians that the conservative West and powerful River Valley should have had a significantly higher family dominance of officeholding than the radical East. That the urban towns should have the least family dominance undoubtedly reflects the fact that many rich and powerful families lived in each of them and were too numerous for a small clique to dominate the officeholding structure.

Perhaps historians will be surprised only by the conclusion that Connecticut's small towns had a higher rate of family dominance than the large ones. Recent work drawing on evidence from throughout New England has suggested that small towns had a more egalitarian officeholding pattern with less family dominance than any other type of town.[21] However, while Connecticut was included in this generalization, most of the evidence for it came from other colonies and much of it came from small towns settled during the eighteenth century. Extended family units and hence family oligarchies did not have time to build up in eighteenth-century towns, most of which were small, but seventeenth-century small towns had demonstrably more family dominance in the town's most important office than any other size towns. The factor that would lead eighteenth-century small towns to be less family dominated was their newness, not their smallness. Undoubtedly three to five families in the old towns distinguished themselves with the attributes colonial men looked for in leaders—longevity in the town, education, wealth, and ability—and did not face the competition for distinction which was somewhat more prevalent in medium and large towns and much more prevalent in urban ones. Of course, the five leading families of small towns comprised a much larger percentage of the town's population than the five leading families in other towns. It is also understandable why, if families were least dominant in urban towns, it does not follow that selected individuals would also be least dominant. Major leaders with exceptional wealth, power, and ability emerged in the urban towns, and, while they did successfully transfer much of this luster to their children, they were never able to transfer as much as the exceptional man in other towns.[22] The exceptional urban families constituted a much smaller percentage of the immediate population and the population contained a higher proportion of leadership potential. Urban dwellers may also have had a different set of intellectual assumptions and a different psychology about elections than nonurban populations.

When oligarchy rates are measured by average terms per deputy for the entire period 1701–1780, the factor of a river location inclined a town to be higher than average, a western location to be average, and an eastern location below average. The river, the western, and the eastern town averaged 8.7, 7.2, and 6.7 terms per deputy. Old towns settled before 1675 averaged 7.6 terms per deputy compared to the 7.3 of late seventeenth-century towns. This latter difference for the two different settling periods of the seventeenth century was not very great and indicates that settlement date was not a major factor for oligarchy as measured by average term rates. Reinforcing this conclusion, towns founded between 1700 and 1735 had as high an average per deputy as towns founded in the seventeenth century. Hence, while early settlement inclined a town toward high rates of family dominance, it did not incline it necessarily to a more oligarchic officeholding pattern when the oligarchy rate is measured by a different method. Indeed, the difference between old and late seventeenth-century towns of 7.6 and 7.3 can be explained by the factor of size better than the factor of settlement, since the old towns contained the five urban towns which all had much higher averages. Size factors also affected towns differently in average term rates than in family dominance. The least family-dominated towns, the urban ones, had the highest rate of 8.2 terms per deputy, compared to rates of 7.6 for both the small and medium towns and 6.8 for the large towns. It was not factors such as geography or founding dates that made the urban towns lead the large towns in averages by this wide margin; both groups drew evenly from the River Valley, the West, and the East, and all but one of both groups were founded prior to 1675. Small towns with the highest rates of family dominance had only average oligarchy rates when measured by average terms in office.

Oligarchy as measured for town types by turnover rates conforms totally to the picture formed from average term measurement. While 44 percent was the average turnover rate for the entire period 1701–1790, the river towns had the least turnover, 39 percent, while the eastern towns had the most, 52 percent, and the western ones had the average, 44 percent. When size factors were measured, the small and medium towns had approximately the average, with 43 percent and 45 percent, while the urban ones had the lowest, 37 percent, and the large towns had 57 percent. The age of towns did not affect their turnover of deputies. The same size towns drawn from all three locations, the East, West, and River Valley, but from different time periods had the same turnover rates.

The best single method of measuring changes in oligarchy indices for types of towns over the period 1701–1780 is to compare the average terms per deputy for the initial 20-year period 1701–1720 to those for the final period 1761–1780. As we have seen, the averages for all towns were precisely the same for these two periods but this disguises major changes occurring in some types of towns. No significant change occurred in the way geography affected average terms. However, when size factors were measured, deputies both from urban and large towns increased their tenure dramatically in the Revolutionary years, from 5.6 and 4.4 in 1701–20 to 7.0 and 5.9 in 1761–80. Correspondingly, tenure in medium towns declined slightly from 5.8 to 5.4, and in small towns declined sharply from 6.0 to 5.1. At first it appeared that old seventeenth-century towns increased their oligarchy rates while late seventeenth-century towns decreased, but the averages were distorted because the old towns included most of the urban and large towns with their rising rates, and the late towns included mostly medium and small towns. When small towns founded in both periods of settlement were compared, the tenure of a deputy's office in both decreased sharply. Thus geographic and age factors did not affect increases or decreases in the tenure of office index of oligarchy in the years 1701–1780, but the size factor did; the large towns, both urban and nonurban, grew more oligarchic, and the medium and small towns grew less so.

When oligarchic change is measured by turnover rates per decade, four town types show a clear trend: large towns declined from turnover rates of 70, 67, and 66 percent for the first three decades of the century to 41, 51, and 53 percent for the three decades between 1760 and 1790; small towns increased their turnover rates from 39, 40, and 40 percent to 45, 40, and 48 percent; medium towns decreased their turnover rates from 44, 49, and 49 percent to 41, 47, and 43 percent; and river towns increased their turnover rates from 36, 38, and 36 percent to 39, 44, and 45 percent for these decades. The trends in changing turnover rates for large and small towns reinforce the picture from average terms measurement, while the increasing turnover rate for river towns suggests a decline in the rate of oligarchy which the average terms measurement did not show. The medium towns' decrease in turnover rates when coupled with the contrary phenomena of a slight decrease in average numbers of terms per deputy suggests that one cannot say whether their degree of oligarchy was increasing or decreasing and can only say that while the total number of terms per officeholder was declining, more officeholders had consecutive terms.

CONCLUSIONS

In summation, the pattern of officeholding of deputies to the Connecticut General Assembly, which this writer sees as basically oligarchic with a strong family dominance, did not change on an overall basis over the first 90 years of the eighteenth century. The pattern fluctuated greatly, however, and clearly correlated to events such as military and political wars. Military wars accompanied discontinuity in the assembly and political wars accompanied continuity. While changes occurred around the immediate Revolutionary years, when these changes were placed in a longer perspective the Revolution did not perceptibly alter patterns of deputy officeholding. Factors of geography, size, and age did affect the officeholding patterns of towns and great differences existed among types of towns.

It is difficult to say, however, as historians have tried to do, which size of towns was most oligarchic and which was least. The degree of oligarchy of different sized towns depends on whether one measures family oligarchy, exceptional individual oligarchy, or average deputy oligarchy. For example, the urban towns might be called the most oligarchic since they had the highest average terms per deputy and the lowest turnover rates or they might be called the least oligarchic since they had the lowest degree of family dominance. Another example of the difficulty of categorizing towns by size can be seen in the large towns which had the lowest average terms per deputy and the highest turnover rates but were increasing the average terms per deputy rapidly and decreasing the turnover rates.

The geographical factor, however, was consistent. Eastern towns were continually less oligarchic in all tests than were western or river towns. Age also was consistent within a given measurement. When measuring family dominance the older the town, the higher the rate of family dominance; yet when measuring average terms per deputy, individual dominance, and turnover rates, settlement dates made no difference.

Just as single-town studies warn their readers that their single towns may not be typical, so the general patterns presented here have many

Table 7
Tendencies of Town Types to be Higher, Lower, or Same as Averages for All Towns

Variable	Select Few Individual Dominance	Family Dominance	Oligarchy measured by Average Terms and Turnover rate[a]	Oligarchy Increasing or Decreasing[b]
East	Lower	Lower	Lower	Same
West	Higher	Higher	Same	Increasing
River	Higher	Higher	Higher	Decreasing
Urban	Same	Lower	Higher	Increasing
Large	Lower	Same	Lower	Increasing
Medium	Same	Same	Same	Same
Small	Higher	Higher	Same	Decreasing
Old 17th/before 1675	Same	Higher	Same	Same
Late 17th/after 1675	Same	Lower	Same	Same
New 18th/before 1735	Same[c]	Lower[c]	Same	Same

[a] Theoretically the average-terms-per-deputy rate and the turnover rate could not agree and one could be higher than the average and one could be lower, but since this never actually occurred the measurements are not separated for this chart.
[b] This is determined by comparing the average terms per deputy rate for 1701–1720 with 1761–1780 and the turnover rates for 1701–20, 1711–20, and 1721–30 with 1761–70, 1771–80, and 1781–90. For medium towns one measure was slightly increasing and one was slighty decreasing. Hence, they balanced each other and "same" is more accurate than "increasing" or "decreasing."
[c] Based on projections of incomplete data.

exceptions and any one town might not fit them. Similarly, these patterns were not necessarily the same for other major or minor officers. However, despite these warnings, this present study hopefully shows that when precision and detail are employed, one can make more secure statements about colonial and Revolutionary society and politics than when one uses isolated quotes, single measurements and single variables, and limited samples. When the methodology and the terminology are clearly defined, when a whole complex of variables is measured, and when the conclusions do not claim more than the sample justifies, meaningful judgments can be made.

From a variety of specialized studies such as the foregoing, a picture of local elites in New England is becoming well enough developed to take on some rather clear outlines. More than any other work, Edward Cook, Jr.'s extraordinary study of officeholding, *The Fathers of the Towns* (1976), has given this picture focus and breadth. Conclusions about the polity of Connecticut towns mesh almost perfectly with the typology developed by Cook. Both Cook's work and the above analysis of General Assembly officeholding in Connecticut suggest that: urban towns tended to produce the most upward mobility and the most provincial leaders and they diminished the importance of family connections; secondary towns had more stable elites in which family connections played a greater role; and small towns had oligarchical, family-dominated elites but these elites served poorly as springboards to positions of power beyond the local community.[23]

Six

Patrician Leadership and the American Revolution: Four Case Studies

Critics of quantitative methodology argue that analyses of data must be placed in an appropriate intellectual context. Otherwise, they are mere sterile numbers devoid of real significance. Few social historians disagree. Nor do social historians disregard the ability of individuals to affect changes in the direction of historical events. Social historians, however, are inclined to discount the power of individuals to redirect or overcome forces that have deep roots in the economic, social, or intellectual bedrock. Rather, they believe that individuals who affect change through dynamic leadership usually are people who personify or reflect values current in society. A biography of a leader, therefore, is not only a study of one person, it is a study of society's values as they are refracted through public perceptions of the leader.

The following chapter identifies four crises in New England during the Revolution and examines the singular role one leader played in defusing each crisis. Each of the four leaders possessed an unusual capacity to bridge deep divisions and appeal to conflicting groups. Each of them also shared a similar background and public image.

The first exposure most new students of American history have to problems of scholarly interpretation invariably centers on the modern chestnut "conflict or consensus." Is American history the product of a long series of battles between diametrically opposed forces reflecting a society with deep internal divisions or of a slow evolutionary liberal process of change reflecting a society in essential agreement? A general weariness with the debate seems to be setting in but the historical profession has so far been unable to formulate a new paradigm to replace the old one.

One problem bedevils both the consensus and the conflict historians of the American Revolution. Proponents of the consensual model, no matter how much they emphasize the shared experience of the Revolutionaries, cannot dispel from most minds the conviction that at the very least geographic disputes between East and West, agricultural countryside and commercial urban areas, seacoast and backcountry, or river valley and uplands, split the Revolutionaries. Given the wide acceptance by historians of one of these splits in most colonies, it is hard to imagine that there would not be political divisions. Yet, while the conflict historians score this basic telling point, they cannot explain what held the Revolutionaries together enough to enable them to be so successful. Given internal conflict, why did the Revolutionary movement not disintegrate into warring factions? Why was one insurrection, Shay's Rebellion, the only serious internal challenge to the orderly process of fighting a war and forming a nation? When this cohesion is juxtaposed with the evidence of serious divisions, we seem to be left with the conclusion that the Revolutionary movement had some conflict and some consensus—enough of one to make the road from colony to nation bumpy, but enough of the other to ensure a safe arrival at the destination.[1]

One of the means of resolving the conflict–consensus debate about the Revolution lies in understanding the leadership roles of a few wealthy patrician whigs. In the New England colonies, for example, deep divisions existed that were serious enough to weaken the cohesiveness of society. But at critical moments in each colony's history, when events threatened to rip it apart, a wealthy patrician associated in the strongest possible sense with the colony's governing elite managed to emerge as a conciliatory unity figure who could avert the tragedy of a true civil war. Recent quantitative studies of leadership shed valuable and needed light on subtle shifts and trends that may have occurred or started in the Revolution. But one could measure 10 percent drops in the social origins of leaders *ad infinitum* and still miss the crucial importance of these men whose vital statistics would not significantly affect a quantitative model.[2] For their decisive roles only a qualitative analysis will suffice.

An understanding of a basic tension in colonial New England society is crucial to this qualitative analysis. From their seventeenth-century roots as Englishmen and covenanted Puritans living in homogeneous nucleated agricultural villages, all the experience of New Englanders had taught them to prize unity and fear conflict. It is clear, however, that since at least 1700 the social structure of New England, growing more pluralistic with every decade, militated against social harmony. Immigration and emigration, the differentiation of communities ranging on a scale from old settled urban areas to new frontier towns, growing disparities in social and economic classes, acute religious ferment, and the rise of economic individualism, all combined to shatter the organic unity within each colony. Yet, while the reality disappeared or perhaps never existed, the goal lingered on and a gap emerged between New England's ideas and practice. Contending "factions," as contemporaries said, characterized New England from at least the Great Awakening onward and created a society in the words of one historian, of "antipartisan theory and partisan reality."[3]

As the Great Awakening religious struggles blended into the pre-Revolutionary struggles of the 1760s, it seemed to many New Englanders that society could not survive the conflicts. The Revolutionary generation, fighting for freedom from one tyranny, was sufficiently wise, however, to realize that repressing conflict would not eliminate it. Rather than suppress what would only rear up again, they sought leadership that would have sufficient wealth, ancestry, and dignity to inspire awe and respect, unchallengeable credentials as whig friends of liberty but moderate, compromising natures, and the delicate ability to cater to the middle classes while all the while maintaining a social distance clearly above them. In short, a wealthy patrician, Revolutionary but moderate, aloof but sensitive to the people, was the ideal leader to balance all the tensions in society—a father figure, a tender patriarch, who like all fathers was not arbitrary and severe but knew more than his children and had deep concern for them.[4] Such men emerged in the crucial moments of the Revolution in Massachusetts, Connecticut, New Hampshire, and Rhode Island: John Hancock, William Pitkin, Meshech Weare, and Joseph Wanton.

JOHN HANCOCK AND THE FIRST GUBERNATORIAL ELECTION IN MASSACHUSETTS

The most sophisticated consensus historian of the Revolution in Massachusetts, Richard D. Brown, in his work on the relationship between the Boston Committee of Correspondence and the towns, while emphasizing essentially the shared convictions of eighteenth-century Massachusetts men, does admit that pre-Revolutionary era divisions did surface in a "court" and "country" party that emerged in 1739 in a dispute over economic policies.[5] The labels "court" and "country" were replaced by "Tory" and "Whig" a generation later. The most recent conflict historian of Massachusetts in this era, Stephen Patterson, in his book on Revolutionary politics, argues that the conflict in late colonial Massachusetts imposed itself upon the Revolution and did not end with the separation of the loyalists from the patriots. Patterson believes that deep sectional, ideological, and class conflicts over the direction of the new state resulted in five bitter years of struggle among the revolutionaries that saw the partisan rejection of one proposed constitution in 1778 and the near rejection of another in 1780. Middle-class agrarian westerners in Patterson's view fought for democratic reforms against an eastern merchant-dominated elite who resisted all attempts to alter the nature of society and government.[6] Though many historians would be unwilling to accept the ideological and class characteristics Patterson attributes to the conflict, few would deny that at least a naked power struggle raged between the East and the West. Robert Taylor's definitive study of western Massachusetts during the Revolution shows that westerners "had a mind of their own" that grew increasingly distrustful of the eastern seaboard after the decision for independence was made.[7] The other serious scholar of western Massachusetts, Lee Newcomer, while trying to maintain a consensus overview, is forced to admit that a populist wing centering in the Berkshire Mountains adjacent to the province of New York dissented vociferously from the eastern Revolutionary leadership. Newcomer tries to submerge the conflict as "strife within an oversized family" but the evidence he amasses speaks louder than his consensual conclusions and shows that the West bitterly blamed the "locusts and cankerworms" in the East for a variety of ills.[8] Richard D. Brown agrees that the divisions over the constitutions pitted East against West as both regions vied for control of the new government.[9]

Division was so deep that probably a majority of Massachusetts' freemen opposed the constitution of 1780 and only gimmickry in the method of ratification resulted in its adoption.[10] With such entrenched antagonism one would expect that the first election fought for control of the new government under the new constitution would be a political bloodletting. Surprisingly, almost miraculously considering the background, John Hancock secured election as governor, the most powerful executive position in the new nation in 1780, by the resounding triumph of 9,475 votes to the 888 for his nearest rival, James Bowdoin. No historian has adequately explained the popularity Hancock enjoyed in both the East and West that resulted in this deluge of approval. With such conflict over power how can one account for such consensus over leadership?

A confluence of circumstances made John Hancock such a popular and unifying figure that the governor's chair could not possibly have been filled by any other. Foremost among these circumstances was his prestigious ancestry. His grandfather, John Hancock, a minister, achieved such fame for his piety and godliness in a society which was still fundamentally Puritan and prized these as its highest attributes that he was known as "Bishop Hancock." His father, also named John, and also a minister, fell short of similar fame only by a premature death. John, the patriot, was raised by his uncle, Thomas Hancock," America's wealthiest merchant. No other Massachusetts man had as formidable a combination of piety and wealth in his ancestry.[11] "King Hancock," as he was dubbed, had wealth and economic power sufficient to cause the normally skeptical John Adams to accept at face value the exaggerated statement that "not less than one thousand families were, every day in the year, dependent on Mr. Hancock for their daily bread."[12] The naming of Hancock in Hampshire County Massachusetts in 1776 testifies to the family's esteem.

Not only Hancock's economic power and ancestral piety inspired awe in the electorate; his highly visible aristocratic living style commanded the attention of all. This was not a generation that looked for republican simplicity in its leaders. Hancock was a grandee and never tried to hide it. He traveled in an elegant coach drawn by six horses and attended by four servants—his coach and entourage were used to convey the first French ambassador when he presented his credentials to the Continental Congress—seemed to be addicted to beautiful and elegant clothes, always insisted upon his social due as New England's foremost aristocrat and a senior Revolutionary statesman, and made a "hobby [of] the dinner table."[13] Hancock's whole person was the antithesis of the simple yeoman Revolutionary. Radical egalitarians like Samuel Adams may have condemned these trappings as contrary to what they perceived the Revolutionary spirit to be but the masses did not. To them Hancock was risking one of the greatest fortunes and reputations in the colonies in order to make people free from oppressive power. Not only did every aspect of Hancock's bearing impress them but the fact that he had so much to lose—that he risked so much—made his commitment all the more meaningful. The Reverend Thatcher, Hancock's pastor, expressed this when he preached that Hancock's combining of "a fortune superior to any" with such ardent patriotism "rendered him the idol of his fellow citizens."[14] Instead of his regal bearing costing him popularity, it occasioned it by making clear to all just how important a man had committed himself to the movement.

Hancock had other assets that commended him to the people as the proper leader of the Revolution in Massachusetts. Though his commitment to liberty was clear and known to all, after all one of the most celebrated pre-Revolutionary events involved a British custom's attack on a Hancock ship, the Liberty, Hancock's cautious personality always caused him to adopt moderate compromise views around which discordant Revolutionaries could group. Virtually every scholar who has examined Hancock's Revolutionary career concludes that he was a "trimmer" who never took a hard position on either side of any debate. He trimmed between the apprehensive merchants worried over losing their fortunes and the inflamed populace which demanded total adherence to the nonimportation agreements. Intellectually inferior to most of the members of the Continental Congress, Hancock's saving grace as President was his ability to mediate between bitterly antagonistic factions and maintain unity. The adoption of the Massachusetts Constitution of 1780 and of the Federal Constitution of 1787 in Massachusetts owes much to his ability to compromise opposing views. Many elite contemporaries condemned Hancock's invariable fence-straddling and most historians have considered it his most serious weakness. His "vacillating" and "chameleon" character usually is ascribed to his love of popularity and his ambition to be governor.[15] A composite negative picture has emerged of a man too weak to take any stand that might cost him the approval of the masses.

The people of Massachusetts, however, did not perceive Hancock's constant compromising to be a character flaw but instead saw it as the virtue of a man who tried to heal society's wounds. If Hancock's goal was to retain popularity and be the leader of his native province, he was phenomenally successful. The people of Massachusetts, respectful of his wealth, ancestry, and piety, impressed by his devotion to liberty and the risks he ran for it, and grateful for the moderating role he played between the forces threatening to tear their society apart, saw him as the one man they could rally around and trust with the care of their new government. Hancock's overwhelming election as governor in 1780 transcended all internal differences and prevented Massachusetts from degenerating into two warring camps. A leader like Samuel Adams who lacked noted ancestry and personal wealth but who was known for his devotion to republican simplicity and purity of principle never could command the popular support in Massachusetts that Hancock did. Historians may be impressed by Adams' credentials as a Revolutionary but to Massachusetts men he was too "middlin'" to inspire great respect and too controversial and partisan to be trusted with the new government. Adams would increase the society's divisions and aggravate its wounds while Hancock could close and heal them.

WILLIAM PITKIN AND THE STAMP ACT ELECTION IN CONNECTICUT

Connecticut, famed as the "land of steady habits," experienced a steady erosion of this virtue throughout the eighteenth century.[16] The fundamental agreement of Connecticut society on most matters of importance that had characterized the seventeenth century ended when economic ambition fueled by land fever engendered controversy both at the colony and local level. The Great Awakening which affected Connecticut more than any other colony resulted in the formation of two clearly defined factions fighting for control of the colony. The New Lights, proponents of the revival, drew their strength primarily from the eastern part of the colony which was its most recently settled area, and seemed to stand for a new order in Connecticut society emphasizing individualism and anti-authority impulses. The Old Lights, drawn primarily from the older towns of the colony in the West, viewed the new religion as "enthusiastic," which was akin in today's language to vulgar, feared its leveling tendencies, and tended in their more exaggerated statements to stigmatize it as anarchic. Amidst the viciously partisan struggles in the 1740s and 1750s which intruded into all aspects of public affairs and which horrified everyone, the Old Lights managed to maintain a tenuous hold on the governorship, an elected position in Connecticut, and on the assistants' council, which was the upper house of the legislature and collectively advised the governor on all matters of state.[17]

As in Massachusetts, the struggles of the era of the Great Awakening fastened themselves on the pre-Revolutionary debates in Connecticut.[18] The most climatic and crucial moment in Connecticut's Revolutionary years came early in 1766, when the New Lights ousted the Old Lights from the governorship and the assistants' council in a political battle fought over the Stamp Act. The Old Lights had, like all Connecticut men, opposed the passage of the Stamp Act but as men with a commitment to law and order they agreed to uphold the Act once it became law. The New Lights, more devoted to purity of principle and less devoted to accepting authority, asserted that the Act should never be obeyed. Connecticut's Sons of Liberty opposed the Act by peaceful petition, a newspaper and pamphlet campaign, and even by physical attacks on men implementing the law. It seemed to most sober Connecticut men that violence might engulf the entire colony and prevent the East and West from ever again acting in harmony or agreeing upon the essentials of government. When Governor Thomas Fitch, an Old Light, and three assistants took the oath in November 1765 to uphold the Act, the New Lights intensified their attempts to drive these "enemies of liberty" from the government. In the elections of spring 1766, William Pitkin replaced Fitch as governor by "votes too numerous to count" and all three assistants were defeated. The New Light triumph was complete and historians acknowledge the driving of the Old Lights from power and William Pitkin's election as Connecticut's internal revolution. The triumph of Pitkin and the New Lights, however, did not exacerbate the existing tensions, but presaged the end of the severe warfare between the East and West that had threatened to destroy Connecticut's homogeneity. Though political fighting did not immediately end, never again was it as vitriolic or destructive, and as anger began to recede it was clear that Connecticut had successfully weathered a severe storm.

Pitkin's name is not as familiar to schoolchildren as Hancock's, but he occupied much the same position in Connecticut as Hancock did in Massachusetts.[19] In a colony known for its propensity to revere a few select old families and trust them with its leadership, the Pitkin claim to ancestral superiority could hardly be surpassed. Both William's grandfather and father, William Pitkin I and II, had been assistants to the governor and had probably only missed being elected governor by premature deaths. The Pitkins were the only family to have two close relatives serving together in the assistants' council since the Winthrops had in the seventeenth century. The family, large and concentrated almost entirely in Hartford, dominated the politics of the capital town during the eighteenth century. As large landowners with interests all over the colony, major merchants engaged in the import–export trade, and particularly as owners of many mills on the Connecticut River, the Pitkins collectively and individually appeared to "middlin'" men as gentlemen of great fortune.

William, the governor, had a long career in Connecticut politics before his Revolutionary election and was deputy governor during his rival Fitch's governorship. As a Hartford town leader, deputy to the General Assembly, assistant to the governor, Chief Justice of the Supreme Court, and deputy governor, William always appeared to be a moderate, conciliatory politician. His devotion to the New Light version of religion during the Great Awakening and to liberty in the early 1760s could not be questioned, yet Pitkin never seemed to be controversial or under attack as most New Light leaders were. He was at his best when sorting out some thorny local problems as an arbiter appointed by the General Assembly, and once, in an almost unparalleled case, he resolved a bitter local town dispute in the capacity of a private person requested to arbitrate by both contending parties. Pitkin drafted petitions to his fellow magistrates in humble and respectful language and managed miraculously to appear to rise above the partisan battles of the era while all around him his Connecticut contemporaries flayed away at one another. He was, in short, a man of renowned piety, ancestry, wealth, and accomplishment, judicious and conciliatory, and yet firmly attached to the cause of liberty.

The New Lights never seriously considered anyone else as their candidate to oust Fitch in 1766. Connecticut had its equivalent of Samuel Adams; Eliphalet Dyer, the fiery purist from Windham, was identified far more than Pitkin with the most ardent spirit of the pre-Revolutionary movement.[20] Connecticut men perceived, however, that a purist or upstart could not heal the colony's wounds while a moderate politician respected by all would have a soothing effect on the colony and would lower the political intensity instead of raising it. No other New Light possessed the stature and character necessary to ease Connecticut government into the hands of a friend of liberty with a minimum of trauma and discord.

Pitkin, like Hancock, enjoyed unusual popularity and survived successfully all future attempts by Fitch to regain the governorship. The only criticism leveled by contemporaries accused him of pandering to the wishes of the masses. An anti-New Light ballad written shortly after his death chided Pitkin metaphorically for steering the ship of state with too close an attention to the crew and of trying to "accomplish every measure by a how do you do, with a decent bow, and a shaking of hands forever." His Old Light adversaries never fully perceived that it was the very combination of his elite image with his attempt "to please the seamen" that made Pitkin the leader Connecticut turned to when its society seemed to be coming apart.

MESHECH WEARE AND THE GRAFTON COUNTY
REVOLT AGAINST NEW HAMPSHIRE

New Hampshire politics, controlled to a strong degree by a small oligarchy of wealthy Portsmouth merchant families, was remarkably free of serious divisions until the ruling elite committed itself to supporting the Townshend Acts. The ground swell of protest against the Acts and the colony leadership which supported them abated somewhat with repeal in 1770 but the anti-court fervor did not disappear. Four factors combined in the years after 1770 to weaken the hold the ruling elite had on the populace's loyalty: the proselytizing activities of the Anglicans, which were supported by the government; the presence of British troops marching across the colony, which rekindled old fears of a standing army; the fiery example of Massachusetts; and Governor John Wentworth's loss of influence in England, which made him unable to disregard English policy that adversely affected New Hampshire and compelled him to enforce unpopular legislation. Until the outbreak of hostilities between the colonies and England, however, sectional, ideological, and class divisions did not emerge. Instead, a government clique backing unpopular policies was arrayed against an increasingly angry citizenry.[21]

When in response to the military events in Massachusetts, Governor Wentworth fled New Hampshire in the summer of 1775, most of the colony's ruling oligarchy left also. In the power vacuum created, internal divisions surfaced that pitted merchant against farmer, creditor against debtor, radical against moderate, and in particular the South, the East, and the seaboard against the North, the West, and the interior. The divisions manifested themselves most seriously in

1781 when thirty-five Grafton County towns in the northern interior Connecticut River Valley, angered because they could not get their desired share of representation in the new state government, seceded from New Hampshire and joined the forces that were involved in negotiating with the Continental Congress for the creation of a new state—Vermont. Ultimately, after a tense year during which internal warfare threatened to break out, the Grafton County towns returned to the fold. With this crisis over, the divisions receded and New Hampshire entered the post-Revolutionary period as a reasonably unified state.[22]

The man who more than anyone else held New Hampshire together and ended the northern secession movement was the state's first president, Meshech Weare. Weare, a wealthy landowner from Hampton Falls, came from a family "justly proud" of its ancestry that had long been associated with New Hampshire leadership. His grandfather, Nathaniel Weare, had been one of the greatest men of the province and had led the much-gloried overthrow of the tyrant Governor Cranfield; his father, also Nathaniel, was Hampton's most illustrious citizen and a prominent member of the colony's assembly. Meshech, destined to political leadership by virtue of birth, was elected the moderator of a town meeting at age twenty-six and six years later succeeded his father as deputy to the General Assembly. He was elected successively auditor and clerk and was made speaker at the age of forty-one in 1752, all unusual positions for a young man in a society known to revere age. Weare led the colony's delegation to the Albany Conference on the Plan for Union in 1754 and served as a justice of the Superior Court on the eve of the Revolution. Few men in New Hampshire could lay greater claim to a place of respect. His home was a sumptuous mansion, he paid the largest tax in his home town of Hampton Falls, he owned land in sixteen towns, and a town, Weare, chartered by Governor Benning Wentworth in 1764, was named after his family.[23]

Weare possessed personal assets to match his ancestral, political, and economic ones. At an early age he had an "appearance of genius" and later won prizes for academic excellence while at Harvard. Weare studied divinity and showed signs of being a great preacher. He only turned away from a career in the ministry because, as a friend wrote, he felt "impelled to give up clerical pursuits for the care of his estates and public service, by circumstances of family life, inheritance of estates, and the ready desire of his fellow townsmen to employ him in civil matters." Even after deciding against a career as a minister he preached as a guest in many pulpits around his home. Every historian who has written of him stresses what one called his "amiable and discreet deportment." The words "cautious" and "moderate" occur frequently in descriptions of Weare, showing him to have been a man of exceptional judiciousness.[24]

Despite his cautious nature, Weare became known as a friend of liberty by the time of the Stamp Act debate and as an ardent patriot when he wrote and published poetry against the Tea Act. In New Hampshire's second provincial congress, called to deal with the Revolutionary crisis, Weare emerged as the unquestionable leader of the moderate whigs and was chosen president of the third congress. When most of New Hampshire's elite leaders abdicated their power and discord engulfed the state in factional fighting, Weare was almost everyone's choice to head the new government. Under a new constitution he was elected the President of the Council, the state's chief executive position. Jeremy Belknap, New Hampshire's first comprehensive historian, described Weare's popularity as unrivaled in the history of the colony, and a more recent historian quoted one observer as remarking that Weare "acquired so much popularity his countrymen expected salvation from his wisdom or arm alone."[25]

It would not be too much of an exaggeration to argue that perhaps New Hampshire's salvation, if salvation can be defined as staying intact as a political unit, came from Weare's wisdom alone. Cautiously, he used his prestige and great popularity to bring stability to the state. He halted the rampant inflation by persuading the assembly to levy heavy taxes; these provided money to support the war effort. When the new Revolutionary government seemed on the brink of falling apart, Weare championed constitutional reform and arranged for the transfer of executive power to the Committee of Safety of which he and two other men were the chief members. In particular, Weare acted as a calming influence on the radicals among the Revolutionaries and kept them from initiating measures that would have ripped the new state apart into warring parties. Finally, under another new constitution, as the first President of New Hampshire, Weare personally rode over the White Mountains in the dead of winter to contain the Grafton County Revolution. Bloodshed between Grafton County and the rest of New Hampshire could easily have occurred. Troops were authorized to quell the rebellion, but forebearance of the new state government under Weare delayed the development and a political solution was arranged. The final compromise came when Weare, who was both old and ill, retired as Chief Justice of the Superior Court and arranged for a Grafton County man to replace him.[26]

Weare's devotion to the Revolutionary cause, caution and moderation, and great popularity, are the qualities always singled out by New Hampshire historians. His contemporaries, mindful of these qualities and their role in guiding New Hampshire from colony to state, were also impressed that someone with Weare's wealth and position in society would risk both in such an uncertain venture. As one wrote, "truly sensible I am that you have sunk a fortune and exposed a large family to danger of being ruined."[27] The assets that to a later and more socially democratic nation would seem artificial, wealth and family, were the very qualities that, combined with Weare's natural leadership and moderation, gave him the popularity to lead New Hampshire through deep divisions that could have resulted in civil war and the dismemberment of the state.

JOSEPH WANTON AND THE ENDING OF THE WARD–HOPKINS CONTROVERSY IN RHODE ISLAND

The factional and contentious nature of Rhode Island society and politics was legendary in colonial New England; eighteenth-century citizens of New Hampshire, Massachusetts, and Connecticut referred to Rhode Island as "Rogues' Island" or "the land where people think otherwise." The prospect of "Rhode Islandism" coming to their colony was a horrible specter guaranteed to frighten inhabitants of the old Puritan colonies.[28] Factions were more developed toward political parties in Rhode Island than in any other mainland colony except New York. For the twenty years before the Revolutionary period two well-defined political machines, one led by the Wards of Westerly and Newport and the other by the Hopkins of Providence, vied for control of the colonial government. The struggle, bitter and steeped in vituperation, aroused Rhode Island into a semiannual frenzy. All serious students of Rhode Island's past agree that the vicious divisions were rooted in a contest between two different geographical sections and had no ideological overtones; power, wealth, patronage, and personal ambition fueled the fight and not differing visions of the good society.[29]

While the rest of New England assumed that Rhode Islanders gloried in dissent and loved every contentious minute of it, the discord was always deplored, especially by those most intimately involved in fomenting it. Even Rhode Island men, famed for their political infighting, bemoaned partisan activity, feared combinations to gain office, and shared the eighteenth-century quest for unity and the public good. Both the Ward and the Hopkins factions feared the colony would be torn apart and not survive the struggle. Both sides were continually sending forth compromise proposals to end the fighting and bring some semblance of peace to the strife-ridden society.

Suspicion between the two sides overcame the early attempts at a compromise solution, but the divisions that emerged between mother country and colonies in the 1760s added a new urgency to the campaign for internal unity. As the Revolutionary crisis grew more grave in the late 1760s, by mutual agreement factional fighting had to come to an end. Both Stephen Hopkins and Samuel Ward, while unalterably opposed to each other, also unalterably opposed encroachments on Rhode Island's liberties by Parliament. As Rhode Island's first important historian wrote, "the famous controversy . . . ceased forever in the presence of a more momentous struggle." Governor Stephen Hopkins proposed, from a position of strength, to end the feud by a compromise that would remove both himself and Samuel Ward from active officeholding and put the governorship in the hands of a man mutually acceptable to both. Accordingly, in April of 1768, Josias Lyndon was chosen governor as a compromise candidate but the compromise was shortlived and political warfare blazed again because Lyndon could not keep in the good graces of both factions.[30]

The election of Joseph Wanton to the governorship in 1769 proved to be the event which ended the Ward–Hopkins controversy as a significant force in Rhode Island politics. Under the conciliatory leadership of Wanton, the colony enjoyed six years of relative stability and most Rhode Islanders approved their governor's firm protest against British imperial policy. Historians may now argue that Wanton was a candidate of the Hopkins factions, but contemporaries did not see him as a stalking horse for anyone and perceived him as someone who rose above the petty partisan battles.[31] His moderate image had widespread appeal and Wanton, burying Ward in the election, even won a majority in Ward's home town and power base, Newport, and in the adjacent towns of Middletown and Portsmouth. The Wards' closest allies in Providence, the Browns, supported Wanton, and the coalitionist spirit and movement overwhelmed the Ward family who did not accept it but were not strong enough to continue the fight.

After Wanton's election, Rhode Island was never again threatened with disunion during the Revolution and the colony whose name was a symbol of divisiveness declared independence and fought the Revolution without widespread internal dissent.[32]

Joseph Wanton, a merchant prince from Newport, was descended from a family of colonial governors; his father William, his uncle John Wanton, and his cousin Gideon Wanton all had occupied the governor's chair and his son, Joseph Junior, had previously been a deputy governor. The family, engaged in extensive shipbuilding and the West Indian trade in the eighteenth century, had first amassed a fortune as privateers in the late seventeenth century and then been co-opted into the Newport elite. Wanton, a Harvard graduate, had an "amiable disposition, elegant manners, and handsome person" and enjoyed such perquisites of a gentleman as expensive clothes and a sumptuous table. He early showed himself to be a patriot but, known not to like bitter fights, he did not thrive on controversy as so many politicians seemed to—clearly he was a moderate. As governor, he steered a course between the extreme "sons of liberty" and "sons of tyranny" and did his best to mediate all divisions. His best was very good—Wanton had virtually no opposition while in office and Rhode Island enjoyed six years of internal concord which were unparalleled in its past.[33]

Wanton led the opposition to the imperial policies up to the final moments before hostilities broke out and was an ardent enough patriot that the British suspected him of complicity in the scuttling and burning of a revenue ship off the Rhode Island coast. Yet, in the final analysis, Wanton could not bring himself to renounce his loyalty to the king and direct military operations against the British regular army. Shortly after his election to a seventh term in May 1775, he walked out of a room to be conveniently absent when the Revolutionaries seized his trappings of office. Because of Wanton's immense popularity and past patriotism, the whigs did not install his successor until seven months after he was deposed and gave him every opportunity to reconsider and take back the governorship. An old and sick man, Wanton opted out of the struggle rather than make war on his king, but in contrast to his hated counterpart in Massachusetts, Thomas Hutchinson, Wanton lived out his life in his home colony as a respected figure.[34]

Although technically a Loyalist, Wanton did more to secure Rhode Island's unified response to the Revolution than any whig. Nor did his deposition (abdication?) mean the elevation to the governor's chair of any out-of-power rabble-rouser. Wanton's deputy governor, Nicholas Cooke, also a wealthy merchant and a moderate, was confirmed as the new governor.[35]

CONCLUSION

The careers of John Hancock, William Pitkin, Meshech Weare, and Joseph Wanton, suggest that neither the consensus nor the conflict model alone can successfully explain the Revolution in New England. Each of the four colonies at some point in the Revolutionary years experienced a geographical division bitter and deep enough to push the imperial struggle into the background and potentially split the colony in half.[36] Yet, each colony managed to group around one figure and form a relatively unified whole to wage a revolution, fight a war, and create a stable government. These four men were merely the most visible examples of a widespread model of leadership. A recent essay that analyzed the attributes of the ninety-nine most important leaders of 1776 and 1787 reveals that their collective identity resembled the British peerage more than the American yeomanry.[37] Hancock, Pitkin, Weare, and Wanton had an abundance of the qualities society looked for in its leadership and had the rare opportunity and ability to make the most of these qualities. Other men of the same type preceded and succeeded them.

As intellectual historians have shown, the goals of colonial society, concord and harmony, were ideally attained through nonpartisan activity. By the fourth decade of the nineteenth century, a contrary world of institutionalized division had emerged where partisan activity was the accepted norm. Long before this world of normalized discord could be legitimized by Jacksonian rhetoric, it had emerged *de facto* in the colonial world out of the attempts by one area of a colony to capture control of the colony's government.[38] The naked realities of electing a government gave rise to deep divisions. Embryonic institutions were created to respond to these divisions long before the social values of pre-industrial man allowed him to accept them. The lack of acceptance made the divisions seem all the deeper and more treacherous and made men search desperately for a real consensus to match their ideological world. When the Revolutionary divisions between the mother country and colonies emerged, each of the colonies looked for saviors to prevent society from disintegrating. Wealthy patricians like Hancock, Pitkin, Weare, and Wanton, men of patriotism and moderation, men above the people but loved by the people, men with long familial histories of leadership, were the natural figures for Revolutionary society to turn to in an anachronistic attempt to realize a beleaguered communal ideal.

III

SOCIAL DIVISIONS

Seven

COLLEGE STUDENTS AND NEW ENGLAND SOCIETY: A QUANTITATIVE PORTRAIT OF YALE GRADUATES IN COLONIAL AMERICA

Harvard and Yale occupied unique positions in colonial New England. A degree from either virtually guaranteed a young man preferment in society, business, or government. The founders of both schools intended them to be bastions of orthodoxy that would sustain the "New England way" and combat dissent, secularism, and licentiousness. While no one envisaged either college as a seminary, religion was central to their purpose. Foreign to their purpose was any sense that they should encourage or even tolerate among students and faculty liberal inquiry into the values and beliefs of society.

Instead of acting as bulwarks against division and contention, however, Harvard and Yale sometimes played active roles in promoting controversy. Harvard's battle with the orthodox leadership of Massachusetts at the turn of the eighteenth century has become a familiar part of the story of Puritan declension. Connecticut conservatives founded Yale in the early eighteenth century partly because they no longer trusted Harvard with the education of their sons. By mid-eighteenth century, Yale, too, flirted with heterodoxy.

The following chapter discusses changes in the composition of the student body at Yale between its founding in 1702 and 1780. As Connecticut society grew more heterogeneous over the course of the eighteenth century so did Yale's student population. At the outbreak of the Revolution, Yale graduates could be found in most occupations and on both sides of most political and religious disputes.

Despite the proliferation of colleges in the nineteenth century and the widespread faith in the efficacy of a college education for success in the twentieth century, a college degree was more respected in colonial New England than at any time or place since in America. Undoubtedly the increased widening of opportunities for a college education which the nineteenth and twentieth centuries have witnessed is partially responsible for this phenomenon: scarcity bred awe and abundance bred familiarity. But scarcity and abundance alone do not account for the esteem or lack of esteem in which college graduates were and are held. The colonial South had many fewer college graduates than New England, and yet the Bachelor's degree never commanded the respect there that it did in New England. Puritans attached substantial respect to education, and the college graduate who had reached the top of the educational structure reaped the benefit of that respect. A college graduate in New England could look forward to a successful life in a position of leadership with but little chance of failure. As a recent study of leadership has shown, the degree of success for college graduates varied cyclically with economic opportunities.[1] But even in classes that were in a disadvantaged position in these cycles, most of the graduates lived lives of achievement.

Given the fact that a college graduate almost automatically joined the leadership pool in New England, it is surprising how little hard data we have on the student bodies at New England's two major colonial colleges—Harvard and Yale. Impressionistically we know that a large percentage of the graduates became ministers; many of them were from the geographically proximate area; some entered the medical and legal professions; most stayed in New England; more were orthodox Puritans than religious dissenters; and more became Revolutionaries than Loyalists during the Revolution. However, no precision can be attached to any of these statements and, more importantly, none of these qualitative statements about the student body measure change over time. Both Harvard and Yale experienced great change and growth over the colonial period. It is reasonable to expect that as they became more secular, diversified their curriculum, responded to the intellectual and political currents of the times, and constantly increased in numbers of students, the relative dimensions of all the above statements would be affected.[2] And these dimensions are important for the history of early New England. They tell us who was most likely to be able to go to college and have enhanced oppor-

Table 8
Places of Origin of Yale Graduates

	1702–10	1711–20	1721–30	1731–40	1741–50	1751–60	1761–70	1771–80
	N–21 %	N–55	N–132	N–173	N–205	N–282	N–305	N–328
Connecticut	61.90	89.08	73.48	75.72	74.15	74.47	78.03	82.62
Massachusetts	23.81	3.64	17.42	9.83	13.66	16.67	18.36	14.02
New York	14.29	1.82	1.52	10.40	9.27	4.97	2.95	3.05
New Jersey		1.82	3.79	0.58	1.46			
Rhode Island			2.27	1.73	0.49	3.19	0.66	0.30
Pennsylvania				1.56				
N. Hampshire				0.58				
Vermont					0.49			
Delaware		1.82						
N. Carolina					0.49	0.35		
England		1.82	1.52			0.35		

period, and forty-three Connecticut students spurned Yale to graduate from Princeton. Moreover, every colony on the mainland except
Georgia and Rhode Island provided at least one Princeton graduate.

The difference in the pattern between Yale and Columbia on the
one hand and Princeton on the other hand can be attributed primarily to their religious orientations. Yale represented the Congregational establishment of Connecticut and Columbia represented the
Anglican establishment of New York, while Princeton represented
the evangelical spirit of the Great Awakening that cut across colony
lines. As a symbol of Yale's provincial base and Princeton's inter-
colony one, all of Yale's colonial presidents were Connecticut-born
ministers, while Princeton named four successive presidents from
outside New Jersey. The experiences of Brown and the University of
Pennsylvania reinforce this conclusion. Although only partial data
are compiled for these two schools, both of them attracted many
more out-of-colony students than Yale and Columbia, and both were
much more liberal and less identified with any particular orthodoxy.
A secondary reason for the different patterns of origins was that a
Princeton, Brown, or Pennsylvanian education cost substantially less
than one at Yale or Columbia, but this advantage for out-of-colony
students must have been largely offset by the high cost to travel to
and from a distant school.

In its patterns of student recruitment, Yale was following the tradition of Oxford and Cambridge, both of which attracted most of
their students from nearby areas. However, the increasing provincialism of Yale contrasts to the declining provincialism experienced by
most of the colonial colleges in the 1760s and 1770s.[9] Within Connecticut, despite circumstances that one might logically think would
give an advantage for an education to young men from more urban
towns, only a slightly higher percentage of the Yale graduates entered
from large- and medium-sized towns than from small country towns.
In the two decades from 1761 to 1780, approximately 21 percent of
the Yale graduates entered the college from Connecticut's five largest
and 23 percent entered from the ten next largest towns. The five
largest towns comprised 16 percent of the colony's population in
1774 and the ten next largest comprised 21 percent of the population. Thus, living in an older, more developed town did give a young
man a slight advantage in securing a college education, but the over-
representation of the large and medium towns was only marginal.
Although we do not have precise data on population distribution by

towns for the first half of the eighteenth century, it appears from estimates that at no time in Yale's colonial history were the more urban towns grossly disproportionately represented at Yale. In 1720 the largest five towns and next largest ten towns comprised at least 50 percent of the colony's population, and students from these towns comprised about 57 percent of Yale graduates. As the small country towns increased in number and in their percentage of the total population, the percentage of the Yale graduates who entered from them increased proportionately. Thus, Yale was not a college primarily for the sons of the elite from the trading centers. Young men from small rural towns had nearly as equal an access to a Yale education as their more urban peers.

If most Yale graduates came from Connecticut, a substantially lower number stayed there after graduation as the percentage of those staying in Connecticut decreased as the century progressed. Every decade after 1711–1720 witnessed a steady decline in the percentage of Connecticut-born Yale graduates who performed their life's work in their home colony. The greatest change occurred in the decade of the 1740s. In the 1730s, 131 Yale graduates were born in Connecticut and 115 died there. In the 1740s, 152 Yale graduates were born in Connecticut but only 118 died there. By 1771–1780 nearly half of Yale's graduates left Connecticut after graduation, and the colony and new state became a substantial exporter of college-trained men. In absolute terms, out of 271 men born in Connecticut who were graduated from Yale in that decade, 110 moved somewhere else.

Yale graduates from 1771 to 1780 ended up in every one of the original thirteen states but Delaware and in such farflung places as Poland and France. The largest number of migrants, however, went to New York State—both New York City and the upstate frontier region, and to the new state of Vermont. These three areas offered economic opportunities for ambitious young men, New York City in commerce and upstate New York and Vermont in land. In this migration, Yale graduates were following patterns of Connecticut society in general. The decade of the 1740s which witnessed the start of the trend toward outmigration by Yale graduates was the decade in which the last of Connecticut's unused lands was settled. Between 1760 and 1790 Connecticut experienced a sizable outmigration because of pressures of declining land supplies on a dense population, and the population declined by approximately 66,000 from what

Table 9
Distribution of Yale Graduates by Size of Connecticut Towns

	1702-10 #---%	1711-20 #---%	1721-30 #---%	1731-40 #---%	1741-50 #---%	1751-60 #---%	1761-70 #---%	1771-80 #---%
Large	5	14	36	31	40	40	48	58
*	41.67	28.57	37.11	23.48	26.32	19.05	20.17	21.27
Medium	2	14	28	50	44	53	69	45
**	16.67	28.57	28.87	37.88	28.95	25.24	28.99	16.42
Small	5	21	33	51	68	117	121	171
***	41.67	42.86	34.02	38.64	44.74	55.71	50.84	62.41

* Large   (five towns comprising 16% of Connecticut's population in 1774).

** Medium   (ten towns comprising 21 % of Connecticut's population in 1774).

*** Small   (fifty-six towns comprising 63% of Connecticut's population in 1774).

Totals of Large, Medium and Small Towns:

1702-10: 12	1721-30: 97	1741-50: 152	1761-70: 238
1711-20: 49	1731-40: 132	1751-60: 210	1771-80: 274

might have been expected through normal growth. Not all of this number left the state, as economic circumstances undoubtedly reduced the natural population increase. But at the minimum, half of this number of 66,000 did migrate out of the state.[10] Still, the rate of Yale graduates migrating was higher than the rate of the general population. It seems that Connecticut exported her poorest inhabitants who sought land to sustain themselves and her most educated inhabitants who sought to capitalize on their intellectual skills. Princeton, the one college where the geographical dispersion of graduates has also been studied systematically, placed alumni in every one of the colonies, but, as we have seen, Princeton students were recruited from further afield.

In light of the increasing number of its graduates who left Connecticut, Yale's influence, it seems safe to say, progressively expanded over an ever wider geographic area. Connecticut and its neighbors in New England and New York still of course absorbed the vast bulk of Yale graduates, but by the end of the last decade of the colonial period, Yale graduates could be found in every part of the Atlantic world. What sort of leadership did these graduates provide for Connecticut and for the other areas into which they moved? An analysis of the occupations of Yale graduates reveals some striking changes.

Yale was never a seminary in the strictest sense of the word. Its graduates did not go directly into the ministry but almost always studied two or three years with a minister before receiving a call to a vacant pulpit.[11] Yet, a high percentage of Yale graduates in the early decades of the eighteenth century did enter the ministry. This percentage declined steadily over the course of the eighteenth century from 73 percent and 66 percent in 1702–1710 and 1711–1720 to 36 percent and 27 percent in 1761–1770 and 1771–1780. A Yale graduate in the early eighteenth century had nearly a three out of four likelihood of becoming a minister, but by 1780 this likelihood had declined to a one out of four. This trend is not surprising given the secularizing trends in society and education in general, but the degree to which the secularization made its impact on the careers of Yale graduates is dramatic and provides testimony to the deep-seated changes occurring in the Puritan world.[12]

The percentage of Yale graduates pursuing careers as farmers and merchants stayed relatively the same throughout the colonial eighteenth century. A larger percentage of Yale graduates became physicians after 1720 than previously, but this percentage increased only

Table 10
Places of Death of Yale Graduates

	1702–10 N = 29	1711–20 N = 51	1721–30 N = 115	1731–40 N = 167	1741–50 N = 198	1751–60 N = 268	1761–70 N = 306	1771–80 N = 308
Connecticut	68.97	74.51	72.17	69.70	59.60	59.70	54.88	52.10
Massachusetts	17.24	5.88	13.04	10.30	7.07	17.91	18.86	13.92
New York	10.34	7.84	3.48	10.30	11.62	8.58	11.11	15.86
New Jersey	3.45	9.80	1.74	2.42	8.59	1.12	1.68	0.65
Rhode Island			2.61	1.21	0.51	2.61	0.34	1.29
Pennsylvania			0.87	1.21	1.52		0.34	1.29
N. Hampshire			0.87	1.21	2.02	2.99	2.69	0.97
Vermont					0.51	2.24	3.37	4.85
Delaware				0.61				
N. Carolina			0.87	0.61	1.01	0.37	0.34	0.32
S. Carolina					1.01			0.32
Mississippi					0.51		0.67	0.32
Illinois					1.01			0.32
Maine						0.37	1.01	
Louisiana							0.34	0.32
Michigan							0.34	0.32
Georgia							0.67	0.97
Ohio							0.67	1.29
Indiana								0.65
Maryland								0.32
Wash. D.C.			0.87	1.82	1.01	0.37	0.67	0.97
Nova Scotia						0.75		0.65
New Brunswick					1.52			0.32
Quebec			0.87					
Ontario								
Cape Breton							0.34	
Haiti						0.37		
Buca						0.37		
St. Croix								0.32
France								
Poland								0.32
West Indies			0.87			1.12	0.34	0.65
England		1.96	1.74	1.61	1.52	1.12	1.01	

slightly between that date and 1780. The legal profession increased the most as a career choice for Yale men, and in the last decade under study sixty-three graduates became lawyers, only twenty-four less than the eighty-seven men who became ministers. One can contrast these figures to those of the sixty graduates who had become ministers between 1702 and 1720 and the five graduates who had become lawyers in that same period. Much of the rest of the decline in the percentage of graduates becoming ministers was taken up by a wide array of occupations, as the Yale graduating classes developed an increasingly diversified career profile.

No members of the classes between 1702 and 1720 became permanent teachers or administrators, but sixteen and twelve men did so, respectively, from the classes graduating between 1771 and 1780. The classes for that decade also produced druggists, career soldiers, manufacturers, writers, and an editor, surveyor, and banker. After 1731 about 5 percent of Yale graduates did not settle on a permanent career but were simply designated as "prominent citizens" by their biographer. Over the course of the colonial period, Yale was evolving from a Puritan college which trained leaders for the church toward a modern elitist college which trained people for varied opportunities in all walks of life. The transformation was by no means complete— 27 percent of Yale graduates between 1771 and 1780 did become ministers—yet the profile of graduates' careers was moving closely toward that of the modern college. It would not be inaccurate to assert that at its beginning Yale graduated future clergymen and a few other types of leaders, and by the end of the colonial period it graduated leaders a portion of whom were clergymen. The secularization process at Yale can be placed in sharper relief by contrasting the percentage of its graduates becoming ministers with Princeton's. On the eve of the Revolution nearly 50 percent of Princeton graduates became ministers. The evangelical impulse behind Princeton's founding clearly attracted a student body more religiously zealous than Yale's.[13]

Along with the decline in percentages of ministers in the Yale graduating classes came a correspondingly sharp increase in the number and percentage of political leaders. Since ministers in New England were precluded from occupying both the pulpit and an elected office, the decline in the percentage of ministers created a larger pool of graduates eligible for political office. From the classes of 1711– 1720 only 17 percent of Yale graduates held a political office, where-

Table 11
Occupations of Yale Graduates

	1702-10 N = 38	1711-20 N = 50	1721-30 N = 108	1731-40 N = 139	1741-50 N = 193	1751-60 N = 249	1761-70 N = 308	1771-80 N = 318
	%	%	%	%	%	%	%	%
Minister	73	66	57	47.9	46.9	35.5	35.8	26.9
Farmer	8	6	9	6.25	4.6	9.3	14.07	7.1
Physician	5	6	10	9.7	17.2	12.8	14.0	13.3
Merchant	10	12	7	13.9	10.4	14.8	14.2	13.3
Prominent Citizen	2		2	4.8	6.3	5.8	1.0	5.6
Lawyer	2	6	9	6.9	9.4	11.6	16.2	19.5
Student		2						
Druggist		2			0.5	0.7	0.3	1.5
Teacher			2	0.6		0.7	0.6	
Administrator			1	2.1	2.6	0.7	0.6	
Mariner			2	0.6		0.7	0.6	3.7
Manufacturer/ Industrialist							0.3	
Soldier								0.6
Writer								0.3
Editor								0.3
Surveyor								0.3
Banker								0.3

as by 1771–1780, 40 percent of them did. However, the percentage of nonministers among the Yale graduates who held a major political office remained approximately the same for the entire period; slightly over half of those who did not enter the ministry became political leaders. Ministers, of course, while not holding office, frequently exercised considerable political power both by being sought out for advice by politicians and by influencing the voting of their congregations. This power, obviously indirect, was progressively being exchanged for direct power as more and more of a percentage of Yale graduates became major political officeholders.

Table 12
Political Leaders among Yale Graduates

1702–10	1711–20	1721–30	1731–40
N = 18	N = 50	N = 108	N = 139
%	%	%	%
33.3	16.6	20.7	25.4

1741–50	1751–60	1761–70	1771–80
N = 193	N = 249	N = 308	N = 318
%	%	%	%
25.11	38.4	32.2	39.93

Both the religious and political world of Connecticut and the rest of the colonies underwent profound changes in the eighteenth century. Two great events, the Great Awakening of the 1740s and the Revolution, mounted extraordinary challenges to the homogeneity and relative tranquility that characterized Connecticut at the time of Yale's founding. The Great Awakening shattered any pretenses Connecticut may have had that it was a colony uniform in faith, and the Revolution forced men to choose between making war on their king or becoming known as traitors to their native land. In both the rending of the Congregational establishment and of the British Empire, Yale graduates played conspicuous roles.

Before the Great Awakening and the Revolution, however, the growth of Anglicanism challenged the orthodoxy of many Yale graduates. Despite the fact that its founders intended Yale to be a bastion of Puritan orthodoxy and a contrast to the more liberal Harvard, religious dissent figured prominently in Yale's early history. The most noted example was the announcement in September 1722 by President Timothy Cutler and four Yale tutors of their conversion to Anglicanism. Cutler revealed his apostasy at the annual commencement, and a shocked board of trustees required all subsequent presidents and tutors to assent to the Saybrook Confession, the platform of Congregational orthodoxy.[14] Despite this affirmation of Yale's religious commitment and Cutler's replacement by a staunch member of Connecticut's religious establishment, Yale was graduating an increasing number of Anglicans by mid-century. From 1721 to 1770 approximately 20 percent of Yale graduates declared for Anglicanism either before or after graduation. This percentage did decline slowly, however, for the two decades after 1750 and declined abruptly to 10 percent in 1771–1780. This decline was related to the opening in New York City of Columbia, offering young area men with an inclination toward Anglicanism a college close to home that was congenial to their religious leanings. Still, the Anglican presence among Yale graduates was significant. Almost all of the other graduates remained within the Puritan persuasion and were either Congregationalists or Presbyterians. Only seven Yale graduates in the entire period identified themselves as Baptists, and, aside from ten members of the Sandemanian sect among the graduates of the classes between 1751 and 1760, few others deviated from Puritanism.

Within Puritanism, however, little unity was evident as the Great Awakening divided the Puritan world into New Lights, proponents of the Awakening, and Old Lights, its opponents. Since most of the Puritan graduates who died after the fury of the Awakening had subsided were identified merely as Congregationalists or Presbyterians, we do not know on which side of the Awakening they positioned themselves. However, many of the graduates of the classes between 1702 and 1750 were identified as either New Lights or Old Lights, and it is clear from the data on them that Yale produced sizable numbers on both sides of the controversy with a slightly larger percentage of religiously conservative and Old Light graduates. Primarily the split between New Lights and Old Lights among Yale graduates reflects the fairly even split of society at large and secondarily it reflects a change in the allegiance of the college's strong-willed president during the Great Awakening struggles. Thomas Clap changed, for political purposes, from being a staunch Old Light to being a moderate New Light.[15] No clear trends over time can be identified in the split between the Old Lights and New Lights, but the division of graduates between these two opposing positions, when coupled with the sizable percentage of Anglicans, shows that Yale did not turn out graduating classes uniform in belief. Indeed, the religion of Yale graduates contained a fair diversity. Yet, this diversity did not range too widely and did not embrace groups on the radical edges of the Protestant spectrum such as the Baptists. Anglicanism, though a dissenting religion to Puritans, was sober and conservative dissent. The division among Yale graduates was primarily between those accepting many of the Arminian trends in Protestantism, the Anglicans and the Old Lights, and those insisting on the purity of the Puritan emphasis on Grace, the New Lights.

Although an analysis of Yale graduates shows them to be generally moderate or conservative religiously, the college has earned the reputation of being a "seminary of sedition," in the words of Louis Leonard Tucker one of its historians, because of the political activity of its students in the Revolutionary years. Tucker argues that less than 2.5 percent of Yale graduates became Loyalists. Yale students in the years of pre-Revolutionary agitation boycotted British imports and took active parts in demonstrations, and in the military years of the Revolution they fought in the defense of New Haven. Several historians have argued that the curriculum's emphasis on the classics at both Yale and Harvard inclined the students to a whig view of politics.[16] Identifying Yale as a hotbed of radicalism, however, is problematic for two reasons. First, it is difficult to label the revolutionists "radicals" inasmuch as the great majority of Connecticut supported the Revolution and being a whig meant swimming with the Connecticut tide. In fact, it took considerably more independence of mind to support the Loyalist position than the Revolutionary one. Second, the quantitative evidence on the allegiance of Yale graduates is by no means complete. While the number of Yale men who declared for the crown is a relatively small percentage of the total number of graduates, one has to remember that a sizable number of Yale graduates had died by 1776. It would accordingly be an obviously gross distortion to calculate the percentage of Loyalists by dividing the number of Loyalists into the number of graduates. Moreover,

Table 13
Religious Affiliation of Yale Graduates

	1702–10 N = 17 %	1711–20 N = 26 %	1721–30 N = 45 %	1731–40 N = 53 %	1741–50 N = 85 %	1751–60 = 98 %	1761–70 N = 105 %	1771–80 N = 79 %
Congregational	5.88		6.67	10.20	25.51	47.96	51.52	50.0
Old Light	52.94	30.77	28.89	20.41	13.25	7.14	13.13	18.75
New Light	11.77	34.62	11.11	28.56	10.84	7.14	1.01	3.75
Presbyterian	23.53	26.92	22.22	18.37	25.51	11.22	10.10	7.50
Anglican	5.88	7.69	24.44	18.33	21.69	19.39	18.18	10.0
Baptist			2.22				2.02	5.0
Unitarian				2.04				
Sandemanian				2.04		6.12	4.04	
Methodist							1.01	1.25
Other						1.02	3.4	1.25

many of the living Yale graduates took no active role in the Revolution. To assume that uncommitted graduates supported the Revolution would be ignoring the problem of fence sitters and secret Loyalists who feared to declare their allegiance.

The existing evidence would indicate that a higher percentage than 2.5 did support the crown. If one examines the 412 Yale graduates whose Revolutionary affiliations were clear—that is, those who took an active part on one side or the other—78 percent were Revolutionaries and 22 percent were Loyalists. Moreover, these percentages change with the decade of graduation. Approximately one-third of Yale graduates with known affiliations who graduated prior to 1760 were Loyalists, as opposed to only 13 percent who were so from the classes graduating after 1760. This should not be surprising as revolution usually appeals more to the young than the old. The degree of Loyalism is much less if one divides the number of declared Loyalists into the number of graduates living at the outbreak of the Revolution and puts all nonactivists into the Revolutionary column. Even with this distortion, however, the percentage of Loyalists was as high as fifteen for the classes graduating between 1751 and 1760 and only in the decade 1771–1780 does the figure go below 2.5 percent. All of this does not mean, of course, that Tucker is wrong. Yale did produce many more Revolutionaries than Loyalists, but the percentage of Loyalists was not inconsequential. The Yale student body was diverse enough in its intellectual life to graduate men who thought differently about the Revolutionary movement. The percentage of Loyalists among Yale graduates does not appear to be lower than the percentage of Loyalists among the population of Connecticut. Yale contrasts sharply with Princeton where only 3 percent of the graduates became Loyalists and is comparable to Harvard where 16 percent did.[17]

The data in the Yale biographies also allows us to make some statements about the personal lives of Yale graduates and compare them to those of the general population of New England. Our demographic knowledge of New England is increasing rapidly but we still do not have a profile of the population's vital statistics that can command widespread agreement among historians. Yet, it is clear that Yale graduates lived longer, married later, had fewer children, and remarried slightly more often than did other New England men. The mean age of death for Yale men was about 61; the age at marriage was slightly more than 27; the number of children per married graduate

Table 14
Loyalism among Yale Graduates

	1731–40	1741–50	1751–60	1761–70	1771–80
	%	%	%	%	%
Loyalists*	10	10	15	7	2
Loyalists**	33	27	37	17	8

*Loyalists: figured as a percentage of the graduating classes

(adjusted for deaths)

**Loyalists: figured as the percentage of those who took an active

part in the Revolution.

was slightly over 6; and the percentage of graduates marrying more than once was about 25. The respective figures for the general population of New England were approximately 56, 26, 6.6, and 17.[18] When looked at in a time series, none of the vital statistics on Yale graduates showed any clear trends, as the figures varied irregularly over the eighteenth century. The absence of a long-range trend should not be surprising. As noted earlier, P. M. G. Harris, who has studied the chances for success of Yale and Harvard graduates, shows that these chances varied cyclically and did not sustain any clear trends.[19] Success rates varied because of short-run economic opportunities which, of course, would also affect the vital statistics of the graduates.

Two items of personal data that are surprising are the rate of geographical mobility and the high mean age of the graduates. Yale graduates averaged only one move after their initial move away from New Haven. But since no similar data for the general population exists to compare with the Yale graduates, it may well be that most of New England experienced a low rate of geographical mobility. At any rate, despite the fact that many of them moved away from Connecticut, most Yale graduates once settled in a position did not move frequently. As with the other vital statistics, the figures for the rate of geographical mobility follow no trends over time. The mean age of graduation for Yale students, despite the prevalent belief among historians and folk culture that colonial graduates were substantially younger than modern college graduates, was not that different from today's graduates. The classes through 1740 were younger, averaging 19.5 years, but after that date the average age climbed to about 21.3 years. This figure is identical to the one for Oxford graduates whose mean age at graduation in 1735 was 21.3 and moving slowly upward. The median age at graduation at Princeton in the pre-Revolutionary years was also 21.[20] A few extraordinary examples of youthful entrants to Yale, such as John Trumbull, who satisfied the entrance requirements at age 7½, have apparently misled historians into thinking that the Yale student body was much younger than it actually was.

What conclusions can we draw about colonial Yale and its graduates from the foregoing data and analysis? Yale seems to have been a curious mixture of provincialism and cosmopolitansim, of orthodoxy and diversity.

In recruitment of students, Yale obviously exhibited its most provincial tendencies, drawing upon Connecticut and its immediate environs for the vast number of its students. This pattern was not weakened by the expanding intellectual currents of the colonies and the eighteenth-century western world. Rather, as other opportunities for college education widened with the founding of more colleges, Yale increasingly drew upon geographically proximate young men for its student body. Yet, the pattern of recruitment must be juxtaposed to the sizable and ever-increasing percentage of Yale graduates who settled in areas distant from Connecticut to pursue their careers. Yale and Puritan influence were being diffused over a widening area by this process.

Yale graduates in most ways seemed to exemplify the orthodoxy of New England and turned their backs on radical dissent. A large percentage became ministers, most remained Puritan, and most followed or led their countrymen in becoming proponents of independence from England. However, the percentage of ministers among the graduates declined with each decade; the occupations of the graduates became progressively diverse; graduates increasingly became political leaders; a sizable percentage of the graduates became Anglicans; the graduates divided over the split in the Puritan world brought on by the Great Awakening; and a significant minority of Yale graduates became Loyalists. Hence, while Yale graduates displayed a substantial commitment to the New England way of life,

Table 15
Vital Statistics of Yale Graduates

	1711-20	1721-30	1731-40	1741-50	1751-60	1761-70	1771-80
Number of Moves	1.0	0.6	1.69	0.9	0.63	0.94	1.11
Age at Graduation	18.8	20.5	19.42	21.69	20.94	21.22	21.34
Age at Death	56.5	59.8	63.15	59.26	62.71	61.59	61.28
Age at Marriage	26.3	26.5	27.83	27.11	26.17	27.71	28.21
Number of Children	5.9	6.5	7.84	6.53	5.92	6.05	5.62
Number of Marriages	1.3	1.3	1.3	1.3	1.25	1.14	1.24

they also displayed a significant diversity in careers, religion, and political orientation.

When our picture of Yale graduates is developed, it reveals a portrait of a maturing college whose features, although distinctly altered by age and experience, retained much from its youth. Continuity and change both characterized the profile of graduates, and this is no paradox. Although Yale became larger, more widespread in influence, more secular, and more diverse intellectually, all of which point to the emergence of a modern institution of higher learning, we should not lose sight of the fact that at the end of the colonial period it was still substantially what its founders envisioned it to be—a "School of the Prophets" designed to educate Connecticut youth as leaders for society. New England society itself was growing in population, becoming more diverse intellectually and religiously, undergoing secularization, and sending its sons and daughters out to populate the centers of commerce and the frontiers. Lawyers among Yale's prophets were nearly as numerous as ministers; the prophets showed an increasing tendency to disagree; and their views were being heard in increasing numbers in distant places. These changes, however, all reflect the symbiotic relationship between Yale and New England society. Yale may not have been a seminary of Puritan religion at the end of the colonial period, but it remained a lyceum of New England culture and testified to the continuing vitality of New England intellectual life.

Eight

Emerging Urbanism and Increasing Social Stratification in the Era of the American Revolution

The growth of urban centers occasioned the most visible change to the map of colonial New England. A landscape of woods, cleared fields, isolated farmsteads, and agricultural villages characterized the seventeenth century. Boston and Newport, Rhode Island, provided the only major exceptions to this pattern and even these two centers of trade reflected the roughness and simplicity of the frontier. Other large towns such as Providence, Rhode Island, or Salem, Massachusetts, differed more by degree than by kind from the several hundred small towns in New England at the beginning of the eighteenth century.

By mid-century, however, over a dozen genuine urban centers had emerged. They increased in size, complexity, and grandeur at an extraordinary pace between 1750 and the beginning of the Revolution. These cities assumed important economic and political functions different from the surrounding towns. And, urban functions created an urbane society. New England became divided between those who experienced life in the country or village and those who experienced it in the city. Moreover, within the cities sharp divisions also emerged. The fortunate enjoyed luxuries, diversions, and cultural opportunities; the unfortunate learned to live with periodic unemployment, segregated and substandard housing, and loss of esteem.

This chapter explores the effects of growth on the social structure of Connecticut's five most important urban centers.

Historians agree that urbanization is a crucial factor in the modernization process. Traditional historians acknowledge the presence and importance of urban units in the American colonies, as well as the growth in their size and numbers in the preindustrial early national period. But these traditional historians contend that cities only became a major factor in American life with industrialization in the second half of the nineteenth century. Historical sociologists usually argue that in nonurban, preindustrial society, social positions were highly visible and stratification was clear and unambiguous.[1] In the European context, manorial society, of course, provides the classic example of this. Industrialization and urbanization, the sociologists contend, created the modern middle class, rendered individuals anonymous, blurred the clearly defined social positions, and modernized the social structure. The forces of urban demography, a dynamic economy, and technological innovations significantly raised mobility and lessened stratification. These empirical trends in society that accompanied urbanization and industrialization, the argument continues, have been in turn accompanied by a democratization of behavior patterns and a change in ideology toward greater egalitarianism.

In America, the transition from ruralism and stratification to urbanism and egalitarianism seems to correspond to this rough outline of development. One can select points along a chronology that would show the decline of stratification which accompanied the rise of urbanism. The extremely hierarchical societies one associates with Puritan New England and with seignorial New York, Maryland, and South Carolina failed to last intact into the eighteenth century. In the 1740s and 1770s, the catalytic forces of the Great Awakening and the Revolution challenged doctrines of acceptance of authority and superiority and further weakened the social hierarchy. The nineteenth century administered the *coup de grace* through the innovation of political parties, the opening of the West and, finally, massive urbanization and industrialization. The only major exceptions to this pattern of development before the era of the "Robber Barons" were the aberrations of slavery and the plantation South. Historical theorists would argue that this trend, though somewhat common to all of western society, also manifests itself in a unique American social structure. Although in the twentieth century all of western society may be becoming more similar, the colonies and the new nation throughout the nineteenth century constantly became less European and more American in a fashion that could be demonstrated as a continuum on a straight line.

Many recent social historians, however, argue as I will that neither the line from great to lesser stratification, nor the line from European to American, has been straight. Moreover, the colonial portion of the eighteenth century witnessed an empirical reversal in the continuum. The American colonies between 1700 and 1776 experienced a sharp growth in urbanization accompanied by a growth in social stratification that constantly grew toward approximating the English norm. Cities in preindustrial America, even though they produced upward and downward social mobility, sharpened rather than blurred social distinctions and positions. The crucial urbanization that made these heightened social distinctions meaningful to the colonists occurred not only in the five cities, Boston, Newport, New York, Philadelphia, and Charlestown, whose importance has been recognized by most scholars—these cities were too exceptional to be meaningful to most colonists—but in the large number of emerging secondary urban units.[2]

The importance and nature of secondary urban units has escaped widespread notice because most historians mistakenly thought that population numbers were the key to defining urbanization. Historical geographers recognize that although population may be a characteristic of urbanization, population density and social and economic function are much more important criteria.[3] Albany and Savannah, for instance, had populations of 4,000 or less in 1775 but were clearly urban because they had well-defined business districts, served as distribution and collection centers for hinterlands, had a wide range of occupational specialization, and concentrated much of their population in one small area.[4] Farmington, Connecticut, on the other hand, had more than double the population of either Albany or Savannah. Yet Farmington would as clearly not qualify as an urban unit because it had no well-defined business district, little mercantile activity, was peopled almost entirely by farmers, and its population was scattered over 200 square miles. Nor did legal incorporation as a city always serve as a sure test of urbanization. There were between 25 and 45 legally incorporated cities in the colonies, mostly in the middle colonies, many of which were genuine urban units. In the South, and particularly in New England, however, many settlements which were legally only villages or towns functioned as urban centers. Since only Royal authority could charter a municipal corporation, the New England charter colonies had no power to create legal cities; because municipal incorporation meant a large degree of freedom from outside control, the Royal colonies in the South had no disposition to create them.[5]

Notwithstanding the definitional problems, even the areas traditionally thought to be nonurban experienced a massive growth in secondary urbanization in the eighteenth century. Portsmouth, New Hampshire; Salem, Medford, and Marblehead, Massachusetts; and Providence, Rhode Island, all competed with Boston and Newport as central places for northern and eastern New England.[6] In Connecticut five secondary urban units. Hartford, Middletown, New Haven, New London, and Norwich, began to challenge Boston and New York's ability to tap southern New England as a cask with spigots at either end.[7] In Pennsylvania a major increase in western colonial urbanization occurred after 1730 with the establishment of Lancaster and Wilmington, Easton, Harrisburg, Chambersburg, and Gettysburg also challenged Philadelphia's domination of Pennsylvania, although none could compete within 50 miles of Philadelphia without being destroyed by its gravitational pull.[8] Many units, small by population size, functioned as urban units throughout the nontidewater lower South. Norfolk, Virginia, with a population less than Farmington, Connecticut, served as the major emporium on the mainland for trade with the West Indies. Cabinpoint, Urbana, Dumfries, Richmond, Falmouth, Fredericksburg, and Alexandria, Virginia, all functioned as major distribution and collection centers.[9] Annapolis and Baltimore belie the notion that urbanization made little progress along the Chesapeake.[10] Everywhere one looks in the colonies in the mid-eighteenth century, preindustrial central places were emerging for primarily economic reasons. In 1770 only 7 percent of the American population lived in urban units, but the percentage was growing sharply and playing a disproportionately important role in the colonies.[11]

Sociologists clash over the causes of social stratification. Functional sociologists argue that stratification results when any social, economic, or occupational differentiation occurs. They believe that stratification has its roots in men's persistent search for differences among themselves and their equally persistent tendency to evaluate these differences. Those opposed to functionalist theory contend that differentiation is a natural condition of mankind and should not be equated with stratification which occurs only when the differences of one generation are passed on to the next generation intact. To the nonfunctionalist, only inherited differentiation or differentiation that is long-enduring involves meaningful stratification. However, all sociologists would agree that the longer a differentiated hierarchy exists, the more it stratifies.[12]

All historians and historical sociologists agree with the folk culture that eighteenth-century American society was significantly less stratified than Georgian England. Few scholars, however, recognize that over the course of the colonial eighteenth century the gap between the two social structures narrowed perceptibly. In the colonies, differentiation of position increased at a rapid rate and the tendency of the social and economic oligarchies created by this differentiation to perpetuate themselves also increased. The increase in stratification and the tendency to approach the English model occurred most discernibly in the emerging urban units and will be illustrated hereafter by an examination of Connecticut's five urban centers—Hartford, Middletown, New Haven, New London, and Norwich.

Connecticut's five cities exercised a political and economic influence grossly disproportionate to their populations. While comprising less than 10 percent of the colony's total population, they produced 40 percent of the governor's councilors elected between 1700 and 1784. Five of the nine governors in this period were from the five cities. Of Connecticut's seven most important military leaders during the Revolution, five resided in the five cities and a sixth had spent four years at Yale in New Haven. An examination of a list of Connecticut's 54 leading merchants in this period, reveals that 41 of them, or 76 percent were from the five centers.[13]

Connecticut underwent an economic revolution at mid-century in which it changed from primarily grain-growing subsistence farming to large-scale production of livestock and increased manufacture of handicrafts for export. After a decline in the standard of living between 1718 and the 1740s, a strong upsurge of business activity occurred in the late 1740s. The five cities led, controlled, and benefitted from the economic revitalization.[14] Trade—particularly the West Indian trade—increased dramatically. The number of ships utilizing these ports tripled; both exports and imports increased dramatically between 1756 and 1774.[15] The five cities, led by the merchants of New Haven and Norwich and the ships of New London, controlled almost all of this trade. Hartford and Middletown became the collection depots and distribution centers for large agricultural hinterlands. The importance of all five cities as central places can be seen by the networks of highways leading from them into the backcountry.[16] Although they had been increasing constantly in function and complexity, it was the boom of the 1740s and 1750s that transformed these centers from "sleepy towns" to provincial cities. Not content merely to control Connecticut's interaction with the great merchants in over twenty West Indian ports, the five cities increasingly vied with Boston and New York in the direct European trade.[17] That this effort was largely unsuccessful does not detract from the grandeur and expansiveness of the cities' aspirations or the reality of their achievements.

The array of shops, goods, services, and social pleasures available in the highly developed business districts of these mid-eighteenth-century cities was impressive. Nearly every known commodity in the western world could be obtained on the seven or eight commercial streets in Hartford. Wigmakers, watchmakers, barbers, harness-makers, brazers and pewterers, apothecaries, grocers, dry goods merchants, jewellers, printers, and artisans of every kind plied their trade and sold their wares. Ten taverns and fourteen inns with colorful names like "Bunch of Grapes," "Old Fortune of War," and "The Harp and the Crown," made sure that Hartford residents and visitors did not have to go far to quench their thirst. Newspapers advertised goods from Holland, Geneva, France, The Indies, and India. The ladies of Hartford, wives of future patriots of republican simplicity, frequented the shop of Marie Gabriel "a mantuamaker and milliner from Paris." Their husbands discussed vintage years for grapes while browsing in newly opened winestores. The elite women of these cities, worried that their attire might be out of fashion, quickly copied styles described by recent travelers to Boston or New York. The outlandish jewelry, parasols, peacock fans, awkward hoops, and especially the hair dressings worn by the ladies of Norwich drove one man to publish a poem in a newspaper satirizing the calash.

> "Hail, great Calash. O'erwhelming veil,
> by all indulgent heaven,
> to calling nymphs and maidens stale,
> in sportive kindness given.
> Safe hid beneath the circling sphere
> unseen by mortal eyes,
> the mingled heaps of oil and hair,
> and wool and powder lies."

Men also carefully cultivated their coiffures. When Samuel Edwards of Hartford died, he left, besides his large amounts of elegant clothes, a "noted wig," "best bob wig," and "natural white wig." The social life of these elegantly attired urbanites also reflected a growing sophistication and love of the mindless but enjoyable pleasures usually associated with leisurely life in English cities. At a wedding dance in Norwich, ninety guests danced 92 jigs, 52 contra dances, 45 minuets, and 17 hornpipes. Dancing clubs, formed in all of the cities, kept late hours and exhausted their members. Young men and women even dared violate the law and meet on the street on Sunday for social occasions.[18]

While the faddish and foppish elite shopped in the cities, the number of people who could not afford even decent middle-class clothes, and who had no reason to feel merry about anything, was increasing. In the half-century preceding the Revolution the gap between the wealthiest and poorest members of society increased in absolute and perhaps in relative numbers. The transition from a frontier environment to an urban stage was accompanied by a growing differentiation of economic classes.[19] Boston, the most economically differentiated community in New England, became an urban area where "merchant princes and proletarians" characterized the eighteenth-century social order. The destitute could be seen in its streets as they tried desperately to avoid its "filthy, dark, crowded, and oderiferous" poorhouse.[20]

Connecticut's cities differed only by degree from Boston. While the average employed, nonskilled urban proletarian earned only £25 per year, Daniel Lathrop of Norwich managed to bequeth £500 each to Yale University, Norwich's treasury, and the city's first ecclesiastical society.[21] The living expenses of many of the cities' gentlemen totaled as much as £700 per year, while other families, even with several members employed, struggled to survive on less than $50 a year. The periodic unemployment of numerous unskilled workers and mariners in the cities also caused many to slip below the income required to support a family in a "middlin'" manner.[22] In the wake of economic disparities residential neighborhoods became segregated and differentiated according to wealth and occupation. The residential patterns reflected hardening class lines.[23] Economic opportunity was present in the northern cities to a much greater extent than it had been previously, but the opportunity to exploit it became more socially determined and increasing numbers of young men were destined to fail.[24]

In addition to the growing social and economic differentiation, the century-long homogeneity in religion and ethnicity disappeared. A more cosmopolitan pluralism emerged in Connecticut's cities. The fight over the Saybrook Platform in the early years of the eighteenth century and the mid-century factionalizing during the Great Awakening shattered the unity of the Congregational church.[25] The fighting over the Great Awakening, bitter in most towns, was most virulent in Connecticut's urban areas. Although only one-half of Connecticut's towns spawned separatist parishes during the Awakening, all five cities did. In each city, with the exception of Hartford, the religious dissension reached extraordinary heights and resulted in deep, angry contention.[26] The urban communities lost a higher percentage of converts to the Anglican Church than did many of the small towns that surrounded them. Anglicans also had greater success in office-holding in urban areas than in rural regions, and Anglicanism no longer was a crushing burden for aspirant officeholders.[27] Catholicism also increased its numbers, and Jewish worship even appeared in New Haven. This plurality of worship reflected an increase in the settlement of new nationalities in the five cities. Spanish, Portuguese, French, Irish, Dutch, and West Indians emigrated to Connecticut's cities. Previously only an occasional French Huguenot or Protestant New Amsterdam Dutchman kept the population from being totally Congregationalist-English.[28] Most of the non-English came to the cities to promote commerce and hence joined the mercantile class. While non-English merchants usually did not become elected leaders in the communities, they did become influential and moved in the best social circles.

The growing differentiation and stratification in Connecticut's cities was reflected in their governments and political patterns. The selectmen increasingly became executive officers who functioned as supervisors over a burgeoning list of lesser officers.[29] The numbers of officers elected by the town meetings increased from approximately twenty-five at the beginning of the century to over one hundred in three of the cities by the end of the colonial period. Greater distinctions separated the selectmen from the lesser officers. Moreover, the town meetings grew less active and allowed the selectmen more discretionary power to govern. Instead of democratizing officeholding patterns, as is emphasized in "consensus" accounts of eighteenth-century politics, each city experienced a growth in the degree of oligarchy among officeholders.[30] Rotation of office, which had characterized the election of selectmen before 1740, gave way to patterns of increasing reelection.[31]

By the late eighteenth century these emerging urban centers had began to look more like English provincial cities and less uniquely American. It was the cities, of course, that led the American resistance to the British imperial policies; ironically, these cities, at the moment of their rebellion, approximated the English urban and elite social structure more than at any time in their previous existence. Even the demographic factors of birth rates, death rates, and marriage ages deviated less from the English norm and began to be affected by the hardening of class lines and lessening of mobility and economic opportunity. One scholar recently suggested that as absurd as it sounds, America may have been becoming just another "overcrowded" old world society by 1776. Other scholars refer to the "Anglicization" of late colonial culture. These judgments, with regard to the urban areas, are convincing. Political and economic power, as well as social prestige, were becoming concentrated in a small number of men and families. The elitism of the seventeenth-century Puritan village had coexisted with feelings of unity and communalism within a homogeneous community. Classes had existed but they were bound together in a whole unit. The eighteenth-century cities became sufficiently heterogeneous and differentiated to destroy, or badly wound, unity. Classes emerged that felt little in common with each other.[32]

Other indicators suggest that the colonies were closer to the English norm and more aware of the Atlantic world than they ever were before, or would be again, until World War I. In the seventeenth century each of the colonies had been exceptionally distinct, but in the eighteenth century, as each copied the English model, they became more similar.[33] English imports per capita into the colonies increased steadily throughout the eighteenth century and at a greater rate of increase than other imports. Carriages graced city streets in increasing numbers. The fox hunt even made its appearance in Charlestown and probably in Newport.[34] The bar and bench, the medical profession, and the military styled themselves more along the lines of their old world colleagues.[35] Even the Puritan church grew so Anglicized—in ways such as using melodies and notes in its singing—that purists stigmatized it as the "Catholick" Congregational Church. Jonathan

Edwards, the greatest American religious thinker of the eighteenth century, was more a European theologian who owed little to the Mathers or Stoddards but much to Locke, Newton, and Hobbes.[36]

The number of newspapers in all of the colonies grew from Boston's one in 1704 to 48 widely scattered journals in 1775. Almost all these journals concentrated their news on nonlocal stories. Reflecting their growing cosmopolitanism, each of Connecticut's five cities commenced the publication of newspapers by the end of the colonial period. The content of the news stories was heavily English and European.[37] Other sophisticated attributes of Connecticut's five cities can be seen in the growth of large personal libraries and book stores, and in the creation of regular post offices. The major public buildings constructed in the late colonial period had the dignity of well-constructed brick Georgian architecture. An unusual example of the decline of the wilderness conditions in Connecticut's cities can be seen in the widely heralded killing of the "last rattlesnake" in Norwich. By the outbreak of the Revolution the five cities had large public grammar schools, and Yale University in New Haven enrolled the large number of 200 students. The great demand for domestic servants caused the appearance of a slave market in Middletown in the 1760s.[38]

Most of the Anglicization or Europeanization occurred without concious thought, but at times the desire to copy English society was given overt expression. John Trumbull, the young Yale poet, wrote an immensely popular poem printed in New Haven called "The Progress of Dullness," in which Tom Brainless and Dick Hairbrain competed for the love of Miss Simper.[39] Through these characters Trumbull condemned American society and urged it to be more like the sophisticated English society he admired. Conversely, European visitors invariably expressed amazement at the similarities between the cities of the old world and the new. Some American cities even displayed such unwanted attributes of European cities as growing health problems, increased crime, and soaring taxes, although generally Connecticut's urban centers did not.[40]

The Revolutionary experience did not end the trend toward the Anglicization of the cities. Connecticut's five urban areas became aware of themselves as entities distinct from their fellow towns and decided to seek incorporation as legal cities. Throughout the eighteenth century in Connecticut, and in every other colony, differences between farm inhabitants and city dwellers surfaced with increased regularity and urgency.[41] In Connecticut's five cities the conflict became acute because each town was an amalgam of an urban business district that was surrounded by outlying farms within the same legal unit. Each of the five towns contained large numbers of farmers, often a majority, whose needs were antithetical to the business community and who often blocked projects which the business community regarded as essential.[42] As early as 1771 New Haven appointed a committee to investigate incorporating the business district of the town as a separate city.[43] Because the Revolutionary War destroyed the commerce of the militarily exposed ports of New Haven and New London, and because Hartford, Middletown, and Norwich, rapidly increased their business districts' commerce by acting as major entrepots, all five centers were convinced at the end of the war that they could only safeguard their mercantile interests by becoming incorporated cities. The Revolutionary War also caused merchants and farmers to conclude that fundamental differences separated urban and rural areas. Few of the surrounding farmers opposed the drive for incorporation and in 1784 the business districts of the five areas acquired standard English municipal government consisting of a "Mayor, Aldermen, Common Council, and Freemen." The only basic difference between the five new city governments and English municipal corporations was that the membership of freemen in the Connecticut cities was quite large; hence, a meeting of their freemen was a large deliberative body while in the English cities the membership was very restricted.[44] Each of the new cities still remained a part of the original towns and still took part in town government.

Connecticut's five acts of incorporation were not unique in the new states. During the Revolutionary shakeup, a wave of incorporations, beginning with Richmond, Virginia, in 1782 and Charleston, South Carolina, in 1783, brought the legal status of other American cities in line with their economic status. The regulation of commerce, the sole reason for incorporation in Connecticut's cities, dominated the incorporation acts and the business of the five cities during their first years. To underscore that largeness of population need not be a criterion for definition of an urban area, none of Connecticut's new cities, when separated from the town's farmers, had more than 4,000 inhabitants.[45]

The growing synthesis between political, social, and economic power in the five cities did not immediately end during the Revolutionary period. Political officeholding was more oligarchic than ever and family prestige, as an important political factor, was at a high point during the Revolutionary years, but undoubtedly the seeds were sown for the destruction of a few families' monopoly of office-holding.[46] The peak of a political cycle was reached during the Revolutionary years. The party battles of the 1790s and of the early nineteenth century, unleashed by Revolutionary forces, ended total dominance of major officeholding by the rich and well-born. However, while the synthesis between power and wealth ended a half-century after the Revolution, the concentration of wealth in the hands of a few and the growing economic stratification continued in Connecticut and in the other cities of the new states. If one looks ahead to the distribution of the nation's wealth in 1861, the ongoing trend can be substantiated.[47] In the immediate Revolutionary years, Hartford's, Middletown's, and Norwich's crucial commercial roles in the provisioning of the Revolutionary armies assured that their commerce would increase, the trend in their increasing importance would be accentuated, and no democratization would occur in their distribution of wealth.[48]

In conclusion then, it appears clear that the colonies did not enter their national existence entirely as a rural, homogeneous unstratified society with only a handful of urban pockets. A century-long trend toward secondary urbanization and toward social stratification that approached English norms preceded the Revolution and in some ways was intensified by it. In Massachusetts, in the thirty years after the Revolution, much of rural society exchanged its values for ones that at first had appeared only in Boston and then in a few secondary centers.[49] Heterogeneity, cosmopolitanism, and organizational variety, which were once found in the cities, began to make their inroads in rural Massachusetts' "Peaceable Kingdom" and soon became a generalized feature of the new state's society. Voluntary associations, which usually are indications of more sifting going on within the social strata, rose sharply in rural society. Small western towns, settled in the half-century after the Revolution, dreamed of becoming great urban communities and hoped to be known as the "Athens of Ohio," or of Tennessee. Settlements never seemed content to remain rural or sleepy towns. They built grand hotels and chartered colleges as indications of their urban aspirations and pretensions.[50] Urban society and urban values were expanding far before any large-scale industrial development. Anglicization was not ended by the Revolution but also continued apace. The rhetoric of post-Revolutionary society may have argued against English models of behavior but the growth in the concentration of wealth, in commerce, in the poor classes, in cosmopolitanism and urban values, and the love of things English during "The Federal Era," all show that in reality, if not in ideology, the trend toward urbanization and stratification survived the Revolution and continued into the national period.

HISTORIOGRAPHICAL DIVISIONS

SAMUEL ADAMS' BUMPY RIDE: RECENT VIEWS OF THE AMERICAN REVOLUTION IN MASSACHUSETTS

Unlike previous chapters, this concluding one, an historiographical analysis of recent writing on the Revolution in Massachusetts, contains no research in original sources. My survey of other scholars' original research, however, suggests few of them can avoid dealing with the question of divisions. Probably, the monographic approach creates a propensity to overstate differences among individuals, classes, and regions. One often finds what one looks for in research. Biographies, analyses of the urban poor and crowds in the street, case studies of local communities, all tend to emphasize the unique contributions or points of view of their subjects. As the number of subjects grows, so does the number of differing experiences.

Nevertheless, the disputatious factions of Revolutionary Massachusetts have not been invented by historians—they were real. And, their conflicting goals and loyalties often derived from economic interest, ideology, class, and geography. Merchants and farmers, conservatives and reformers, gentlemen and mobs, easterners and westerners, at times found themselves opposing each other nearly as much as they opposed English policy and English military force.

Massachusetts's role in and importance to the Revolution were far greater than those of any other colony. Many loyalists believed serious anti-British agitation originated with a cabal of Boston malcontents intent on destroying good government. Conspiratorial-minded patriots rooted the attack on their liberties in the murky, corrupt plots of a self-serving Boston junta currying favor with imperial authorities. British policymakers, long after civil war had exposed the strength of Revolutionary sentiments throughout the colonies, clung to their reassuring delusion that Massachusetts had artificially fomented the crisis and manipulated other colonies into rebellion. From the 1760s to the present, Massachusetts's leaders have been identified as the Revolution's leaders. Samuel and John Adams, James Otis, John Hancock, and Thomas Hutchinson loom over the events of the Revolution and their names have become household words. Only Virginia's three great leaders, George Washington, Thomas Jefferson, and Patrick Henry, and Pennsylvania's, Benjamin Franklin and Joseph Galloway, rival those of Massachusetts for recognition. Neither Virginia nor Pennyslvania, however, can equal Massachusetts in supplying icons to the Revolution. The sloop Liberty, the Boston Massacre, the Boston Tea Party, the Massachusetts Government Act, the Battles of Lexington, Concord, and Bunker Hill, and Shays' Rebellion are the signposts that mark the road to and from revolution.

Almost all professional historians, although willing to acknowledge the preeminence of Massachusetts in the pre-Revolutionary agitation, would probably agree that the primacy of the Bay Colony has been exaggerated. Nevertheless, Revolutionary Massachusetts has received scholarly attention nearly proportionate to its visibility in the popular mind. Heroes and villains require explanations for their behavior; their personalities and motives become historically newsworthy. Icons require explication and elaboration to retain their celebratory quality. The very sources used by modern historians lend themselves to scholarly overindulgence. The flamboyant actions of Massachusetts's leaders, mobs, and towns created a self-sustaining body of written records. New Englanders had the highest literacy rate in the colonies and their town meeting records surpass in bulk and detail the local political records of any other region. Even the presence of so many colleges and universities in Massachusetts with large faculties and libraries has enhanced its attractiveness as a subject. For at least a half-century, the art of serious historical writing has been dominated by the professoriat; and there are a lot of professors in New England and wonderful research facilities to attract visiting ones.

As everyone no doubt suspects, these prefatory remarks serve a purpose beyond merely describing how high the mountain is that I am trying to climb. They get me off the hook, at least partially I hope, for the things this chapter does not do, and they attempt to justify those things it does do. I wish to concentrate my attention on the major works published primarily in the last two decades, and I do not wish to discuss in detail earlier work or the torrent of recent short articles and unpublished theses. To review all the secondary literature on Massachusetts's Revolutionary experience would obscure the forest in an effort to identify every tree.

GENERAL TRENDS

Since the publication of Carl Becker's *The History of Political Parties in the Province of New York, 1760-1776* (Madison, Wis., 1909), American historians have seemed unable to escape dealing with the largest issues of the Revolution in terms prescribed by him. As iconoclastic a scholar as Becker would probably be appalled to know that for three-fourths of a century, historians have debated his proposition that the events of the 1760s, 1770s, and 1780s constituted both a war of independence and a social revolution in which differing social and economic classes vied for control of the Revolutionary resistance and settlement. To be fair to the historical profession, the questions raised by Becker are basic and profound; and the debate has been refined, taking some unusual and productive twists and turns along the way. To be fair to the spirit of honest self-examination, however, no one since 1909 has matched the conceptual audacity of Becker's eighteen-page first chapter. Professional historians use differing sets of terms to identify the opposing sides in this debate—Whig vs. Progressive, Consensus vs. Conflict, Neo-Whig vs. New Left—but the essential historiographical outlines remain the same. One wonders how much intellectual energy and vitality has been expended defending or attacking Becker's thesis that might have been more profitably spent elsewhere. I had hoped to be able to say that I would avoid participating in the consensus–conflict dialogue. Alas, I cannot. The nature of the secondary literature will not allow its omission.[1]

Within the general framework so bemoaned above, some exciting new areas of investigation have been opened that have produced much and promise to produce more. Brilliance has not disappeared from the ranks of Revolutionary historians, it has just been confined. Often, historians have tried to break outside the consensus-conflict limits only to find reviewers and subsequent scholars searching their work for signs of whether it should be assigned to one camp or the other. Historiographers seem to resist anyone breaching the perimeter. In particular, six new types/methods/conceptual patterns are worth brief mention before we move to Massachusetts. They are not mutually exclusive and many studies fall within two or more of these categories.

(1) Ideology. Probably the most influential book of recent years, Bernard Bailyn's *The Ideological Origins of the American Revolution* (Cambridge, Mass., 1965), attracted everyone's attention to the notion that the Revolutionaries filtered a complex body of oppositional whig, classical republican, and Enlightenment ideology through their own experiences as an outpost of the British Empire and focussed their thought on the crises of the pre-Revolutionary years. Lockian ideas of the social compact and formal English constitutional theory which previously had been regarded as the ideological well-springs of the Revolution became, under Bailyn's pen, just a part of a much more eclectic world view held by colonists. Gordon Wood's *The Creation of the American Republic, 1776–1787* (Chapel Hill, N.C., 1969) similarly drew together the diverse strands of thought after the Revolution that were woven together in the writing of the state and federal constitutions.[2]

(2) Religion. Although part of the ideological matrix described by Bailyn and others, religious thought and the colonists' religious background has received a special emphasis. Edmund S. Morgan's "The Puritan Ethic and the American Revolution," *William and Mary Quarterly*, 3d Ser., XXIV (1967), 3–43 tied the Revolutionaries to their seventeenth-century past as reformers with a mission to purify the world and suggested that the secular qualities of the Revolutionary generation had been overemphasized. Alan Heimert's *Religion and the American Mind: From the Great Awakening to the Revolution* (Cambridge, Mass., 1966) shows clear connections between religious radicalism and the antiauthority impulses of the 1760s.[3]

(3) Localism. No area of colonial and Revolutionary historical writing has increased as rapidly in size and explanatory importance as local history. Most of the first major studies stopped short of the Revolution and concentrated on the colonial period but many of them commented implicitly on the Revolution and increasingly, as the *genre* matured, its practitioners explicitly analyzed the Revolution from a local perspective.[4]

(4) Lower Classes. Since Jesse Lemisch first turned that felicitious phrase, "The American Revolution Seen from the Bottom Up,"

during the turbulent 1960s, historians have been following the lead of their European predecessors in trying to capture the essence of life at or near the bottom of the social structure.[5] The roles of sailors, crowds, debtors, the unemployed, and so forth have been integrated into a revolutionary movement previously populated by merchants, lawyers, gentlemen, and substantial landowners. Jackson Turner Main's pioneering *The Social Structure of Revolutionary America* (Princeton, N.J., 1965) was the point of departure for much of this scholarship although it has been largely superceded by those it helped inspire.

(5) Colonial Background. Revolutionary historians, of course, have always emphasized the colonial period to a substantial degree: the rise of the assembly, the development of royal government, the imposition of trade regulations, and so forth have figured prominently as institutional preconditions for the imperial crisis. Recently, however, demographic, economic, and social historians have identified in the colonial past changes and trends in society that may have created some of the underlying societal preconditions for revolution. Kenneth Lockridge's essay, "Social Change and the Meaning of the American Revolution," *Journal of Social History*, IV (1973), 403–439, was the first of many to argue that population growth, a dwindling supply of available land, and other economic difficulties created tensions in colonial society that made it rife with dissatisfaction and ripe for rebellion.[6]

(6) Previously excluded groups. Many groups mentioned previously only in passing have begun to receive serious historical attention. In particular, loyalists and women, two large populations who had been viewed in the past primarily passively and in relationship to the patriot movement—loyalists were wrong or misguided: women sewed and suffered—are being studied on their own terms.[7]

The expansion of substance in the above six categories has been accompanied by an expansion or elaboration of historical methodologies. The greatest development has been in the increasing reliance on quantitative data and statistical analysis but this should not obscure other alterations in approach that are nearly as significant. Virtually abandoned in the revolt against the Turner thesis, historical geography has again assumed a status of legitimacy. Town, county court, parish, probate, and land records probably now exceed colony archives in their use as sources. And, social science theory, particularly from the disciplines of anthropology and psychology, is assuming a new importance.

All of the above is providing a richer picture of the American Revolution as a far more complex subject than anyone previously imagined. In Massachusetts, our perspective of the Revolution, prior to the last two decades, has been unduly limited despite the massive amount of secondary literature. Too much has focussed on too little. If Massachusetts dominated the Revolutionary era, Boston dominated Massachusetts, the Caucus dominated Boston, and Samuel Adams dominated the Caucus. Thus, Cass Canfield, a journalist–historian, thought it appropriate to entitle his book, *Sam Adams's Revolution.* Published by a serious press, Harper and Row, the book unabashedly asserts that the title is appropriate because "without Sam Adams there would have been no Declaration of Independence on July 4, 1776."[8] Canfield is unintentionally exaggerating a theme less baldly stated but implicit in much of the writing about pre-Revolutionary Massachusetts. The secondary literature of the past two decades, however, has eroded that reductionist proposition to the point where it is no longer tenable even in muted form. Samuel Adams was important; the Caucus was important; Boston was important; but other individuals, other groups and classes, and other communities were also important and are receiving the attention not only that they deserve but that we need if we are to understand what happened in Massachusetts between 1763 and 1789. I wish to discuss the Revolution in Massachusetts by looking at the work of historians who have viewed it from four perspectives: (1) from the top down—the role of leaders; (2) from the bottom up—the role of the lower classes; (3) from the center—The General Court and Boston; and (4) from the hinterland—the other towns and regions in the colony. These categories are in some ways confining; the work of most historians fits in more than one. For the sake of orderly analysis and brevity, however, I will assign (but I hope not consign) each of the works to one of them. Once the four views are developed, they can be superimposed on each other for a fuller picture.

FROM THE TOP DOWN

More than that of any of the Revolutionaries, Samuel Adams's reputation has undergone the most striking reinterpretation in recent years. Largely shunted to the sidelines by nineteenth-century historians, Adams moved to centerstage in the first half of the twentieth century but the role he played was hardly flattering. A wily agitator, seen to be suspecting British plots everywhere, Adams manufactured crises when there were none and orchestrated resistance when there should have been reconciliation. Unhampered by a concern for truth or ethical scruples, Adams became a "pioneer in propaganda" in the title of John C. Miller's biography. Clifford Shipton's entry on him in Sibley's *Harvard Graduates* further embellished the duplicity of a leader committed to revolution at any cost because of his own personal failures and neuroses.[9] A variety of scholars in the early 1970s, however, began to question both Adams's influence and malevolence. This new view had its best statement in an article on Adams by Pauline Maier that was subsequently expanded and appeared as a chapter in her book, *The Old Revolutionaries: Political Lives in the Age of Samuel Adams* (New York, 1980), which should have laid to rest forever the myth of "Sam Adams's Revolution" and with it the pejorative implication that the Revolution was somehow manufactured.[10] Maier shows Adams to be an austere man, deeply rooted in his Calvinist past and committed to a vision of republican virtue. Despite enhancing Adams's character, ironically Maier's work diminishes his relative importance, although in a further irony she uses his name as a label for the pre-Revolutionary decade. According to Maier, Adams "controlled" neither the crowds in the street nor the Boston Town Meeting, did not bully other leaders into submission, and did not advocate independence in the 1760s. Adams groped his way toward revolution reluctantly as the only alternative he could accept when imperial reform proved impossible.

The "other Adams," John, has received even more attention recently than his cousin, although our picture of him has not been altered as dramatically. Since the opening to scholars of the Adams' papers in the 1950s, several biographies or book-length studies of his thought or character have appeared. The first of these, Page Smith's two-volume study published in 1962, does not, as Smith frankly admits in the preface, "materially alter the picture" we already had.[11] Adams had been treated by scholars consistently as an ambitious but honest, dour but decent, conservative but revolutionary, introspective intellectual haunted by a sense of duty. Smith's biography supports this view and is the most detailed account of Adam's life.

John Howe, Jr.'s analysis of Adams's political thought is more insightful and interpretive. Howe argues that the maintenance of order and stability obsessed Adams all his life. Anchored in this conservatism, Adams's specific thought changed, Howe believes, in response

to changes in society. Although stubborn and unswerving in his commitments to deeply felt beliefs, the John Adams that emerges from
Howe's pen is an adaptive man able to modify his thought as a result
of his experience.[12]

The image of a brooding, duty-conscious John Adams has often
been contrasted with the picture of his supposedly vocal, wily cousin
Samuel. Peter Shaw's study of John's character read in conjunction
with Maier's reinterpretation of Samuel, shows the two cousins had
much in common. John Adams also derived his essence from the
moralistic past of his seventeenth-century ancestors, Shaw argues.
Full of self-doubt, John was nearly as austere as Samuel, and sought
a state of grace the way the Puritans had through continual self-
examination. He had, in Shaw's words, a "lonely struggle with ambition" and courted popularity as a recognition of his worth but also
courted unpopularity as a sign to himself of courage and integrity.[13]
Both John and Samuel Adams emerge as much misplaced Puritans as
they do properly cast revolutionaries. Both disciplined themselves
through self-denial, despised luxury and excess, feared venality and
corruption, and suspected it in their opponents.

A third Adams, John's wife Abigail, has long been regarded as the
most important and influential woman in Revolutionary and early
national America. With the rise of women's history, Abigail has
achieved a new prominence. Lynne Withey's sympathetic and charming biography of Abigail shows her life to have embodied a tension
between domesticity and feminism. Essentially very conservative,
convinced that a woman's place was in the home, Abigail nevertheless could not suppress her indignation at injustices accorded the
poor, slaves, and women. A loyal wife and domineering mother,
she prodded her husband to "remember the ladies" when reforming
government and society and inculcated a spirit of inquiry in her
children.[14]

All three Adamses believed Thomas Hutchinson, the last royal
governor of peacetime Massachusetts, to be the most villainous actor
in the Revolutionary drama. Neither Bernard Bailyn nor William
Pencak, his two recent biographers, would agree.[15] One finishes reading Bailyn's sensitive moving account of Hutchinson's life with a
tremendous sense of sympathy and an admiration for his virtues. No
other piece of historical literature can rival this biography in portray-
ing individual tragedy in the Revolution. As unswerving as any of the
Adamses, Hutchinson shared with them to a substantial degree the

whig fear of unchecked power. To Hutchinson, however, the greatest danger came not from imperial policy but from home-grown demagoguery within Massachusetts. Published in 1982, eight years after Bailyn's book, Pencak's analysis of Hutchinson's political and social thought argues that the loyalist–historian formulated a comprehensive, consistent, and personally satisfying conservative philosophy of politics and history. Calling Huchinson, an American Burke, Pencak reasserts the connection between loyalism and classical conservatism that American historians once wrote of and Canadian ones still do. If Bailyn tries to place Hutchinson on the conservative side but within the whig spectrum, Pencak tries to place him in a separate ideological camp. Both scholars, however, rehabilitate his character and both admire his impressive intellectuality.

The other major new biography of a Massachusetts loyalist, Carol Berkin's *Jonathan Sewall* (New York, 1974), is equally sympathetic to a less well-known man. Born to an impoverished branch of a prominent family, Sewall worked his way up the ladder of Massachusetts politics through ability, industry, and a capacity for leadership acknowledged by all. Rebellious as a student and young man, Berkin argues that Sewall became a victim of his own success and his loyalty to friends. Developing a conservative sense of authority and at home in the factional politics of mid-century, Sewall never seemed to understand fully that great principles were at stake in the 1760s and 1770s and that the battles of those days were not just a continuation of politics as usual. Cautious and optimistic at first, Sewall was forced into exile in England and, like his friend Hutchinson, succumbed to depression. Sewall eventually migrated to Canada, an unhappy man whose life was blighted by events whose meaning he could not comprehend.[16]

James Otis and John Hancock, Boston's other two well-known patriots, still await modern biographers. The brief treatments of Hancock in recent books on other aspects of the Revolution, suggest that the enduring view of him expressed in three earlier biographies as a "vacillating and chameleon" seeker of popularity may require some revision.[17] Otis's career and political thought have been re-examined in part by John J. Waters, Jr., in his *The Otis Family in Provincial and Revolutionary Massachusetts* (Chapel Hill, N.C., 1968), and in an article by James R. Ferguson, "Reason in Madness: The Political Thought of James Otis," *William and Mary Quarterly*, 3d Ser., XXXVI (1979), 194–214. Waters attributes the seemingly erratic twists and turns of Otis's Revolutionary career to his mental instability, personal quarrels with Hutchinson and John and Samuel Adams, and to the constant jockeying for position that took place in the court–country politics of the colony government. Ferguson sees amidst Otis's rambling and at times incoherent writings a consistent tension between the doctrine of natural law and the concept of sovereignty. Early in the 1760s when he emphasized natural rights, Otis supported the patriot's cause; when he later emphasized the sovereignty half of his political equation, he supported royal government.

Charles W. Aker's *The Divine Politician: Samuel Cooper and the Revolution in Boston* (Boston, 1982) attempts to bring a hitherto less publicized leader into the forefront of the Revolutionary movement. Cooper, pastor of the Brattle Street Church, the wealthiest and most influential church in Boston, was the friend and minister of John Hancock, John Adams, James Bowdoin, and several other patriot leaders. Akers's characterization of Cooper as a sensitive, pragmatic, conciliatory man who tried to heal the divisions in Massachusetts society through soothing sermons and personal charm is convincing. And, Cooper undoubtedly did play more of a role in the years after independence was declared, particularly in promoting the French alliance, than posterity has credited him with. Yet, the evidence available does not move Cooper into the first rank of Massachusetts's leaders.[18]

Another Revolutionary, however, Elbridge Gerry, not forgotten but certainly moved away from center stage since his death, does deserve the more prominent role his biographer George Billias assigns him.[19] The most important Massachusetts leader who did not make Boston his home during the years of pre-Revolutionary agitation, Gerry lived in Essex County and is remembered primarily for lending his name to devious methods of drawing election district boundaries and for his alleged obstructionism in refusing to sign the federal constitution drafted in Philadelphia. In the most definitive of any of these biographies being discussed, Billias persuasively argues that a republican ideology suffused all of Gerry's actions and writings and that Gerry's pursuit of his vision of republican virtue required him not to sign the constitution even though he had played an influential role in drafting parts of it. Gerry emerges as an immensely likeable man in Billias's book and seems to be the happiest and most personally untroubled patriot leader. Along with John and Samuel Adams, Gerry shared the Puritan conception of public virtue and fear of luxury and excess. Unlike them, however, he managed to pursue austerity without becoming dour.

The only recent historian to compare explicitly the personalities of several of Massachusetts's leaders, Peter Shaw, did so in *American Patriots and the Rituals of Revolution* (Cambridge, Mass., 1981) published five years after his book on John Adams's character. Shaw also looks at the crowds in Boston during the Revolution and concludes that the speech and writings of both patriot leaders and followers show them to be irrationally angry at English leaders and loyalists whom they regarded as father figures unfairly limiting their growth and curbing their personal independence. Like most children, of course, the patriots had been taught to revere their fathers and they tried to resolve the tension in their anger/respect ambivalence, Shaw argues, through excessive zeal. Shaw's work is careful in many ways and provocative throughout but the parent/child revolt theory does not tell us much about the Revolution. Revolutionaries often identify a mother country as an unfair parent: why did this anger manifest itself when it did? Why was Hutchinson the target? Why were certain issues identified and others not? As Charles Royster writes in a review of Shaw's work, "to diagnose is not necessarily to explain."[20]

FROM THE BOTTOM UP

Historians of Revolutionary Massachusetts surprisingly lagged behind those of some other colonies in direct and systematic examinations of the role of the lower classes. Many scholars allude to artisans, sailors, poverty, small farmers, and crowds, but the first major study focussed on class was Allan Kulikoff's "The Progress of Inequality in Revolutionary Boston," *William and Mary Quarterly*, 3d Ser., XXVII (1971) 375-412. Taking as his point of departure an article by James Henretta which contended that wealth distribution had become more skewed over the course of the pre-Revolutionary eighteenth century, Kulikoff argues that the trend toward greater inequality increased dramatically in Boston during the Revolutionary years.[21] Not only did the rich get richer, they also became more politically dominant. Poverty became a pressing issue as the Revolution progressed and economic and social divisions became more pronounced. Kulikoff, however, did not believe that the widening gap between classes necessarily led to political divisions and he believed it certainly did not lead to political violence.

Since 1971, several historians have published articles along the lines established by Kulikoff, but most of them did not connect their societal analysis with the political events of the Revolution.[22] Three recent books, however, do connect class divisions to Revolutionary action: Dirk Hoerder, *Crowd Action in Revolutionary Massachusetts, 1765-1780* (New York, 1977); Gary B. Nash, *The Urban Crucible: Social Change, Political Consciousness, and the Origins of the American Revolution* (Cambridge, Mass., 1979); and David P. Szatmary, *Shays's Rebellion: The Making of an Agrarian Insurrection* (Amherst, Mass., 1980). Taken together these three books constitute a major contribution to our understanding of the role of the people at the bottom of the social structure.

The most combative by far of the three, Hoerder's analysis of the crowd, argues that political agitation in the streets reflected the basic divisions in Massachusetts society identified by social historians. Colonial crowd action was rare, according to Hoerder. When it occurred, it was used, as Pauline Maier has argued for the colonies as a whole, not as a means of challenging community norms but as a means of enforcing them. During and after the Stamp Act riots this changed, Hoerder contends; the riots of the 1760s, he believes, "activated latent economic grievances" and the elite became increasingly frightened by forces in the street that defied control.[23] After troops sent to Boston dampened crowd action there, it grew in intensity in the countryside where it proved even more difficult to control. Both inside and outside of Boston, according to Hoerder, local grievances frequently overshadowed ones against imperial policy.

Hoerder's sympathies are with the crowd and he makes no attempt to conceal his ideological commitments. He does not use the term "mob" because it has a pejorative connotation; he seems to dislike all of the Revolutionary elite leaders; and he does not like the term "inarticulate" that historians frequently apply to the lower classes—they were articulate, historians have not tried to hear what they said. The stridency and tone of Hoerder's work will probably diminish somewhat the thoughtful consideration that its substance deserves. L. Kinvin Wroth, for example, argues in a review that it is "ahistorical and value laden;" Hoerder's "focus is confined and pre-ordained," and "finding economic differences he [Hoerder] presumes social conflict."[24]

Nash's *The Urban Crucible* examines links between social divisions and political behavior in three colonial cities: Boston, New York, and

Philadelphia. It has several chapters specifically on Boston, however, and this material by itself would be sufficient for a medium-sized monograph. Though agreeing in general with Hoerder and sharing his sympathies, Nash is much more judicious and restrained. He paints a picture of poverty and working-class anger in Boston that spread and intensified after Boston's economy languished in the years following the Seven Years War. Added to economic class divisions, Nash argues, were religious ones. The religious revival of the mid-eighteenth century became a class-specific movement supported by the lower classes and opposed by the middle and upper ones. Revivalists preached an antientrepreneurial message suffused with communalism and a concern for economic and social justice. Nash believes that these divisions profoundly affected the origins of the Revolution because they provided the anger for tinder that was necessary to fuel revolutionary fire. Nash is much more sophisticated than Hoerder in discussing the relationship between the laboring people and leaders. Many of the leaders did not try to gull the people and laboring men often looked to sympathetic leaders such as Samuel Adams or James Otis to express their views. On the other hand, crowds in the street were not "frenzied with liquor and dancing like puppets" on the leading strings of men above them.[25] Nash, however, encounters the same basic problem that Hoerder could not solve: the link between class division and political action must be largely presumed. Little evidence exists to make a direct connection between poverty and politicization.

Szatmary's account of Shay's Rebellion is the only major piece of history from the bottom up that is written about events primarily outside of Boston. He assembles a mass of quantitative data on the Regulators in the Massachusetts backcountry and finds, not surprisingly, that they were small, debt-ridden farmers, Congregationalists, and frequently ex-Revolutionary soldiers. The Shaysites did not turn lightly to "social banditry," Szatmary contends, but tried for two years to secure relief to no avail. Even after taking up arms, they did not become wild-eyed fanatics but planned their campaigns, picked specific targets, and were purposeful and restrained in using violence. Only after being suppressed ruthlessly by the eastern merchant interest did the rebellion turn radical and lash out indiscriminately at the social and economic elite.

Shays's Rebellion has previously engendered a certain amount of sympathy among historians, but Szatmary's account will occasion both more sympathy and more respect for Massachusetts's Regulators. In many ways their plight sounds similar to that of today's farmers who are squeezed by debt into radical anticommercial activity. In Hampshire County, the Court of Common Pleas heard nearly 3,000 debt cases in the two years of 1784 and 1785. Nearly one-third of the county's male population over sixteen years of age was involved. Seizures of property enraged farmers; fear of the debtor's cell ran deep. Szatmary further argues that the rebellion was more than an economic class war: it represented two differing world views arrayed against each other. The farmers who rebelled saw themselves defending a rural, communal, family-based, agrarian way of life against an ever-encroaching commercial society threatening its existence. This clash of world views is plausible, even probable, but little evidence is adduced in its support.

An aesthetic problem that bedevils lower-class history in all fields is equally troublesome in the work of each of the above: Kulikoff, Hoerder, Nash, and Szatmary. In an effort to write about *all* of the people, individuals disappear to be replaced by tables, charts, and percentages. In most instances, this is virtually inevitable and is just one of the prices social historians have to pay. Alfred Young's charming biography of a shoemaker turned soldier moves away from quantitative data and probes the mind of a Revolutionary from near the bottom of the social scale.[26] Young is given the source material to do so because his subject, a man with the unlikely name of George Robert Twelve Hewes, became recognized as a hero fifty years after the Revolution and had several lengthy interviews recorded. Young's story of the radicalization of Hewes is a good companion piece of work to read in connection with Hoerder's account of the radicalization of the crowd. Hewes was in many of the crowds Hoerder describes.

In general, historians of the bottom part of Massachusetts society have securely established two propositions: (1) real social and economic divisions characterized town and countryside and the plight of the poor was getting worse; (2) crowds, working class people, and poor farmers played active roles in the Revolution and these roles were not entirely directed by the elite. The nature of the connections between these two conclusions, however, has not been specified with any degree of certainty. With Shays's Rebellion a connection does seem to be more self-evident but even in this case going beyond the obvious relationships requires a leap of faith.

FROM THE CENTER

Robert E. Brown's *Middle-Class Democracy and the Revolution in Massachusetts, 1691-1780* (Ithaca, N.Y., 1955) remains the most aggressive statement ever published by a serious historian arguing that the Revolution was a war of independence and contained few or no elements of internal social conflict. Belligerent, unsystematic in research design and collection, and oblivious to contrary evidence, Brown's book is capable of being picked apart in dozens of places. It is, however, a monument on the historiographical landscape; many historians seem to feel that although outrageously overstated, Brown's overall thesis is more right than wrong. And, until recently, most scholars have felt constrained to deal with his argument that colonial Massachusetts was a functioning democracy that fought a war with England to preserve its democratic institutions and patterns of government that the English were trying to destroy with a new imperial policy.

Richard D. Brown's *Revolutionary Politics in Massachusetts: The Boston Committee of Correspondence and the Towns, 1772-1774* (Cambridge, Mass., 1970), a careful and judicious book, endorses in essence the Brown thesis. Richard D. Brown's meticulous research into the connections between the Boston Committee of Correspondence and the committees of the towns leads him to argue that Boston did not create, dominate, or manipulate the towns' responses to imperial policies. The several hundred towns of the Massachusetts countryside were as prepared to defend their liberties as Boston was and the varied nature of the towns' opinions indicates that no central body controlled the patriots' opinions. The Boston committee may have provided much of the original stimulus to move towns to action, but the localities played an increasingly active role in both the resistance to England and in the forming of a new state government and constitution. Once awakened, towns determined patriotic policy as much as they reacted to Boston's suggestions for it.

Richard D. Brown feels that the countryside and Boston could unite because they shared to a remarkable degree a consensus on what Massachusetts had been and what it should be. He admits that differences, of course, had existed in late colonial Massachusetts over the land bank, currency issues, factional fighting in the General Court, and several other issues; differences existed after independence over the Constitutions of 1778 and 1780 and over financial matters.

Nevertheless, Brown argues, court and country factions united on most imperial matters, and party politics as we now define them did not exist. Neither truly democratic nor oligarchic, colonial and Revolutionary Massachusetts embodied a premodern view of politics and society that enabled it to realize a substantial degree of harmony and enabled its citizens to cooperate effectively during the Revolution. In essence, Brown diminishes Boston's role in the Revolution and diffuses the responsibility widely throughout the province.

Stephen Patterson's *Political Parties in Revolutionary Massachusetts* (Madison, Wis., 1973) provided the first major challenge to the views of the two Browns. As Patterson's choice of title suggests, he believes that political parties existed in the colony and state legislatures and were based on geographical, economic, and ideological differences. Massachusetts's citizens may have hated the idea of political parties and believed in the intrinsic good of harmony and consensus, but, according to Patterson, reality belied belief and a generation of "antipartisan theory and partisan reality" characterized the background to the Revolution. During the Revolution, the sectional split became more pronounced. Patterson does not compile social and economic data to establish his claims of class division but relies rather on the manifestations of these divisions in voting patterns in the General Court. If Massachusetts was so united on basic issues, he asks, why did it fight so heatedly over the Constitution of 1778 and ultimately reject it? Why was Massachusetts the last of the original thirteen states to adopt a constitution?[27]

Patterson wears no ideological blinders and does not crudely overstate his case or ignore contrary evidence. He admits that the country party neither advocated economic redistribution of goods nor articulated notions of class conflict. But, he argues, the countryside did think that the rise of commerce on a grand scale was corrupting their society, and they did advocate reform through self-sacrifice, the abandonment of the pursuit of luxury, and a restoration of their sense of old-fashioned virtue. At the highest level in Boston, according to Patterson, the various splits among the leaders reflected their positions in favor of or against the reforms of the country party. The consequence of internal strife in Revolutionary Massachusetts, Patterson believes, lay in the creation of a more modern view of politics which accepted the legitimacy of conflict: partisan theory matched partisan reality.

William Pencak's *War, Politics, and Revolution in Provincial Massachusetts* (Boston, 1981) challenged Patterson's neo-Progressive view in the first modern narrative of the political history of the Revolution in Massachusetts. Mincing few words, Pencak is as combative in this remarkable *tour de force* as Hoerder was on the opposite side of the spectrum in his analysis of crown action. According to Pencak, the Revolution was a "true peoples' revolt" and "the product neither of personal elite squabbling, a paranoid fear of British tyranny, nor class conflict." War, Pencak argues, was the most basic political fact in colonial Massachusetts between 1689 and the Revolution. It continually produced problems: inflation, high taxes, recession, social disorder, and other forms of suffering. England seemed unable or unwilling to comprehend or care about the devastating effects of nearly a century of military conflict and, Pencak believes, shamelessly used Massachusetts as an imperial pawn. After enduring generations of this treatment, Massachusetts, tired of being sacrificed to the interests of an ungrateful mother country, "rose almost unanimously" against royal government. The Revolution was, Pencak writes, a "reasonable response to severe, undeserved burdens."[28]

Pencak does not hide behind the walls of rhetoric but attacks head-on the work of Patterson, Hoerder, Nash, and other neo-Progressives. To Patterson's argument that political parties existed in the General Court, Pencak says that systematic roll call analyses suggest they did not. Further, he believes Patterson overestimated the amount of rivalry among elite factions in Boston. To Hoerder's and Nash's contention of significant class conflict exemplified by crowd action against the wealthy, Pencak replies that there was almost a complete absence of mob violence against wealthy Revolutionaries: it was exclusively directed against loyalists or suspected loyalists. Although Pencak agrees with Hoerder and Nash that crowds became increasingly active in the Revolutionary era, he believes they continued to operate primarily as an extension of the institutional structure. By Pencak's count, ninety-four Boston merchants belonged to the Sons of Liberty, making it a community organization not a working man's crowd. Much of the rhetoric in Boston referring to the people in the street as hooligans, Pencak says, came from loyalists doing all they could to discredit the patriot cause and to spread fear of anarchy.[29]

Pencak's work is provocative and courageous. Compared to its closest interpretive counterpart, Robert E. Brown's book published a quarter-century earlier, it is a model of careful research and honest argument. Reviews are fulsome in praise for his accomplishment, but many believe that Pencak has not found divisions because he has looked in the wrong places. His focus on high provincial politics, for example, does not allow him to comment extensively on events in the countryside. His examination of manifest political events diminishes his appreciation of social, religious, and ethnic differences. And, the voting rolls of the General Court still await a definitive analysis before the existence of parties can either be confirmed or denied.

Before moving from Boston to the hinterland for our views of the Revolution, four legal/constitutional histories that provide a perspective different from more traditional history require mention. The most important of them, William E. Nelson's *Americanization of the Common Law: The Impact of Legal Change on Massachusetts Society, 1760–1830* (Cambridge, Mass., 1975), argues that a conception of consensus sustained pre-Revolutionary laws whereby juries determined almost all considerations of fact, law, and issue. During the Revolution, Nelson believes, tensions already straining this consensus became more pronounced and the court system proved unable to function properly amidst the growing divisiveness. A new system emerged based not on consensus but on law codes imposed by judicial authority. Complementing this argument, Ronald M. Peters, Jr.'s *The Massachusetts Constitution of 1780: A Social Compact* (Amherst, Mass., 1978), argues that the opposing legal positions in the formation of a new constitution pitted those who wished to enshrine in it the conception of individual rights versus those who favored popular sovereignty. Thus, the heart of the debate was between those who wished to protect the individual and those who wished to protect society. From a textual examination of the constitution, Peters concludes that the latter prevailed and that the form of the new government reflects an anachronistic attempt to maintain a waning colonial conception of society and law. Peters's analysis of the political theory embedded in the constitution makes an important contribution to our knowledge of it, but forcing the document into one or the other of the two categories seems ahistorical. The constitution was built on compromise not on an either/or basis that included one principle to the near exclusion of the other.

John Phillip Reid's *In a Defiant Stance: The Conditions of Law in Massachusetts Bay, the Irish Comparison, and the Coming of the American Revolution* (University Park, Pa., 1977) is as eclectic and provocative as its title suggests. Reid makes an obvious but often un-mentioned point that, although the laws of Massachusetts were suffi-cient to maintain the royal government's prerogative, the conditions of enforcing the law were inadequate since the courts were partially under the colonists' control. Hence, no patriot was ever tried and found guilty of treason. The same basic laws were in place in Ireland but enforced by imperial authorities who used the courts to suppress Irish dissent. The Revolution, Reid argues, stemmed not from English tyranny but from permissiveness and laxity. M. H. Smith in *The Writs of Assistance Case* (Berkeley, Calif., 1978) makes much the same point in his study of the first major incident of the pre-Revolution-ary years. He argues that if judged by English precedent, the royal authorities had every right to press the case as they did and were not in the least over-zealous as the colonists claimed they were in not making the writs specific but in using them as a general tool. No doubt both Reid and Smith are correct from a legal perspective; Massachusetts was treated more leniently than Ireland and there was English precedent for imperial actions in the Writs of Assistance case. Too much perspective, however, may be as bad as too little. Telling an unemployed Boston laborer that he was fortunate not to be starving in the Irish countryside would not have been any more effective in relieving his anger.

FROM THE HINTERLAND

Two books that do not explicitly deal with the Revolutionary movement are nonetheless important places to begin to gain an under-standing of the countryside; they provide a context in which to place community studies and have been a point of departure for many historians. Michael Zuckerman's *Peaceable Kingdoms: The New Eng-land Town in the Eighteenth Century* (New York, 1970) maintains that Massachusetts townspeople predicated their social vision on a desire for concord and harmony. Although many scholars dispute Zuckerman's contention that a high degree of local consensus was achieved, almost everyone agrees that it was a deeply-felt goal. Robert Zemsky's *Merchants, Farmers, and River Gods: An Essay on Eight-eenth-Century American Politics* (Boston, 1971) analyzes the politics of mid-eighteenth-century Massachusetts towns. Zemsky agrees with Zuckerman that within towns divisions were few and most towns functioned in a relatively democratic manner. Between towns, however, Zemsky sees divisions reflected in their voting patterns in the General Court. Although primarily geographical, these divisions did not necessarily pit eastern Massachusetts against the West. Rather, Zemsky argues there were five different regions in the colony, each of which had an identifiable pattern of behavior. The divisions may have been partly attributable to class, but location was more important Zemsky believes. And, the divisions revealed anger and serious tensions in Massachusetts.

Van Beck Hall's *Politics Without Parties: Massachusetts, 1780–1791* (Pittsburgh, 1972) studies the voting behavior of all towns in the state in the decade following independence. As does Zemsky, Hall sees bitter intertown political divisions reflected in voting patterns in the General Court. He is more insistent than Zemsky, however, that intertown conflict tended to divide society along social and economic lines. Hall agrees that sectional divisions were important but not as important as ones that derived from community types. The nature of a town's economic development predicted its voting behavior far more than its location, Hall argues. Ironically, divisions based on type of community may have somewhat mitigated sectional conflict because each region in the state had towns with sizable and with negligible commercial development.

Edward M. Cook, Jr.'s *The Fathers of the Towns: Leadership and Community Structure in Eighteenth-Century New England* (Baltimore, 1976), a study of local officeholding, also argues that differing types of communities had differing patterns of leadership. Cook identifies five distinctive types of communities and local polities: In general, the larger and more complex a town was, the more elite and restrictive its politics were. Most importantly for our present purposes, however, Cook sees few changes in officeholding occasioned by the Revolution. The "fathers of the towns," as he calls the local patriarchs of the eighteenth century, by and large survived the Revolution with prestige and positions intact.

The most recent book to continue, in the tradition of Zuckerman, Zemsky, Hall, and Cook, to examine the behavior of many towns in order to arrive at some general conclusions is Gregory H. Nobles' *Divisions Throughout the Whole: Politics and Society in Hampshire County, Massachusetts, 1740–1775* (New York, 1983). Of virtual necessity, Nobles engages in a dialogue with one of the most influential books written in an earlier era on the Revolution, Robert J. Taylor's *Western Massachusetts in the Revolution* (Providence, 1954).

Taylor had argued that in the pre-Revolutionary years a few powerful leaders ruled without challenge over a conservative, quiescent
population of western farmers. The Revolution, according to Taylor,
politicized the farmers who turned their fury on the elite and drove
them from power. Taylor studied the western response primarily
through an analysis of the elite. Nobles focusses instead on local
politics in the two dozen or so towns in Hampshire County and
arrives at somewhat different conclusions than did Taylor. Although
peace and harmony may have been goals in western towns at mid-
eighteenth century, Nobles maintains it was never achieved and, far
from apathetic, small farmers, recently "awakened" in religious re-
vivals and angry over a diminishing supply of land, challenged rule by
the elite in the two decades prior to the 1760s. Nobles argues that
division and tensions arising out of preexisting local grievances fastened themselves upon the politics of the Revolutionary era. Agitation
against the elite did not begin in the 1760s, it intensified. Nobles
agrees with Taylor on the course of development during the Revolution itself. A dual revolution occurred in western Massachusetts
towns: British rule ended and a local elite toppled.[30]

Despite the complaints of many reviewers about a glut of New
England town case studies, only two major single-community studies
of Massachusetts towns during the Revolutionary period have been
published. The first, Benjamin Woods Labaree's *Patriots and Parti-
sans: The Merchants of Newburyport, 1764-1815* (Cambridge, Mass.,
1962), surprisingly is seldom referred to in the literature. The second,
Robert Gross's *The Minutemen and Their World* (New York, 1976),
is widely acclaimed as one of the modern classics of local and Revolutionary history.

As its title indicates, Labaree's book on Newburyport focusses on
the merchant community over a half-century that includes the Revolution. Pathbreaking at the time of its publication, it has suffered the
same relative neglect as Charles Grant's pioneering study of Kent,
Connecticut, published a year earlier. Eclectic in interpretation,
Woods argues that Robert Brown's belief in the widespread nature of
democracy in Massachusetts was wrong; over half of Newburyport's
unskilled workers were disenfranchised on the eve of the Revolution
and a small interconnected elite dominated the town's politics. On
the other hand, Labaree sees no major disputes or political divisions
arising from the social and economic ones. From the beginning, most
of the town including the merchant elite supported the patriotic

movement. The Revolution, however, destroyed the merchant's hold on power not because they were politically attacked but because they lost their economic base. Newburyport's merchants suffered as much during the 1780s as western farmers did and collapsed as a collective entity to be replaced by a new group of entrepreneurs. Although lacking the sophisticated methodological tools developed by historians in the years since its publication, Labaree's work is careful, convincing, and of much value because it is the only detailed study of a seaport other than Boston.

The Minutemen and Their World, a history of Concord during the Revolution, deserves the praise it has received. The beauty of Gross's work is that it combines the best of two traditions: the charming personal view of history as narrative, and the quantitative, demographic view of history as social science. As David Hackett Fischer writes on the book's back cover, "this book is a pleasure to read—so much so that one may easily miss the monumental research upon which it rests." In interpretation, Gross is not as original and for the most part joins debates already in progress. Economic malaise and sectional intratown rivalries produced bitter divisions in Concord prior to the Revolution. Little concerned with the world beyond their own boundaries, Concord's residents found themselves plunged into the imperial debates during the 1770s that at first seemed to end some of their long-standing divisions. Once the war began and new hardships emerged, some of the bitterness resurfaced. No dual revolution occurred in Concord, however, according to Gross. Most Concord residents were moderate whigs, and the elite remained in power throughout the era although traditional deference was weakened and average townspeople developed a penchant for holding their leaders accountable for their actions. Concord also resisted direction from Boston or other outside agencies such as the Continental Congress and jealously guarded its own local prerogatives. No strikingly new picture of the Revolution emerges from Gross's account, but no one else has created such a beautifully textured portrait of a Revolutionary community.

CONCLUSION

Inherently narcissistic, historiography at its best is but a useful service; at its worst it is a tedious recitation of publishing details. To rescue this discussion from the latter charge, I would like to offer six general conclusions about the Revolution in Massachusetts.

(1) Ideology played an important role in the minds of almost all participants, including those at the top and bottom of society and those inside and outside of the centers of action. Whether austere Calvinism, English constitutionalism, philosophical conservatism, eighteenth-century republicanism, New Light revivalism, antientrepreneurialism, or local resistance to outside authority, clusters of ideas crystallized in people's minds and helped shape their responses to events before, during, and after independence. Sometimes articulated and sometimes not, ideas moved individuals, crowds, and communities although no single pattern of thought or motivation prevailed.

(2) The responsibility for the Revolution was diffused over a broad range of individuals, groups, and classes. All towns took part. The Revolution was not Sam Adams's, it was Massachusetts's. The ranks of leaders were not dominated by any one or two individuals. Indeed, the rise in importance attributed to people such as Abigail Adams, Samuel Cooper, and Elbridge Gerry makes one suspect that this diffusion may spread yet more widely. The increasing importance and independence of thought and action attributed to crowds and the various regions and towns of Massachusetts bespeaks an increasing complexity and multiplicity of motivations.

(3) Religious thought and religious controversy played a far more important role in the Revolution than was once thought. Many leaders, and presumably many followers, had a Calvinist view of duty, morality, and human nature that conditioned their reaction to events. The Great Awakening and its political manifestations also conditioned the reactions of individuals and communities.

(4) Pre-Revolutionary patterns of politics fastened themselves on the Revolutionary era. The factional battles and shifting alignments within royal government and local squabbles over town divisions, land availability, and leadership conditioned attitudes toward and stands taken on imperial policy and on resistance to that policy.

(5) A substantial degree of consensus in Massachusetts existed before, during, and after the Revolution. People identified harmony as a goal. Most citizens, including loyalists, thought the new imperial policy unwise. Revolutionaries who disagreed did so peacefully at the ballot box over such issues as the Constitutions of 1778 and 1780. Much of the state recoiled in horror at Shays's Rebellion and the

Shaysites themselves embraced violence reluctantly only after they felt peaceful dissent failed.

(6) Serious divisions did characterize Massachusetts society at all levels and in all regions. Section, regions, and types of communities had differing perceptions of events. Within most towns from Hampshire County to Concord to Boston, divisions were apparent. Debtors and creditors had different solutions to the problems of the new state.

I would like additionally to make the following six observations about the state of historical writing on the Revolution in Massachusetts.

(1) The consensus/conflict debate is still a vital part of the historiography. It has not gone away and probably will not in the foreseeable future. Many scholars still address it explicitly and most do implicitly. Although we know there were many shared values and many divisions in Massachusetts, we do not know the relative weighting and importance of consensus and conflict.

(2) Historians are increasingly tending to place positive constructions on the motivations of participants in the Revolution regardless of their positions or roles. Villains are disappearing from the historical landscape. Revolutionaries, loyalists, merchants, crowds, and even the Shaysites are all being portrayed as individuals or groups with integrity. Samuel Adams may have declined in influence in the writings of recent historians, but he has increased in his stature as a person. One assumes he would prefer his present position as being one of many steadfast fellows instead of being the singular master of deceit and manipulation.

(3) The problem of definition remains serious and causes much unnecessary disagreement among historians. Richard D. Brown, Van Beck Hall, and Stephen Patterson, for example, agree substantially in their description of political maneuvering in the General Court but disagree in their choice of language to apply to this activity. Only to a small extent does this disagreement reflect real substantive differences.

(4) Substantive disagreements do remain, however, and they will only be settled by more research. The degree of upheaval that accompanied the Revolution remains a subject of genuine debate. Which experience—that of Boston, Hampshire County, Newburyport, or Concord—should be used to assess what type of and how much internal revolution occurred? Does an analysis of voting patterns in the

General Court reveal the absence or presence of demonstrable, persistent, partisan activity?

(5) We know a great deal about the Revolution in Massachusetts. A brilliant, rich, general history of Revolutionary Massachusetts could be written entirely from secondary sources.

(6) There are some gaps in our knowledge that would not permit a few parts of the picture in the history to be filled in, and there are some parts of the picture that would be fuzzy. For example, no systematic and comprehensive accounts of loyalism and women exist. No major biographies have been written for leaders in the backcountry. Some Bostonians such as John Hancock and James Otis need a thorough reexamination. And, the nature of the connections between social and economic tensions and manifest political activities must be spelled out more precisely.

With all this water over the historical dam, the various participants in the drama that unfolded in Massachusetts in the second half of the eighteenth century would probably be both amazed and flattered that so many intelligent men and women have spent so much energy and time trying to figure out what they did and why they did it. We know far more about their revolution than they did. A large number of them were just mad as hell at the English; some were mad as hell at the rabble-rousers; others were mad as hell at their neighbors; and some were not mad at all. It has become our task to tell them why they were or were not. Virginia's James Madison may have unknowingly provided the best contemporary explanation of the Revolution in Massachusetts. In *Federalist Number Ten*, Madison wrote that republicanism can best thrive in a society comprised of a vast multiplicity of self-interested individuals, groups, classes, economic interests, regions, and religions. In a society with only a few interests, Madison argued, one or two self-seeking ones can achieve a dominant position and impose a tyranny or create a conflict so deep or sharply focussed that it will lead to civil war. In a society of dozens of competing interests, many of which are defined by ambiguous or overlapping lines, such a sharp cleavage will not occur. A consensus based on compromise will emerge, unplanned by anyone but resulting from these divisions scraping against each other in the day-to-day political, social, and economic marketplace. Colonial Massachusetts was a diverse society: its diversity may have given it the unity to fight a successful revolution.

AFTERWORD: THE FRAGMENTATION OF NEW ENGLAND

In addition to a similar research design, one theme ties the previous chapters together and makes them more of a book and less a collection of essays. Each one describes an increase in the heterogeneity of New England society over the course of the eighteenth century. New England entered the Revolutionary years as a more complex and divided region than it had been seventy-five years earlier.

The change should not be overemphasized. The first settlers of the region, try as they might, were never able to create a truly homogeneous society. Religious dissenters to the Puritan way; dissent within the established church; social, educational and economic class differences; the creation of distinct and separate colonies along the Connecticut River, on the shores of Narragansett Bay and in the Merrimac Valley; and several other factors meant that seventeenth-century New England contained many divisions as, indeed, almost all societies do. Jostling for place in the rough circumstances occasioned by the founding process inevitably widened some of these divisions.

Despite all of this and despite some celebrated incidents such as those involving the Hutchinsonians or the near-hedonists at Merrymount, divisions in seventeenth-century New England society appeared less sharp and bitter than those found elsewhere in the English colonies. The first two generations of New Englanders managed to maintain at least a modicum of cohesion. Religious radicals and conservatives, rich men and paupers, merchants and shoemakers, were all found in the early colonial years; but, in general, seventeenth-century New England was not a society of extremes or of many competing groups. Most inhabitants shared a belief in the same current of the Reformation; poverty was not a serious problem; great estates or economic empires did not exist, and the vast majority of settlers were farmers living in towns of less than one thousand people.

In the eighteenth century, as the New England colonies matured, they became more heterogeneous relative to their condition during the founding years. Whether one chooses to call this change, Anglicization, Europeanization, or normalization—three labels that have been applied to the trend—the process is recognizable in all of them. As they shed their newness, they began to resemble more closely the Old World with its greater distinctions among classes, groups, types of communities, and regions. Economic specialization, the growth of commerce, greater accumulations of wealth, an increase in poverty, the development of political oligarchies, the emergence of urban centers and urbane habits, the settlement of new regions removed from the coast and major river valleys, the secularization of higher education, and an increased complexity in government combined to create a variety of reference points that competed for a New Englander's loyalties. Increasingly in the eighteenth century, colonists could identify themselves as members of several small subgroups of the larger society. Frequently these groups had, or perceived that they had, conflicting interests or aspirations. Success and growth exacted a toll on the Puritan ideal and fragmented the covenanted communities of the seventeenth century.

The degree of fragmentation and the divisions that emerged in pre-Revolutionary society do not seem extraordinary by today's standards. Twentieth-century New England contains far more divisions than did eighteenth-century New England. But today's economic, political, and social divisions have been softened by institutions explicitly designed to restrain their effect, by an intellectual system based on tolerance of or even pride in diversity, and by a shared history of nationhood. None of these cultural devices were available in well-developed form to mitigate the tensions in eighteenth-century society. Present institutions act as instruments of brokerage to diffuse conflict and reduce its threat.

Eighteenth-century New England, however, had some of its own instruments to ameliorate the effects of fragmentation: a residue of the Puritan ethos; traditional English social deference; a substantial degree of openness in the recruitment of new members of the elite; a high standard of living and of economic opportunity; and an intimacy among groups that derived from some firsthand knowledge each had of the other. All of these factors and others lessened conflict. In the long run they worked: fragmentation did not cause fratricide and New England joined with the other mainland colonies to form a nation.

Ironically, the divisions in New England society may have promoted American nationalism. It was not a foregone conclusion that the Revolutionary states would form a nation. Differences among regions were greater than differences within regions. Residents of Connecticut, Massachusetts, New Hampshire, and Rhode Island viewed New Yorkers, Pennsylvanians, Virginians, and Carolinians with suspicion. New Englanders clung tenaciously to their regional identity. But they could not ignore the obvious economic, political, and social distinctions and divisions that had emerged among themselves. This reality may explain partially New England's willingness to subordinate its regional loyalty to a union with the other new states. Had Revolutionary New England been as cohesive as Puritan New England, this union might never have occurred. Divisions among themselves forced and accustomed New Englanders to live in a world of differing beliefs, lifestyles, and aspirations. Few articulated this change. Few wanted to face the truth that the covenanted community no longer existed. But, although the goal of unity was too ingrained to be explicitly abandoned, there was no escape from the effects of the new social reality. New England's diverse social structure helped blur some of the differences between it and the Middle and Southern regions and in the process also helped remove one of the barriers to the creation of the American nation.

At the same time that the increasing divisions in New England were helping to create a national polity based on tolerance and diversity, they were planting seeds of future discord. Between 1700 and 1840—from approximately the end of Puritan New England through the Jacksonian era—American rhetoric increasingly became committed to an ideology of democracy. A variety of circumstances and events occasioned this development during the colonial period, among them the struggle between royal governors and assemblies; frequent elections and partisan fighting for office; a lessening in the authority of religious leaders; English whig and European enlightenment ideas; the Great Awakening and the American Revolution; geographic, social and economic mobility; and a buoyant, increasingly diverse economy. The ideology of the eighteenth century almost always moved in one direction—toward more political, social, and economic equality. The signs and language were ubiquitous. Both implicitly and explicitly, colonists and Revolutionary Americans were told that the gap between the elite and the rest of society was and should be narrowing. Jefferson may have had legal rights in mind when he penned the words "all men are created equal," but to many Americans the phrase bespoke a new era of equality that was no less epochal because its meaning was vague and ill-defined.

The new era of equality, however, may have been more than vague or ill-defined: it may have been illusory if measured by some social indicators. The entrenchment and expansion of slavery in the old and new South is one obvious example of the progress of inequality. The social history of colonial New England provides several other more subtle ones: increases in unemployment, poverty, transiency, and tax revolts; the development of a less-humane system of providing welfare to the poor; an increasingly oligarchical pattern of officeholding; growing distinctions among the upper, middle, and lower classes' social habits and activities; and striking differences between urban and rural life. All of these, at first glance, suggest a gap between rhetoric and reality—a gap that might imply some degree of societal hypocrisy or, at the least, self-delusion. But, a closer look suggests something else. The cleavage between an ideology of increasing democracy and a reality of increasing class distinctions reflects the ambiguity inherent in the definitions of equality and democracy. After the Jacksonian era solidified the American commitment to equality and democracy, it was no longer politically feasible to question either concept in public. A tension emerged, however, between those who interpreted equality and democracy to mean equal opportunity in the marketplace and political arena and those who interpreted the words to mean that some degree of equality of condition ought to prevail in both politics and economics. In western political discourse this tension is often described as a conflict between liberty and equality. Since the Depression and the New Deal of the 1930s, American political parties base their definitions of liberal and conservative on their understanding of the word equality: conservatives argue for a greater emphasis on liberty or equality of opportunity; liberals for a greater emphasis on equality of conditions.

When the social, political, and intellectual histories of eighteenth-century New England are evaluated in light of each other, they suggest that the lines between the two types of equality began to diverge during the late colonial period. Colonists enjoyed increased freedom to choose their occupation, their religion, their place of residence, and their leisure activities. The number of political offices, economic and education opportunities, and consumer goods burgeoned. As the eighteenth century progressed, the likelihood diminished that any white male would accept public rhetoric that told him he could not aspire to political or economic success. Yet, many white males would find themselves further removed from the economic and political leadership than their fathers had been. To a substantial degree, this distance was a simple reflection of the sheer growth in population, the commercialization of the economy, and the ending of a frontier society. The two-sided nature of equality of opportunity, however, became apparent to those who could not succeed in taking advantage of the new freedoms.

There is a great danger in overstating the divergence between the two lines of development. At no time in colonial and Revolutionary New England did people make an enthusiastic, unequivocal commitment to a democratic ideology. Similarly, at no time did economic inequities or political oligarchies develop to a point that approached the extremes of English or European society. In fact, the standard of living continued to rise for most New Englanders throughout the colonial and Revolutionary years, and more New Englanders held a political office in 1790 than at any time in the past. The rising curve of democratic ideals thus was intersected as much by a curve of aspirations that were destined not to be realized as a curve that represented a real decline in condition. Nevertheless, the trends reflected in the gap between aspiration and achievement continued apace into the nineteenth century. the first one peaking with the ideology of Jacksonian democracy and the second one with the polarization of economic classes during the Gilded Age. The clash between equality of opportunity and equality of condition which became so painfully apparent after the Civil War can, with the hindsight provided by social history, be rooted in the pre-Revolutionary eighteenth century. The late colonial period in New England foreshadowed one of the central themes in American history—the tension between mass society and elite rule.

NOTES

CHAPTER 1

1. The only economic history of New England is William B. Weeden's *Economic and Social History of New England, 1620-1789*, 2 vols. (New York, 1890), which is antiquarian. The nearest approaches to professional synthesis are unpublished dissertations by Gaspare John Saladino, "The Economic Revolution in Eighteenth-Century Connecticut" (Ph.D. diss., University of Wisconsin, 1964), and Albert Van Dusen, "The Trade of Revolutionary Connecticut" (Ph.D. diss., University of Pennsylvania, 1948), and chapter five of Robert J. Taylor, *Colonial Connecticut: A History* (New York, 1979). All three are fine pieces of economic history and have been useful for this chapter but fall considerably short of providing a full picture of the development of the economy. Saladino's and Van Dusen's studies are specialized by time and topic respectively, and Taylor's account is more descriptive than analytical and does not discuss in detail changes over time.

2. Percy Wells Bidwell and John I. Falconer, *History of Agriculture in the Northern United States, 1620-1860* (Washington, D.C., 1925), 10-12; Thomas Reed Lewis, Jr., "From Suffield to Saybrook: An Historical Geography of the Connecticut River Valley in Connecticut before 1800" (Ph.D. diss., Rutgers University, 1978), 149-151.

3. Bidwell and Falconer, *Agriculture in the Northern U.S.*, 10-12; Frances Manwaring Caulkins, *History of New London, Connecticut. From the First Survey of the Coast in 1612 to 1860* (New London, 1895), 268; Lewis, "From Suffield to Saybrook," 154-157; Edward Jenkins, "Connecticut Agriculture," in Norris Galpin Osborn, ed., *History of Connecticut in Monographic Form* (New

York, 1925), 307-308; Samuel Orcutt, *History of Torrington, Connecticut . . .* (Albany, N.Y., 1879), 68.

4. Bidwell and Falconer, *Agriculture in the Northern U.S.*, 89; Lewis, "From Suffield to Saybrook," 164; Albert Laverne Olson, *Agricultural Economy and the Population in Eighteenth-Century Connecticut*, Connecticut Tercentenary Series, XL (New Haven, 1935), 7-9.

5. Bidwell and Falconer, *Agriculture in the Northern U.S.*, 19-21, 26-31; Lewis, "From Suffield to Saybrook," 166-170.

6. Bidwell and Falconer, *Agriculture in the Northern U.S.*, 14, 19-21, 25, 28; Olson, *Agricultural Economy*, 2.

7. Chester McArthur Destler, *Connecticut: The Provisions State*, Connecticut Bicentennial Series, V (Chester, 1973), 9; Bidwell and Falconer, *Agriculture in the Northern U.S.*, 97-101; Olson, *Agricultural Economy, passim.*

8. Bidwell and Falconer, *Agriculture in the Northern U.S.*, 98-101, and Chester McArthur Destler, "The Gentleman Farmer and the New Agriculture: Jeremiah Wadsworth," *Agricultural History*, XLVI (1972), 135-153. See Jackson Turner Main, *Connecticut Society in the Era of the American Revolution*, Connecticut Bicentennial Series, XXI (Hartford, 1977), 29, for data on average size of herds. Data on number of domestic animals come from Connecticut Archives, Finance and Currency, 2d Ser., V., doc. 163a, Connecticut State Library, Hartford.

9. Bidwell and Falconer, *Agriculture in the Northern U.S.*, 98-101; Olson, *Agricultural Economy*, 1-9; Howard Russell, "Allium Capa: Three Centuries of Onions," *New England Galaxy*, XVIII (1977), 12-21.

10. Jared Eliot, *Essays Upon Field Husbandry in New England . . .* , eds. Harry J. Carman and Rexford G. Tugwell (New York, 1934), 3, *passim*; Rodney C. Loehr, "Arthur Young and American Agriculture," *Agr. Hist.*, XLIII (1969), 43.

11. Bidwell and Falconer, *Agriculture in the Northern U.S.*, 87; Olson, *Agriculture Economy*, 28-29; Destler, "Gentleman Farmer," *Agr. Hist.*, XLVI (1972), 135-153; Loehr, "Arthur Young," *ibid.*, XLIII (1969), 43-47. See Robert A. Gross, *The Minutemen and Their World* (New York, 1976), 87, 172-173, for an account of the new agriculture in Massachusetts.

12. Destler, *Connecticut, passim*; Saladino, "Economic Revolution," 68.

13. Van Dusen, "Trade of Revolutionary Connecticut," 141; Saladino, "Economic Revolution," 4; J. Hammond Trumbull and Charles Hoadly, eds., *The Public Records of the Colony of Connecticut* (Hartford, 1850-1890), VII, 580-581, XIV, 498, hereafter cited as *Col. Recs. Conn.*

14. Oscar Zeichner, *Connecticut's Years of Controversy, 1750-1776* (Chapel Hill, N.C., 1949), chaps. 3, 4; William S. Sachs, "Agricultural Conditions in the Northern Colonies before the Revolution," *Journal of Economic History*, XIII (1953), 284; James F. Shepherd and Gary M. Walton, *Shipping, Maritime Trade, and the Economic Development of Colonial North America* (Cambridge, 1972), 43-44; Marc Egnal, "The Economic Development of the Thirteen Continental

Colonies, 1720 to 1775," *William and Mary Quarterly*, 3d Ser. XXXII (1975), 204-205, 212; Saladino, "Economic Revolution," 152-158, 232-235.

15. Glenn Weaver, "Some Aspects of Early Eighteenth-Century Trade," Connecticut Historical Society, *Bulletin*, XXII (1957), 25-29, hereafter cited as Weaver, "Connecticut Trade"; Saladino, "Economic Revolution," 113, 13, 23-25; Van Dusen, "Trade of Revolutionary Connecticut," 136-137; Glenn Weaver, *Jonathan Trumbull: Connecticut's Merchant Magistrate* (1710-1785) (Hartford, 1956), *passim*; Carl Bridenbaugh, *Cities in Revolt: Urban Life in America, 1743-1776* (New York, 1955), 263; Zeichner, *Connecticut's Years of Controversy*, 81-82; Robert Owen Decker, "The New London Merchants: 1645-1901: The Rise and Decline of a Connecticut Port" (Ph.D. diss. University of Connecticut, 1970), 30-38.

16. Saladino, "Economic Revolution," 6-8; Van Dusen, "Trade of Revolutionary Connecticut," 146-150; Decker, "New London Merchants," 253-255.

17. Saladino, "Economic Revolution," 6-8; Van Dusen, "Trade of Revolutionary Connecticut," 147; Weeden, *History of New England*, II, 651; *Col. Recs. Conn.*, VII, 580-581.

18. Bruce C. Daniels, *The Connecticut Town: Growth and Development, 1635-1790* (Middletown, 1979), chap. 6; Weaver, "Connecticut Trade," 23-29.

19. Weaver, "Connecticut Trade," 23-29; Main, *Connecticut Society*, 23-24.

20. Decker, "New London Merchants," 77-78; Destler, *Connecticut, passim*; Saladino, "Economic Revolution," 94-95; Weeden, *History of New England*, II, 772. The best account of privateerring in Connecticut during the Revolution is Louis F. Middlebrook, *History of Maritime Connecticut during the American Revolution, 1775-1783*, 2 vols. (Salem, Mass., 1925).

21. Decker, "New London Merchants," 1-2; Saladino, "Economic Revolution," 63-65, 152-158; Van Dusen, "Trade of Revolutionary Connecticut," 389-390.

22. The information on mills and the number in each town is taken from individual town histories, and the citations would demand too much space to be included here. I would be pleased to list the relevant secondary sources for, and share my data with, any interested person.

23. Lewis, "From Suffield to Saybrook," 124.

24. Conn. Arch., 2d Ser., V. doc. 214a; Van Dusen, "Trade of Revolutionary Connecticut," 93; Caulkins, *History of New London*, 83; Bernard Christian Steiner, *A History of the Plantation of Menunkatuck and of the Original Town of Guilford, Connecticut . . .* (Baltimore, 1897), 228-231. Three recent and sophisticated analyses of artisans are Jackson Turner Main, "The Distribution of Property in Colonial Connecticut," in James Kirby Martin, ed., *The Human Dimensions of Nation Making: Essays on Colonial and Revolutionary America* (Madison, Wis., 1976), 64-66; Main, *Connecticut Society*, 9, 21, 38; and John J. Waters, "Patrimony, Succession, and Social Stability: Guilford, Connecticut, in the Eighteenth Century," *Perspectives in American History*, X (1976), 132.

25. J. L. Rockey, ed., *History of New Haven County, Connecticut* (New York, 1892), II, 228; Saladino, "Economic Revolution," 4; Charles R. Stark, *Groton, Connecticut, 1705-1905* (Stonington, 1922), 341-342; Van Dusen, "Trade of Revolutionary Connecticut," 91; Weeden, *History of New England*, II, 576; Glenn Weaver, "Industry in an Agrarian Economy: Early Eighteenth-Century Connecticut," Conn. Hist. Soc., *Bull.*, XIX (1954), 89, hereafter cited as Weaver, "Industry in an Agrarian Economy."

26. *Col. Recs. Conn.*, II, 224 (May 1674).

27. Saladino, "Economic Revolution," 2; Weaver, "Industry in an Agrarian Economy," 86-90; Shirley Spaulding Devoe, *The Tinsmiths of Connecticut* (Middletown, 1968), 3-6.

28. Herbert Keith and Charles Harte, *The Early Iron Industry in Connecticut* (New Haven, 1935), 8-26.

29. Peter Bohan and Philip Hammerslough, *Early Connecticut Silver, 1700-1840* (Middletown, 1970), 6-16, 219-259.

30. Saladino, "Economic Revolution," 14-15. Jackson Turner Main, "The Economic and Social Structure of Early Lyme," in George J. Willauer, Jr., ed., *A Lyme Miscellany, 1776-1976* (Middletown, 1977), 32, shows that the shortage of land occasioned an increase in tradesmen.

31. Joseph Goodwin, *East Hartford: Its History and Traditions* (Hartford, Conn., 1879), chap. 14; A. P. Pitkin, *Pitkin Family of America* (Hartford, Conn., 1887), lxxvi, lxxxvi; Joan Nafie, *To the Beat of a Drum: A History of Norwich, Connecticut, during the American Revolution* (Norwich, 1975), 37-42; Saladino, "Economic Revolution," 55, 164; Van Dusen, "Trade of Revolutionary Connecticut," chap. 14.

32. Ellen D. Larned, *History of Windham County, Connecticut* (Worcester, Mass., 1974), I, 77; Isabel S. Mitchell, *Roads and Road-Making in Colonial Connecticut*, Connecticut Tercentenary Series, XIV (New Haven, 1933), 18; Rockey, ed., *History of New Haven County*, I, 43.

33. Lewis, "From Suffield to Saybrook," 140; William DeLoss Love, *The Colonial History of Hartford* (Chester, Conn., 1974), 187; Mitchell, *Roads and Road-Making*, 13-18; Rockey, ed., *History of New Haven County*, II, 275; Van Dusen, "Trade of Revolutionary Connecticut," 59-357.

34. Lewis, "From Suffield to Saybrook," 140; Mitchell, *Roads and Road-Making*, 21-30; Saladino, "Economic Revolution," 19-20.

35. Lewis, "From Suffield to Saybrook," 177-179; Mitchell, *Roads and Road-Making*, 21-30; Saladino, "Economic Revolution," 19-20. See Michael Chisholm, *Rural Settlement and Land Use: An Essay in Location* (London, 1962), 159, for a discussion of rural transportation systems. Chisholm argues that including communities on a road "justifies quite considerable detours."

36. Shepherd and Walton, *Shipping, Maritime Trade, and the Economic Development*, 43-44, shows that per capita exports from Connecticut in the late colo-

nial period averaged only .53; Main, *Connecticut Society*, 25, shows that the minimum yearly income for an acceptable standard of living was £50 per family. Obviously, then, most Connecticut produce was consumed by Connecticut families. This was also true for Pennsylvania, another major exporter of foodstuffs. See James T. Lemon, *The Best Poor Man's Country: A Geographical Study of Early Southeastern Pennsylvania* (New York, 1972), 180-181.

37. Egnal, "Economic Development," WMQ, 3d Ser., XXXII (1975), 191-222, and Sachs, "Agricultural Conditions in the Northern Colonies," *Jour. Econ. Hist.*, XIII (1953), 274-290.

38. Kenneth A. Lockridge, "Social Change and the Meaning of the American Revolution," in Stanley N. Katz, ed., *Essays in Politics and Social Development: Colonial America* (Boston, 1971), 490-520.

39. These changes were not unique to Connecticut. The Atlantic world's demand for foodstuffs led to a massive increase in their export in all the colonies. See Merrill Jensen, "The American Revolution and American Agriculture," *Agr. Hist.*, XLIII (1969), 111-112; Egnal, "Economic Development" WMQ, 3d Ser., XXXII (1975), 204-205, 212; and Sachs, "Agricultural Conditions," *Jour. Econ. Hist.*, XIII (1953), 284.

40. This is admittedly the highest possible figure of emigrants. The true figure is probably slightly lower inasmuch as higher marriage ages and lower birth rates undoubtedly accounted partially for the decline in the growth rate, as did the dislocation wrought by the Revolution. The outmigration did not end by 1790; many Connecticut farmers in the Federalist and Jeffersonian years sought their future in the Ohio Valley. Richard Thomas Warfle, "Connecticut's Critical Period: The Response to the Susquehannah Affair, 1769-1774" (Ph.D. diss., University of Connecticut, 1972), 4-32.

41. For the price of land see Main, *Connecticut Society*, 27; Ezra Stiles, *Extracts from the Itineraries and Other Miscellanies of Ezra Stiles...*, ed. Franklin Bowditch Dexter (New Haven, Conn., 1916), 191; and Saladino, "Economic Revolution," II. Weaver, *Johnathan Trumbull, passim*, shows how the credit system and debts plagued rich and poor alike.

42. Saladino, "Economic Revolution," 63-68, 150-167, 232-238.

43. For examples of price and wage controls see *Col. Recs. Conn.*, I, 18 (Apr. 1638), 65 (June 1641), II, 325 (Oct. 1677), 244 (May 1674). For information on just price, regulation, and encouragement see Taylor, *Colonial Connecticut*, 97-100, and Saladino, "Economic Revolution," 14-15. On the local quality-control officers see Bruce C. Daniels, "The Political Structure of Local Government in Colonial Connecticut," in Daniels, ed., *Town and County: Essays on the Structure of Local Government in the American Colonies* (Middletown, Conn., 1978), 67.

44. Taylor, *Colonial Connecticut*, 102-103; Bruce C. Daniels, "Money-Value Definitions of Economic Classes in Colonial Connecticut, 1700-1776," *Histoire*

Sociale/Social History, VII (1974), 348-349; Richard L. Bushman, *From Puritan to Yankee: Character and the Social Order in Connecticut, 1690-1765* (Cambridge, Mass., 1967), 117-121.

45. For a cogent discussion by a social scientist of the relationship between the development of an economy and the values of society see Robert A. Nisbet, "The Impact of Technology on Ethical Decisionmaking," in Robert Lee and Martin E. Marty, eds., *Religion and Social Conflict* (New York, 1964), 17-20. See also Horace M. Miner, "Community-Society Continua," *International Encyclopedia of the Social Sciences*, III (New York, 1968), 174-181.

CHAPTER 2

1. Alice Hanson Jones, "Wealth Estimates for the New England Colonies About 1770," *Journal of Economic History* 32 (March 1972), 98-127.

2. Jackson Turner Main, "Trends in Wealth Concentration Before 1860," *Journal of Economic History*, XXXI (1971), 445-447.

3. James Henretta, "Economic Development and Social Structure in Colonial Boston," *William and Mary Quarterly*, 3d Ser., XXII (1965), 93-105.

4. Jackson Turner Main, *The Social Structure of Revolutionary America* (Princeton, 1965), 7-43. The use of terms such as frontier and subsistence does not mean to imply that no commercial farming took place in these areas. Virtually all farms produced some crops for market. Calling a town frontier or subsistence simply means that it tended to produce less for export and more for local consumption than commercial towns did.

5. Jones, "Wealth Estimates," 116.

6. Kenneth Lockridge, "A Communication," *WMQ*, 3d Ser., XXV (1968), 16.

7. Henry Bronson, "Historical Account of Connecticut Currency," *New Haven Colony Historical Society Papers*, vol. 1 (New Haven, 1865), 74. Joseph Felt, *Massachusetts Currency* (Boston, 1839), 49, 50, 92, 93, 96.

8. Carl Bridenbaugh, *Cities in the Wilderness: The First Century of Urban Life in America, 1625-1742* (New York, 1938), 143; Bridenbaugh, *Cities in Revolt: Urban Life in America, 1743-1776* (New York, 1955), 216.

9. Populations for all of the Connecticut towns come from the census of 1774 in J. Hammond Trumbull and Charles Hardley (eds.), *The Public Records of the Colony of Connecticut* 15 vols. (Hartford, 1850-1890), 14 (1774), 486-490.

10. Bridenbaugh, *Cities in Revolt*, 217.

11. Ibid., 217.

CHAPTER 3

1. More attention was paid by colonial scholars fifty years ago to poor relief practices than is today. Marcus Jernegan, *Laboring and Dependent Classes in Colonial America, 1607-1783* (New York, 1931), is the most thorough study of

colonial poor relief, but it contains many deficiencies, not the least of which is an absence of local research. Rhode Island does have a more well-developed study of poor relief than most colonies. See Margaret Creech, *Three Centuries of Poor Law Administration: A Study of Legislation in Rhode Island* (Chicago, 1936). This work contains a wealth of information but suffers from being essentially uninterpretive and insensitive to changes over the colonial period. Still, anyone wanting more details on legislation than this essay provides should consult Creech's work. David Rothman, *The Discovery of the Asylum: Social Order and Disorder in the New Republic* (Boston and Toronto, 1971), is a brilliant analysis of nineteenth-century relief practices and contains two strong background chapters on eighteenth-century thought about welfare. It does not, however, deal with local practice.

2. John Russell Bartlett, ed., *Records of the Colony of Rhode Island and Providence Plantations*, 10 vols. (Providence, 1856-1865), I, 1647, 185-186, hereafter cited as *R.I.C.R.*.

3. Portsmouth Town Meeting Minutes, Jan. 1649; Warwick Town Meeting, Apr. 1660; *Early Records of the Town of Providence*, 21 vols. (Providence, 1892-1915), VIII, June 1681, 95-96. The local records cited in the notes are all located in the respective town and city halls unless otherwise specified.

4. Providence Town Council Minutes, Jan. 1693; Portsmouth Town Council Minutes, Oct. 1710, Nov. 1698, Apr. 1710; Warwick Town Council Minutes, Mar. 1699; *R.I.C.R.*, III, Oct. 1682, 117-118; Rothman, *The Discovery of the Asylum*, 317.

5. See Bruce C. Daniels, *The Connecticut Town: Growth and Development, 1635-1790* (Middletown, Conn., 1979), chap. II; Darrett Rutman, "People in Progress: The New Hampshire Towns of the Eighteenth Century," *Journal of Urban History*, I (1975), 268-292; Kenneth Lockridge, "Land, Population, and The Evolution of New England Society, 1630-1790," *Colonial America: Essays in Politics and Social Development*, ed. Stanley Katz (Boston, 1971), 467-491.

6. See Evarts Greene and Virginia Harrington, *American Population Before the Federal Census of 1790* (Gloucester, Mass., 1966), 62-63, for the data on population. Bruce Bigelow, "The Commerce of Rhode Island With the West Indies Before the American Revolution," (Ph.D. diss., Brown University, 1980), *passim.*

7. The literature on wealth distribution is vast (see Chap. 2 of the present volume). Alice Hanson Jones, "Wealth Estimates for the New England Colonies About 1770," *Journal of Economic History*, XXXII (1972), 98-127; James Henretta, "Economic Development and Social Structure in Colonial Boston," *William and Mary Quarterly*, 3d Ser., XXII (1965), 75-105; Allan Kulikoff, "The Progress of Inequality in Revolutionary Boston," *WMQ*, 3d Ser., XXVIII (1971), 375-412; Jackson Turner Main, "The Distribution of Property in Colonial Connecticut," *The Human Dimension of Nation Making*, ed. James Kirby Martin (Madison, Wis., 1976), 54-104; and John Waters, "Patrimony, Succession,

and Social Stability: Guilford, Connecticut in the Eighteenth Century," *Perspectives in American History*, X (1976), 131-160.

8. For a general account see Howard Peckham, *The Colonial Wars, 1689-1762* (Chicago, 1962).

9. See Syndey V. James, *Colonial Rhode Island: A History* (New York, 1975), 136, 275-280.

10. Portsmouth Town Meeting Minutes, June 1731, Aug. 1744, Aug. 1740, and 1760s, *passim*; Warwick Town Meeting Minutes, Jan. 1765; East Greenwich Town Meeting Minutes, Aug. 1748, May 1754; Cranston Town Meeting Minutes, June 1756; Newport Town Meeting Minutes, Jan. 1763; New Shoreham Town Meeting Minutes, Mar. 1753; Providence Town Meeting Minutes, Aug. 1748; Scituate Town Meeting Minutes, May 1765; South Kingston Town Meeting Minutes, Mar. 1753; Tiverton Town Meeting Minutes, Oct. 1757; Westerly Town Meeting Minutes, Apr. 1752. These examples could easily be expanded.

11. Warwick Town Council Minutes, Feb. 1744; *Digest of 1744* (Newport, 1744), June 1748, 48-51.

12. Portsmouth Town Council Minutes, *passim*; Providence Town Council Minutes, 1774, Jan. 1758. The Providence act symbolized the erosion of personal involvement in the warning out process.

13. Providence Town Council Minutes, Sept. 1770; Warwick Town Council Minutes, 1755, April 1755; South Kingston Town Council Minutes, Dec. 1752; *R.I.C.R.*, III, May 1702, 452; Providence Town Council Minutes, Mar. 1777, Jan. 1759. See also Douglas Jones, "The Strolling Poor: Transiency in Eighteenth-Century Massachusetts, *Journal of Social History*, VIII (1975), 28-54.

14. Portsmouth Town Council Minutes, Jan. 1728, Feb. 1728; Providence Town Council Minutes, June 1723, Apr. 1778, July 1758; Portsmouth Town Council Minutes, Aug. 1773.

15. Portsmouth Town Council Minutes, Oct. 1741; Providence Town Council Minutes, Nov. 1773.

16. *R.I.C.R.*, V, Feb. 1742, 40, Nov. 1742, 57; *Digest of 1767* (Newport, 1767), 197; Warwick Town Council Minutes, Aug. 1757, Dec. 1757, Mar. 1764, Aug. 1782; Providence Town Council Minutes, May 1740, Sept. 1742; South Kingston Town Council Minutes, Jan. 1742; Providence Town Council Minutes, June 1758; Warwick Town Council Minutes, June 1756; Portsmouth Town Council Minutes, June 1756; Portsmouth Town Council Minutes, Mar. 1763, May 1788; South Kingston Town Council Minutes, July 1739.

17. Newport Town Council Minutes, Newport Historical Society, July 1723; Providence Town Meeting Minutes, Jan. 1738, June 1750, Apr. 1754; Warwick Town Meeting Minutes, June 1760, June 1762, Jan. 1763; East Greenwich Town Meeting Minutes, Apr. 1761; Portsmouth Town Meeting Minutes, Apr. 1763; Tiverton Town Meeting Minutes, Dec. 1754.

18. Providence Town Meeting Minutes, Aug. 1763; Providence Town Council Minutes, Dec. 1768; Warwick Town Council Minutes, Sept. 1777.

19. Newport Town Meeting Minutes, Newport Historical Society, Apr. 1760, Jan. 1746, Oct. 1750; Warwick Town Council Minutes, Mar. 1782; Providence Town Council Minutes, Apr. 1776.

20. Bristol Town Meeting Minutes, May 1757; Cranston Town Meeting Minutes, June 1756, June 1761, Feb. 1762; East Greenwich Town Meeting Minutes, Mar. 1779; Newport Town Meeting Minutes, Aug. 1769; South Kingston Town Meeting Minutes, June 1765, Aug. 1771; Westerly Town Meeting Minutes, Apr. 1752. See James, *Colonial Rhode Island*, 306-307, for a discussion of colony taxes on towns and partisan politics.

21. Westerly Town Meeting Minutes, Dec. 1765, Oct. 1769, Feb. 1771, Apr. 1771, June 1771; Newport Town Meeting Minutes, May 1770, Oct. 1773, Jan. 1774; Oct. 1774, Feb. 1775, Sept. 1775; South Kingston Town Meeting Minutes, Jan. 1782, Feb. 1782, Oct. 1782, Mar. 1783, June 1783, June 1784, June 1785, Sept. 1785.

22. The record of Scituate's expenses is found on pages 4, 5, 6, and 7 in vol. V of the Town Council Records.

23. Jones, "The Strolling Poor," 28-54.

CHAPTER 4

1. An exception to this criticism must be made for Michael Zuckerman's excellent analysis of Massachusetts town meetings in *Peaceable Kingdoms: New England Towns in the Eighteenth Century* (New York, 1970), 154-186. Otherwise, analyses of local institutions in New England have not improved upon Edward Channing, *Town and County Government in the English Colonies of North America*, Johns Hopkins University Studies in Historical and Political Science, 2d Ser., X (Baltimore, 1884), 5-58. G. E. Howard, *An Introduction to the Local Constitutional History of the United States: Development of the Township, Hundred, and Shire* (New York, 1889); and Charles M. Andrews, *The River Towns of Connecticut: A Study of Wethersfield, Hartford, and Windsor*, Johns Hopkins University Studies in Historical and Political Science, 7th Ser., VII-IX (Baltimore, 1889). Such seminal studies as Charles S. Grant, *Democracy in the Connecticut Frontier Town of Kent* (New York, 1961); Sumner Chilton Powell, *Puritan Village: The Formation of a New England Town* (Middletown, Conn., 1963); and Kenneth A. Lockridge, *A New England Town, The First Hundred Years: Dedham, Massachusetts, 1636-1736* (New York, 1970), while perceptive in their social, economic, and political analyses, do not attempt an institutional analysis. In *Democracy in Kent*, chaps. 8 and 9, Grant hints at the importance of the problem but does not develop this beyond passing references and skeletal outlines. Historians writing in the nineteenth century spent more time on descriptions of local government. See Frances Manwaring Caulkins, *History of Norwich, Connecticut* (Norwich, 1873), and Elizabeth Hubbell Schenck, *The History of Fairfield*, 2 vols. (New York, 1889-1905). The standard refer-

ence for town government, John Fairfield Sly, *Town Government in Massachusetts, 1620–1930* (Cambridge, Mass., 1930), is not as useful as Channing, Howard, and Andrews. The best recent analyses of New England's local institutions appear in three unpublished doctoral dissertations on colonial Connecticut, but they are based on only a small number of towns and are fragmentary. See Bruce C. Daniels, "Large Town Power Structures in Eighteenth-Century Connecticut" (Ph.D. diss., University of Connecticut, 1970); Bruce P. Stark, "Lebanon, Connecticut: A Study of Society and Politics in the Eighteenth-Century" (Ph.D. diss., University of Connecticut, 1970); and William F. Willingham, "Windham, Connecticut: Profile of a Revolutionary Community, 1755–1818" (Ph.D. diss., Northwestern University, 1972).

2. Historians now recognize that it is incorrect to speak of *the* New England town; major differences existed among types of towns as well as among towns of different colonies. See Edward M. Cook, Jr., "Local Leadership and the Typology of New England Towns, 1700–1785," *Political Science Quarterly*, LXXXVI (1971), 586–608. This chapter relies heavily on four of the older large towns—Farmington, Hartford, Middletown, and Norwich—as primary examples, and on the numerous secondary sources that study either a single town or one aspect of government in several towns. For broader statements that include most towns, my sources are the statutes of the General Assembly, which, of course, applied to all towns, and a sample of 30 towns whose records have been examined. These 30 comprised 36 percent of the colony's 84 towns and included towns of every county, size, function, and age. I have not examined all their operations of government but have catalogued the towns' officers, noted the dates when those men were first elected, counted the number of town meetings, and noted the subjects the meetings dealt with, and examined the records for information on town meeting election procedures.

3. Roy Hidemichi Akagi, *The Town Proprietors of the New England Colonies: A Study of Their Development, Organization, Activities, and Controversies, 1720–1770* (Philadelphia, 1924), 55–59. The colony government was called the General Court until 1698, when it officially divided into two houses and was renamed the General Assembly. Hence I refer to the colony government as the General Court prior to 1698 and as the General Assembly thereafter.

4. "Hartford Town Votes, 1635–1716," Connecticut Historical Society, *Collections*, VI (Hartford, 1897), 21, 32.

5. Anthony N. B. Garvan, *Architecture and Town Planning in Colonial Connecticut* (New Haven, 1951), 68.

6. Middletown Town Meeting Records, City Hall, Middletown, Conn., Feb. 1680, Dec. 1715, and Dec. 1717.

7. Middletown Proprietor Records, City Hall, Middletown, Conn., 1734, *passim*. There is no evidence to indicate how the proprietors' membership was established and how exclusive it was. William Rockwell was both proprietor and town clerk, but he signed his reports in the 1734 meetings records as "proprietors' clerk."

8. Norwich Town Meeting Records, City Hall, Norwich, Conn., Dec. 1717, May 1718.

9. Farmington Proprietor Records, in Farmington Town Meeting Records, Town Hall, Farmington, Conn., I, Apr. 1727.

10. Farmington Recs., Dec. 1736.

11. J. Hammond Trumbull and Charles J. Hoadley, eds., *The Public Records of the Colony of Connecticut* (Hartford, 1850-1890), VII, 379, 137, hereafter cited as *Conn. Col. Recs.*

12. Akagi, *Town Proprietors*, 63-66.

13. *Ibid.*, 46.

14. Richard L. Bushman, *From Puritan to Yankee: Character and the Social Order in Connecticut, 1690-1765* (Cambridge, Mass., 1967), 83-85.

15. Akagi, *Town Proprietors*, 181-182.

16. The standard authorities on New England and Connecticut proprietors believe that many Connecticut towns settled in the eighteenth century experienced contests between resident proprietors and absentee proprietors who still owned land within the town. See *ibid.*, 130-133, and Garvan, *Architecture and Town Planning*, 65-68. In the case of at least one Connecticut town, Kent, this struggle has been exaggerated. In Kent although twenty-five of forty-one men who bought proprietary shares never lived in the town, most of the absentee proprietors sold their shares quickly to residents. Thirty-two of Kent's first forty settlers were proprietors, and even though many Kent settlers complained of being victimized by absentee proprietors, their real aim was to delay payments to the General Assembly or the original proprietors. Grant, *Democracy in Kent*, 15-20.

17. Grant, *Democracy in Kent*, 21.

18. Garvan, *Architecture and Town Planning*, 66.

19. Grant, *Democracy in Kent*, 15; Stark, "Lebanon," 349.

20. David H. Fowler, "Connecticut's Freemen: The First Forty Years," *William and Mary Quarterly*, 3d Ser., XV (1958), 313-315.

21. *Conn. Col. Recs.*, III, 24.

22. Since it was not a requirement for a town selectman to be a freeman, a nonfreeman selectman could theoretically recommend someone for freemanship. It is doubtful, however, that any selectman was ever not a freeman.

23. *Conn. Col. Recs.*, VII, 250.

24. The process is described in Grant, *Democracy in Kent*, 109.

25. Many of the low estimates of freemanship stem from historians' acceptance of Ezra Stiles's remark that only one out of nine Connecticut men could vote. See Oscar Zeichner, *Connecticut's Years of Controversy* (Chapel Hill, N.C., 1949), 8, and George C. Groce, Jr., *William Samuel Johnson, Maker of the Constitution* (New York, 1937), 54. Lawrence Henry Gipson, *Jared Ingersoll: A Study of American Loyalism in Relation to British Colonial Government* (New Haven, Conn., 1920), 19, rejects Stiles's estimate and suggests that freemen

may have numbered slightly higher than 25 percent of the adult white male population.

26. Figures for Farmington are based on calculations made from the Freeman's List, Farmington Recs., 1730; for Norwich see Daniels, "Large Town Power Structures," 134; for Lebanon see Stark, "Lebanon," 208; for Kent see Grant, *Democracy in Kent*, iii; for East Haddam and East Guilford see Chilton Williamson, *American Suffrage from Property to Democracy, 1760-1860* (Princeton, N.J., 1960), 27.

27. Grant, *Democracy in Kent*, iii; Stark, "Lebanon," 208, 209; Daniels, "Large Town Power Structures," Appendix I.

28. Stark, "Lebanon," 217-219; Grant, *Democracy in Kent*, 113.

29. All of Connecticut's early towns were larger than the 36-square-mile township which folk culture enshrines as the typical American town. Farmington, Norwich, Lebanon, and Kent were approximately 100, 96, 77, and 50 square miles, respectively, in 1776. Today eight whole towns and parts of three other towns have been carved from the original Farmington. East Haddam and East Guilford were former societies in other towns, and at 58 and 36 square miles, respectively, in 1776 were smaller than most Connecticut towns. This probably accounts for their higher percentage of freeman.

30. In Farmington Recs. freemen are entered after the Dec. 1691 meeting. Stark, "Lebanon," 205, and Grant, *Democracy in Kent*, 113, also point this out.

31. Middletown Recs., Mar. 1774; Sharon Town Meeting Records, Town Hall, Sharon, Conn., Oct. 1755.

32. The whole process is described in *Conn. Col. Recs.*, IV, II, 12.

33. These numbers are based on Samuel H. Rankin, Jr., "Conservatism and the Problem of Change in the Congregational Churches of Connecticut, 1660-1760" (Ph.D. diss., Kent State University, 1971), 116-117. Also see Bushman, *From Puritan to Yankee*, Appendix I. Hillel Schwartz, in "Admissions to Full Communion in the Congregational Churches of Connecticut" (typescript), Conn. Hist. Soc., Hartford, estimates that the average population of the societies in 1740 was approximately 850.

34. *Conn. Col. Recs.*, VII, 211. Most schools in towns with more than one parish were society schools, although in the larger towns the town meeting administered grammar schools.

35. A good discussion of the structure of a society can be found in Stark, "Lebanon," 151.

36. The best discussion of the controversies that created new societies is in Bushman, *From Puritan to Yankee*, 147-232. Also see Rankin, "Conservatism and the Problem of Change," *passim*.

37. Stark, "Lebanon," 85, 88-92.

38. *Ibid.*, 28.

39. Rankin, "Conservatism and the Problem of Change," 110, 111, shows that the churches managed to retain a great deal of individual autonomy even

under the Saybrook Platform, which was designed to enforce uniformity, through county associations, upon an increasingly pluralistic religious structure.

40. These details of the societies' independence are from Rankin, "Conservatism and the Problem of Change," 110, 111, 150-152, 246, 247, 316, 317.

41. Connecticut's example of town meeting frequency suggests either that the pattern of the increased activity in two Massachusetts towns, described by Kenneth A. Lockridge and Alan Kreider, "The Evolution of Massachusetts Town Government, 1640 to 1740," WMQ, 3d Ser., XXIII (1966), 549-574, was unique to Massachusetts or that the two towns were atypical.

42. Waterbury Town Meeting Records, City Hall, Waterbury, Conn., Dec. 1754; Sharon Recs., Dec. 1763, Jan. 1767, and Dec. 1776; Norwich Recs., Sept. 1716.

43. *Conn. Col. Recs.*, VII, 245.

44. Middletown Recs., 1700-1720, esp. Dec. 1702; Farmington Recs., Dec. 1709; Ridgefield Town Meeting Records, Town Hall, Ridgefield, Conn., Dec. 1722, and 1720s-1750s, *passim*; Norwich Recs., Aug. 1715.

45. Middletown Recs., Dec. 1712, 1717, and 1720; Ridgefield Recs., Dec. 1722, 1749, and 1751; Branford Town Meeting Records, Town Hall, Branford, Conn., Oct. 1781 and 1782; Norwich Recs., Feb. 1702.

46. Farmington Recs., Dec. 1765; Newtown Town Meeting Records, Town Hall, Newtown, Conn., Dec. 1766; Ridgefield Recs., Dec. 1772; Norwalk Town Meeting Records, City Hall, Norwalk, Conn., Dec. 1748, 1752, and 1756; Farmington Recs. Dec. 1702; Norwich Recs., Dec. 1728, and adjourned meeting of Dec. 1728.

47. Bruce C. Daniels, "Town Government in Connecticut, 1636-1675: The Founding of Institutions," *Connecticut Review* (1975), 39-40, points out that the colony government created most of the first town offices and was responsible for the similarity of all towns' institutions. However, Thomas W. Jodziewicz, "Dual Localism in Seventeenth-Century Connecticut: Relations between the General Court and the Towns, 1636-1691" (Ph.D. diss., College of William and Mary, 1974), shows that despite the colony government's formal control, local governments often resisted the direction of the central government, so that the two levels were "partners in localism." Zuckerman, *Peaceable Kingdoms*, argues that Massachusetts's central government closely controlled the towns until the loss of the original charter, whereas both Powell, *Puritan Village* and Lockridge, *A New England Town*, present a model of greater town autonomy in Massachusetts. T. H. Breen, "Persistent Localism: English Social Change and the Shaping of New England Institutions," *WMQ*, 3d Ser., XXXII (1975), 3-28 notes that there was a tension between colony and local authorities. This probably was also true for Connecticut.

48. Andrews, *River towns*, 110-112; *Conn. Col. Recs.*, II, 281, III, 53.

49. *Ibid.*, II, 61.

50. *Ibid.*, III-V, *passim*.

51. Herbert B. Adams, *Saxon Tithing-men in America*, Johns Hopkins University Studies in Historical and Political Science, 1st Ser., IV (Baltimore, 1883), 8.

52. *Conn. Col. Recs.*, V. 324.

53. *Ibid.*, VI, 277, XI, 499.

54. *Ibid.*, VI, 463-464.

55. See election meeting records in Hartford Town Meeting Records, City Hall, Hartford, Conn., 1721-1729, *passim*, and Middletown Recs., Dec. 1737.

56. *Some Early Records and Documents of and Relating to the Town of Windsor, Connecticut, 1639-1703* (Hartford, 1930), Dec. 1642; Fairfield Town Meeting Records, Town Hall, Fairfield, Conn., 1734, 1756, *passim*; Middletown Recs., 1708, 1712-1719, 1720; Derby Town Meeting Records, City Hall, Derby, Conn., Dec. 1707.

57. Farmington Recs., Dec. 1776.

58. *Conn. Col. Recs.*, IV, 32, 455, V, 73, VI, 112, XII, 255, XV, 193-194; Charles J. Hoadley, ed., *The Public Records of the State of Connecticut*, I (Hartford, 1894), 228. Grant's study of Kent strongly supports the conclusions of this paragraph. The Revolutionary effort in Kent was mainly directed by the selectmen. Grant, *Democracy in Kent*, 134, 135. During the Revolutionary years the activities of the town meeting and of the selectmen greatly increased. The Revolution was obviously a "crisis" situation that politicized the town meeting.

59. Hartford Recs., Dec. 1706; Farmington Recs., Dec. 1708; Norwalk Recs., Feb. 1702, Dec. 1709; Farmington Recs., Apr. 1710, Dec. 1736.

60. *Conn. Col. Recs.*, V, 403; Rankin, "Conservatism and the Problem of Change," 169.

61. The importance of plural officeholding and of large family units is well known to historians. See Bruce C. Daniels, "Family Dynasties," *Connecticut's First Family: William Pitkin and His Connections*, Connecticut Bicentennial Series. XI (Chester, 1975), and chapter 5 of the present volume.

62. For the growth of economic inequality see chapter 2 of the present volume and James A. Henretta, "Economic Development and Social Structure in Colonial Boston," WMQ, 3d Ser., XII (1965), 93-105. Alice Hanson Jones, "Wealth Estimates for the New England Colonies about 1770," *Journal of Economic History*, XXXII (1972), 98-127, and Jackson Turner Main, *The Social Structure of Revolutionary America* (Princeton, N.J., 1965), show the economic inequality in the Revolutionary era. For the decline of land availability and its effects see Philip J. Greven Jr., *Four Generations: Population, Land and Family in Colonial Andover, Massachusetts* (Ithaca, N.Y., 1970); Kenneth A. Lockridge, "Land, Population, and the Evolution of New England Society, 1630-1790; and an Afterthought," in Stanley Katz, ed., *Colonial America: Essays in Politics and Social Development* (Boston, 1971), 467-491; and Darrett Rutman, "People in Progress: The New Hampshire Towns of the Eighteenth-Century," *Journal of Urban History*, I (1975), 268-292. For the growth of family influence and oligarchical officeholding see Daniels, "Family Dynasties," "Large Town Office-

holding in Eighteenth-Century Connecticut: The Growth of Oligarchy," *Journal of American Studies*, IX (1975), 1-12, and chapter 5 of the present volume.

63. See Bushman, *From Puritan to Yankee*, and Zeichner, *Connecticut's Years of Controversy*, for these ideological and political currents.

64. Quoted in Perry Miller, *Orthodoxy in Massachusetts, 1630-1650* (Boston, 1933), 186.

CHAPTER 5

1. Benjamin Trumbull, *A Complete History of Connecticut*, 2 vols. (New London: H. D. Utley, 1898), I, 386.

2. The quotations are from Leonard Labaree, *Conservatism in Early American History* (New York: 1948), and Charles Andrews, *Our Earliest Colonial Settlements* (New York: 1933), both quoted in Robert Dinkin, "The Nomination of Governors and Assistants in Colonial Connecticut," Connecticut Historical Society, *Bulletin*, XXXVI (1971), 92.

3. For another view of this "system of little oligarchies," see Herbert L. Osgood, *The American Colonies in the Eighteenth Century*, 4 vols. (Gloucester, Mass., 1958), III, 275-277.

4. Robert Brown, *Middle-Class Democracy and the Revolution in Massachusetts, 1691-1780* (Ithaca, N.Y., 1955), 21-100.

5. Charles Grant, *Democracy in the Connecticut Frontier Town of Kent* (New York, 1961), 122-127; and Dinkin, "The Nomination of Governors," 93-94.

6. The first of these, Oscar Zeichner, *Connecticut's Years of Controversy, 1750-1776* (Chapel Hill, N.C., 1949), antedated Brown by six years. Others are Richard Dunn, *Puritans and Yankees: The Winthrop Dynasty of New England, 1630-1717* (Princeton, N.J., 1962); Robert C. Black, *The Younger John Winthrop* (New York, 1966); and, most importantly, Richard Bushman, *From Puritan to Yankee: Character and the Social Order in Connecticut 1690-1765* (Cambridge, Mass., 1967). The contributions of these historians and others to the "steady habits" literature is surveyed in Christopher Collier, "Steady Habits Considered and Reconsidered," *Connecticut Review*, V (1972), 28-37. While many historians have questioned the apathy and steady habits of Connecticut politics, apparently no one can controvert the fact that few voters turned out in colony-wide elections. For example, after 1740 when Connecticut appeared most turbulent, the highest recorded voter turnout was 27 percent. See Robert Dinkin, "Elections in Colonial Connecticut," Connecticut Historical Society *Bulletin*, XXXVII (1972), 17, 18; and J. R. Pole, "Suffrage and Representation in Massachusetts: A Statistical Note," *William and Mary Quarterly*, 3d Ser., XIV (1957), 582, 583.

This was not because the vast majority of adult white males were disenfranchised, because most were not. Most recent studies find that after the control of freemanship was transferred from the General Assembly to the towns in 1729 there were few impediments to voting registration and a minimum of 70 percent of adult white males qualified for the franchise although only 50 percent bothered to enroll. J. Hammond Trumbull and Charles Hoadley, eds., *The Public Records of the Colony of Connecticut*, 15 vols. (Hartford, 1855-1890), VII (Oct., 1729), 259; Grant, *Kent*, 111; Bruce P. Stark, "Lebanon, Connecticut: A Study of Society and Politics in the Eighteenth Century," (Ph.D. diss., University of Connecticut, 1970), 208; and Chilton Williamson, *American Suffrage, from Property to Democracy, 1760-1860* (Princeton, N.J., 1960), 27.

7. Already cited are Grant, *Kent*, and Stark, "Lebanon, Connecticut." See also William Willingham, "Windham, Connecticut: Profile of a Revolutionary Community, 1755-1818," (Ph.D. diss., Northwestern University, 1972); and Willingham, "Deference Democracy and Town Government in Windham, Connecticut, 1755 to 1786," *WMQ*, 3d Ser., XXX (1973), 401-421. My own unpublished doctoral dissertation, "Large Town Power Structures in Eighteenth Century Connecticut" (University of Connecticut, 1970), and subsequent articles, "Family Dynasties in Connecticut's Largest Towns, 1700-1760," *Canadian Journal of History*, VIII (1973), 99-110, and "Large-Town Officeholding in Eighteenth-Century Connecticut: The Growth of Oligarchy," *Journal of American Studies*, IX (1975), 1-12, deal only with limited samples of one type of town. In his study of Massachusetts, Kenneth Lockridge, *A New England Town: The First Hundred Years* (New York, 1970), dealt only with one town while Michael Zuckerman, *Peaceable Kingdoms: New England Towns in the Eighteenth Century* (New York, 1970), dealt with only 15 of over 200 Massachusetts towns and these were basically of only one type. Dirk Hoerder, *Society and Government 1760-1780: The Power Structure of Massachusetts Townships* (Berlin, 1972), studies officeholding extensively but only in a sample of five towns. The only study of Connecticut that completely escapes this particularism is Bruce Steiner, "Anglican Officeholding in pre-Revolutionary Connecticut: The Parameters of New England Community," *WMQ*, 3d Ser., XXXIV (1974), 369-405, and his scope is limited by his subject.

8. Edward M. Cook, Jr., "Local Leadership and the Typology of New England Towns, 1700-1785," *Political Science Quarterly*, LXXXVI (1971), 586-608, makes this point most forcefully.

9. For a perceptive discussion of changes occurring in society, see Kenneth Lockridge, "Social Change and the Meaning of the American Revolution," *Journal of Social History*, VI (1973), 403-439. Also see John Murrin, "The Legal Transformation: The Bench and Bar of Eighteenth-Century Massachusetts," in Stanley Katz, ed., *Colonial America* (Boston, 1971), 416-449.

10. See for example the groundbreaking work of Jackson Turner Main, "Government By the People: The American Revolution and the Democratization of the Legislatures," *WMQ*, 3d Ser., XXIII (1966), 391-407; Willingham, "Deference Democracy"; and Hoerder, *Society and Government*.

NOTES

9. Brown, *Revolutionary Politics*, 241.

0. Samuel Eliot Morison, "The Struggle Over the Adoption of the Constitu-
of Massachusetts, 1780," *Massachusetts Historical Society Proceedings*, L
6–1917); 353–412.

1. See Herbert Allan, *John Hancock: Patriot in Purple* (New York, 1953),
W. T. Baxter, *The House of Hancock: Business in Boston, 1724-1775*
hbridge, Mass., 1945), 4, 6, 224; and Lorenzo Sears, *John Hancock, the
resque Patriot* (Boston, 1912), 12-15.

2. Adams is quoted in Arthur Schlesinger, *The Colonial Merchants and the
rican Revolution, 1763-1776* (New York, 1918), 354.

3. Allan, *Hancock*, 4; Baxter, *House of Hancock*, 148, 169; and Sears, *Han-
, 176-177.

4. Allan, *Hancock*, 4; Baxter, *House of Hancock*, 308; and Sears, *Hancock,

5. See Allan, *Hancock*, X, 134, 180, 191, 206, 324; Baxter, *House of Han-
, 149, 224, 240; Patterson, *Political Parties*, 71, 72, 87, 132, 185, 186;
esinger, *Merchants*, 255; Sears, *Hancock*, ix, x; and Taylor, *Western Massa-
setts*, 174.

6. For a discussion of "steady habits" and other traits of colonial Connecti-
see Bruce C. Daniels, "Connecticut's Place in the American Colonies: What's in
ckname?" The Connecticut Historical Society, *Bulletin*, XLVIII (1978), 91-96.

7. The best discussion of the whole process is in Richard Bushman, *From
tan to Yankee: Character and the Social Order in Connecticut, 1690-1765
nbridge, Mass., 1967). The secondary literature on the erosion of "steady
its" is summed up and analyzed in Christopher Collier, "Steady Habits Con-
red and Reconsidered," *Connecticut Review*, V (1972), 28-37.

8. See Oscar Zeichner, *Connecticut's Years of Controversy, 1750-1776
apel Hill, N.C., 1949); and Christopher Collier, *Roger Sherman's Connecticut:
kee Politics and the American Revolution* (Middletown, Conn., 1971).

9. An extensive secondary literature does not exist for William Pitkin as it does
John Hancock. The subsequent discussion is based on Bruce C. Daniels, *Con-
ticut's First Family: William Pitkin and His Connections* (Chester, Conn., 1975).

0. See George Groce, "Eliphalet Dyer: Connecticut Revolutionist," *The Era
he American Revolution*, Richard Morris, ed., (New York, 1939), 290-305.

1. This paragraph based on Jere Daniell, *Experiment in Republicanism: New
npshire Politics and the American Revolution, 1741-1794* (Cambridge, Mass.,
0).

2. The only two serious historians of the Revolution in New Hampshire,
le disagreeing on an overall interpretation, agree on the progression of events.
Daniell, *Experiment in Republicanism*, and Richard Upton, *Revolutionary
w Hampshire: An Account of the Social and Political Forces Underlying the
nsition from Royal Province to American Commonwealth* (Port Washington,
Y., 1970). Early New Hampshire is woefully under studied by professional
torians.

11. The period of 1700-1780 was used for the overall period instead of 1700-
1790, since 1700-1780 could be broken into four twenty-year periods and there-
by make for ease in handling the data. It also represents, with the exception of
the last four years, the colonial period of the eighteenth century. Changes occurring in these four years would not affect the significance of the overall colonial
statistics as they would if 14 additional years were included.

The rationale for focussing on the locale, age, size, and function of the towns
and the criteria used in distinguishing them will be explained later.

12. Family was defined to mean all individuals with the same last name. This
undoubtedly involves some error but genealogical validating of this definition
reveals the error rate is insignificant.

13. Steiner, "Anglican Officeholding," stresses the importance of family in
officeholding. It shows that proper family connections could even overcome the
opprobrium of being an Anglican at election time.

14. Zuckerman, *Peaceable Kingdoms*, 278. Zuckerman's conclusions point
out what I mean by the problem of definition. With almost precisely the same
results in turnover rates and longest serving officeholders for Massachusetts that
I find for Connecticut, he believes these patterns mitigate against the existence
of an oligarchy while I believe the contrary. No one can say whose choice of
language fits the data best but a study of twentieth-century state assemblies
shows that they have a turnover rate significantly higher than 50 percent and
that 67 percent of the assemblies have a turnover rate of higher than 67 percent.
Hence they are less quantitatively oligarchic than colonial Massachusetts and
Connecticut. Yet many people complain of local oligarchies in present day state
assemblies. Of course on the other hand one can look at the U.S. House of Representatives where in the first part of the twentieth century political scientists call
a 25 percent turnover rate of its members high and where after great upsets in
1958 and 1964 when the number of "junior representatives" was lamented, still
over 40 percent of the house had served more than ten years. In the 1974 Con-
gressional elections, newspapers remarked on the number of new Congressmen
and the turnover rate was about 25 percent. C. Merriam and R. Merriam, *The
American Government* (New York, 1954), 225; D. S. Alexander, *History and
Procedure of the House of Representatives* (Boston, 1916), 30; Robert Peabody,
"Party Leadership Changes in the U.S. House of Representatives," eds. R. Peabody and N. Polsby, *New Perspectives on the House of Representatives* (Chicago,
1969), 385; *National Observer* (January 18, 1975), 2.

15. See Bushman, *From Puritan to Yankee*, 235-266; Zeicher, *Connecticut's
Year of Controversy*, chaps. II, III, VI, VII, and VIII; Christopher Collier, *Roger
Sherman's Connecticut: Yankee Politics and the American Revolution* (Middle-
town, Conn., 1971), chaps. II, III, and IV.

16. Queen Anne's War broke out in 1702 and lasted until 1713. The official
years of the Seven Years War were 1756-1763 but for New England the crucial
years of the war started with the Albany Conference of 1754 and ended with the

fall of Fort Niagara, Fort Ticonderoga, Crown Point, and Quebec, and the destruction of St. Francis, all in 1759. Similarly the war years of the Revolution started with the spring of 1775. King George's War failed to produce a similar high rate of turnover in the 1740s but it was the shortest and least consequential of the colonial wars and, aside from the assault on Louisbourg and the Cape Breton expedition, did not create much activity in New England. Howard Peckham, *The Colonial Wars: 1689-1762* (Chicago, 1964), 77, chap. 9, and chap. 5. Connecticut's General Assembly only unduly concerned itself with military affairs during King George's War for two years, 1745 and 1746. See *Conn. Col. Recs.*, IX (1744-1750).

17. Steiner, "Anglican Officeholding," 398-403, believes that the spirit of community and the belief in harmony overcame the wounds caused by the inroads of Anglicanism.

18. It would be misleading to look at officeholding patterns but not misleading, of course, to compare who was an officeholder in the 1760s and 1780s, as did Main, "Government By the People" or to compare officeholders immediately before and after independence as did James Kirby Martin, "Men of Family Wealth and Personal Merit: The Changing Social Basis of Executive Leadership Selection in the American Revolution," *Societas*, II (1972), 43-70. Their conclusions for some colonies that the type of officeholder changed would not necessarily be challenged by my data. My data do show, however, that the 15 years prior to the Revolution in Connecticut were unusual in their officeholding patterns. Jack P. Greene in "An Uneasy Connection: An Analysis of the Preconditions of the American Revolution," in Stephan Kurtz and James Hutson, eds., *Essays on the American Revolution* (Chapel Hill, N.C., 1973), 36-37, suggests that in all of the colonies, deference to elites and oligarchical tenure of office was on the rise in the years prior to the Revolution.

19. See especially Philip Greven, Jr., *Four Generations: Population, Land and Family in Colonial Andover, Massachusetts* (Ithaca, 1970), and Kenneth Lockridge, "Land, Population, and the Evolution of New England Society, 1630-1790," and "An Afterthought," in Katz, ed., *Colonial America*, 467-491.

20. The median white population of Connecticut towns in 1774 was 2,168, compared to a median in Massachusetts in 1776 of 1,005. In Connecticut 34 percent of people lived in towns with more than 4,000 as compared to 23 percent in Massachusetts. Steiner, "Anglican Officeholding," 384, note 36. Connecticut created new ecclesiastical societies within towns instead of new towns. Samuel Rankin, "Conservatism and the Problem of Change in the Congregational Churches of Connecticut, 1660-1760," (Ph.D. diss., Kent State University, 1971), 116-117, discusses the proliferation of societies.

21. Cook, "Local Leadership," 588-589 and 602-603. Cook did find that family connections were more important on the colony level than in local officeholding and since I am only measuring colony-level officeholding, this may account for the difference. I agree with his conclusion that family connections were

more important in colony-level leadership than in local go further and say that most different offices had dis ship recruitment and officeholding. See Daniels, "Larg

22. Nevertheless, families were extremely importa and urban towns. Daniels, "Family Dynasties," *passim.*

23. Edward Cook Jr., *The Fathers of the Towns: L Structure in Eighteenth-Century New England* (Baltim shortly after this present chapter was written. For mor the 11 essays in Bruce C. Daniels (ed.), *Power and St American Colonies* (Middletown, Conn., 1986).

CHAPTER 6

1. This moderate view is essentially accurate. Alt historical and accommodates the evidence presented b sensus historians. See Edmund Morgan, *The Birth o 1956), 4-13, 99-101, and *passim.* Morgan argues that th ground, Protestant religion, widespread ownership of p self-government, and love of the English constitution come regional, social, economic, and ideological differen

2. I do not mean to suggest that the recent work which analyzes quantitative changes in leadership durin valuable—it is. Martin's work, however, analyzes only and I believe that my present essay significantly adds to of leadership and the Revolution. Martin and I agree tha a major role in the Revolution. I believe, however, that from an imperial to a local elite should not necessarily be ratizing shift in power. See James Kirby Martin, *Men in mental Leaders and the Coming of the American Revo N.J., 1973).

3. This point is perceptively developed by both Step *Parties in Revolutionary Massachusetts* (Madison, Wis Richard D. Brown, *Revolutionary Politics in Massachus mittee of Correspondence and the Towns, 1772-1774* (C 9-10.

4. Brown, *Revolutionary Politics*, 10, discusses the ideal ruler.

5. Brown, *Revolutionary Politics*, 7.

6. Patterson, *Political Parties*, 71-87.

7. Robert Taylor, *Western Massachusetts in the Revol 1954), 3.

8. Lee Newcomer, *The Embattled Farmers: A Massac the American Revolution* (New York, 1953), 87, 88, 99.

23. Avery Butters, "New Hampshire History and the Public Career of Meshech Weare, 1713 to 1786," (Ph.D. diss., Fordham University, 1961), 5, 11, 14, 30, 40-50, 123; Daniell, *Experiment in Republicanism*, chaps. 2 and 3; Clifford Shipton, "Meshech Weare," *Biographical Sketches of Harvard Graduates*, vol. IX, 590-605; Upton, *Revolutionary New Hampshire*, 14; and William Little, *History of Weare* (Concord, 1888).

24. Butters, "New Hampshire History," 15, 20, 23; Daniell, *Experiment in Republicanism*, 121; Shipton, "Meshech Weare," 596, 597, 604; and Upton, *Revolutionary New Hampshire*, 44.

25. Butters, "New Hampshire History," 122, 123-126, 277; Daniell, *Experiment in Republicanism*, 127, 128; Shipton, "Meshech Weare," 598; and Upton, *Revolutionary New Hampshire*, 44, 45, 53-57.

26. Butters, "New Hampshire History," 203, 269; Daniell, *Experiment in Republicanism*, 124, 125, 130, 150, 151, 161; and Shipton, "Meshech Weare," 598.

27. Butters, "New Hampshire History," 276; and Shipton, "Meshech Weare," 602.

28. Sidney James, *Colonial Rhode Island: A History* (New York, 1975), 296.

29. The best account of the Ward-Hopkins years is in David Lovejoy, *Rhode Island Politics and the American Revolution, 1760-1776* (Providence, R.I., 1958), *passim*. See also Samuel Arnold, *History of the State of Rhode Island and Providence Plantations*, 2 vols. (New York, 1860), II, 245-93; Frank Bates, *Rhode Island and the Formation of the Union* (New York, 1898), 37, 38, 39; James, *Colonial Rhode Island*, 296; and Irwin Polishook, *Rhode Island and the Union* (Evanston, Ill., 1969), 12, 13, 43.

30. Arnold, *History*, II, 281-293; Bates, *Rhode Island*, 39-40; James, *Colonial Rhode Island*, 296; Lovejoy, *Rhode Island Politics, passim*; and Polishook, *Rhode Island*, 12, 13, 43.

31. Lovejoy, *Rhode Island Politics*, 150, 151, argues this.

32. *Appleton's Cyclopedia of American Biography*, VI; Arnold, *History*, II, 281-315; *Dictionary of American Biography*, XIX, 412, Lovejoy, *Rhode Island Politics*, 150-151, 179, 181; and Polishook, *Rhode Island*, 12, 13.

33. Bates, *Rhode Island*, 37, 58; Lovejoy, *Rhode Island Politics*, 179; Polishook, *Rhode Island*, 37; and William Weeden, *The Economic and Social History of New England*, 2 vols. (New York, 1890), II, 583.

34. Arnold, *History*, II, 347-361; *Dictionary of American Biography*, XIX, 412; James, *Colonial Rhode Island*, pp. 319, 346; Lovejoy, *Rhode Island Politics*, 184; and Mack Thompson, *Moses Brown: Reluctant Reformer* (Chapel Hill, N.C., 1962), 115.

35. James, *Colonial Rhode Island*, 346; Matt Jones, ed., "Revolutionary Correspondence of Governor Nicholas Cooke, 1775-1781," *Proceedings of the American Antiquarian Society*, XXXVI (1926), 231-253; Lovejoy, *Rhode Island Politics*, 184; and Polishook, *Rhode Island*, 11, 37.

36. Although possible, it is not certain that meaningful ideological and class differences always accompanied these geographical divisions; historians do not

agree on this and more basic research will have to be done to confirm or disprove that more than sectional differences existed. If ideological class differences did not exist, historians may be tempted to say that there was no *meaningful* conflict in the Revolution since a consensus on ideology existed. They could liken this situation to late nineteenth-century America when two parties agreed upon essentials but still fought viciously for control of the government. However, the fact that the political fights in colonial and Revolutionary America were based so strongly on geography, unlike the party struggles of a later period, shows that at least one important issue was at stake—for which section's benefit was the colony or state to be developed? This is not the same type of issueless conflict as the late nineteenth century indulged in. These divisions could have destroyed the territorial integrity of each of the colony's boundaries or even destroyed the Revolutionary movement itself.

37. Richard D. Brown, "The Founding Fathers of 1776 and 1787: A Collective View," *WMQ*, 3d Ser., XXXIII (1976), 465–480.

38. Most historians would agree that, despite its divisions, New England was much more homogeneous and unified than the Southern Colonies and in particular more so than the Middle Colonies. The success of these two regions waging the Revolution would suggest that the model presented here could also apply to them.

CHAPTER 7

1. P. M. G. Harris, "The Social Origins of American Leaders: The Demographic Foundations," *Perspectives in American History*, III (1969), 186–188.

2. The changes at Yale can be seen by reading three historians whose work consecutively covers the college's colonial experience. See Richard Warch, *School of the Prophets: Yale College, 1701-1740* (New Haven, 1973); Louis Leonard Tucker, *Puritan Protagonist: President Thomas Clap of Yale College* (Williamsburg, 1962); and Edmund S. Morgan, *The Gentle Puritan: A Life of Ezra Stiles, 1727-1795* (New Haven, 1962). For Harvard the changes are described in Samuel Eliot Morison, *Three Centuries of Harvard, 1626-1937* (Cambridge, Mass., 1937).

3. Franklin Bowditch Dexter, *Biographical Sketches of the Graduates of Yale College, With Annals of the College's History, October 1701 to June 1892*, 4 vols. (New York, 1885-1907); and John Langdon Sibley, Clifford Shipton, *et al.*, *Biographical Sketches of Graduates of Harvard University in Cambridge, Massachusetts*, 20 vols. (Cambridge, Mass., 1873-   ).

4. The story of the founding is well told by Warch, *School of the Prophets.*

5. Morgan, *Ezra Stiles*, 359.

6. Beverley McAnear, "College Founding in the American Colonies, 1745-1775," *The Social Fabric*, eds. John Cary and Julius Weinberg (Boston 1975), 70-75.

7. Warch, *School of the Prophets*, 253; and Tucker, *Thomas Clap*, 78, *passim*.

8. James McLachlan, *Princetonians, 1748-1768: A Biographical Dictionary* (Princeton, N.J., 1976), XIX.

9. For the data on Columbia graduates see David C. Humphrey, *From King's College to Columbia, 1746-1800* (New York, 1975), 97; for Princeton see McLachlan, *Princetonians*, XX; and for Brown and Pennsylvania see Beverley McAnear, "The Selection of An Alma Mater by Pre-Revolutionary Students," *Pennsylvanian Magazine of History and Biography*, LXXIII (1949), 430. McAnear argues that the high cost of travel was an important factor influencing students to attend a college near home. See McAnear, "The Selection of An Alma Mater," 431. For Oxford and Cambridge patterns of geographical recruitment see Lawrence Stone, "The Size and Composition of the Oxford Student Body, 1580-1909," *The University in Society*, ed., Lawrence Stone, 2 vols., (Princeton, N.J., 1974), I, 35-36, 58-59. For the changing trends in recruitment see McAnear, "College Founding in the Colonies," 79.

10. For these population movements see Bruce C. Daniels, *The Connecticut Town: Growth and Development, 1635-1790* (Middletown, Conn., 1979), chap. II.

11. Tucker, *Thomas Clap*, 80; and Warch, *School of the Prophets*, 192.

12. See Richard Hofstadter, *Academic Freedom in the Age of the College* (New York, 1965), 176-178, for a discussion of secularization in education in general and specifically at Yale.

13. McLachlan, *Princetonians*, XXI.

14. Warch, *School of the Prophets*, 100-117.

15. Tucker, *Thomas Clap*.

16. Louis Leonard Tucker, *Connecticut's Seminary of Sedition: Yale College*, VIII, "Connecticut Bicentennial Series," (Chester, Conn., 1974), 21, 41-42. For the relationship between whiggism and the curriculum see Lawrence Cremin, *American Education: The Colonial Experience, 1607-1783* (New York, 1970), 135-136. Cremin's and Morison's conclusions about this relationship were brought to my attention by Tucker, *Connecticut's Seminary of Sedition*, 25.

17. McLachlan, *Princetonians*, XXI-XXIII.

18. These figures were arrived at by averaging data from a variety of sources. Edward Wigglesworth argued that the life expectancy of a 21-year-old man in the eighteenth century was 55.22 years. Maris Vinovskis, a skilled demographer, thinks this is slightly too low but is still the best guide we have. At any rate, even if Wigglesworth's calculation was grossly in error, the mortality rate of the general population would still be higher than that of Yale graduates. See Maris Vinovskis, "The 1789 Table of Edward Wigglesworth," *Journal of Economic History*, XXXI (1971), 580, 589. The marriage ages of the population of New England varied with time. The averages I have used are taken from Robert Higgs and H. Louis Stettler, III, "Colonial New England Demography: A Sampling Approach," *William and Mary Quarterly*, 3d Ser., XXXVII (1970), 285; Susan Norton, "Population Growth in Colonial America: A Study of Ipswich, Massa-

chusetts," *Population Studies*, XXV (1971), 445; and Philip Greven, Jr., *Four Generations: Population, Land, and Family in Colonial Andover, Massachusetts* (Ithaca, N.Y., 1970). Norton's and Greven's figures were drawn to my attention by Daniel Scott Smith, "The Demographic History of Colonial New England," *Journal of Economic History*, XXXII (1972), 177. The average number of children per completed family is from Smith, "The Demographic History," 177. The remarriage rate is from Higgs and Settler, "Colonial New England," 286. They give a possible range of from 8.5 to 17 percent and I have used the maximum percentage to contrast to the rate among Yale graduates. Obviously, the minimum percentage would make the contrast even stronger.

19. Harris, "The Social Origins," 186-188.

20. Stone, "Oxford Student Body," 33-57; and McLachlan, *Princetonians*, XXI.

CHAPTER 8

1. The sociological theory upon which this paragraph is based is found in Kurt B. Mayer, "The Changing Shape of the American Class Structure," *Social Research*, 30 (1963), 462-468.

2. The conception of Anglicization of features of Massachusetts' society is discussed in John Murrin, "Anglicizing An American Colony: The Transformation of Provincial Massachusetts," *Colonial America: Essays in Politics and Social Development*, ed., Stanley Katz, (Boston, 1971). The idea of increased stratification is discussed in Kenneth Lockridge, "Land, Population and the Evolution of New England Society 1630-1790," *Colonial America*, ed., Katz, 467-491, and Lockridge, "Social Change and the Meaning of the American Revolution," *Journal of Social History*, VI (1973), 403-439. The importance of the five main colonial centers has been brilliantly chronicled by Carl Bridenbaugh, *Cities in The Wilderness: The First Century of Urban Life in America, 1625-1742* (New York, 1938), and *Cities in Revolt: Urban Life in America, 1743-1776* (New York, 1955). Jackson Turner Main did note over a decade ago that the lesser cities were important and that their social structures "with certain modifications . . . shared the same qualities" as the larger cities. See Jackson Turner Main, *The Social Structure of Revolutionary America* (Princeton, N.J., 1965), 34.

3. See Joseph A. Ernst and H. Roy Merrens, "Camden's Turrets Pierce the Skies! The Urban Process in the Southern Colonies During the Eighteenth-Century," *William and Mary Quarterly*, 3d Ser., XXX (1973), 549-574. Ernst's and Merrens' position is questioned in Hermann Wellenreuther, "Urbanization in the Colonial South: A Critique," *WMQ*, 3d Ser., XXXI (1974), 653-668, but ably defended by their rebuttal in the same issue. See also James T. Lemon, "Urbanization and The Development of Eighteenth-Century Southeastern Pennsylvania and Adjacent Delaware," *WMQ*, 3d Ser., XXIV (1967), 501-542, 520-524.

4. Bridenbaugh, *Cities in Revolt*, 216, 217.

5. Ernest S. Griffith, *History of American City Government: The Colonial Period* (New York, 1938), 71, 72, 97. I shall follow the convention accepted by Carl Bridenbaugh and most American historians of calling urban areas "cities" even though often they legally were not.

6. Bridenbaugh, *Cities in Revolt*, 48.

7. Gaspare John Saladino, "The Economic Revolution in Late Eighteenth-Century Connecticut" (Ph.D. Diss., University of Wisconsin, 1964), 17-20; Robert Owen Decker, "The New London Merchants: 1645-1901: The Rise and Decline of a Connecticut Port" (Ph.D. Diss., University of Connecticut, 1970), 30-38; Rollin G. Osterweis, *Three Centuries of New Haven, 1638-1938* (New Haven, 1953), 75-76; and Frances Manwaring Caulkins, *A History of Norwich, Connecticut* (Hartford, 1966), 309.

8. Lemon, "Urbanization," 502-517.

9. Ernst and Merrens, "Urbanization in South," 558-569; Robert Coakley, "Virginia Commerce During The American Revolution" (Ph.D. Diss., University of Virginia, 1949), *passim*; James H. Soltow, "The Role of Williamsburg in the Virginia Economy, 1750-1775," *WMQ*, 3d Ser., IV (1958), 467-482, 468.

10. Bridenbaugh, *Cities in Revolt*, 216-217.

11. James A. Henretta, *The Evolution of American Society, 1700-1815: An Interdisciplinary Analysis* (Lexington, Mass., 1973), 80-81. Bridenbaugh, in an unfortunately little-used book, *The Colonial Craftsman* (New York, 1950), chapter IV, calls attention to the importance of these secondary units, but his remarks have escaped wide notice.

12. Talcott Parsons is probably the best known proponent of functionalism. See Walter Buckley, "Social Stratification and the Functional Theory of Social Differentiation," *Social Stratification in the United States*, Jack L. Roach, Llewellyn Gross, and Orville Gursslin (eds.) (Englewood Cliffs, N.J., 1969), 17-24. See also Roach *et al.* (eds.), *Social Stratification*, "Introduction," 3.

13. North Callahan, *Connecticut's Revolutionary War Leaders*, Connecticut Bicentennial Series, III (Chester, Conn., 1973), 7-51 *passim*; Thomas Barrow, *Connecticut Joins the Revolution*, Connecticut Bicentennial Series, I (Chester, Connecticut, 1973), 7-44 *passim*; Saladino, "The Economic Revolution," appendices 29 and 30, 425-432. In all of New England, cities always contributed a disproportionate share of the colony offices. See Edward Cook, Jr., "Local Leadership and the Typology of New England Towns, 1700-1785)," *Political Science Quarterly*, LXXXVI (1971), 586-608, 594.

14. Henretta, *The Evolution of Society*, 41; Saladino, "The Economic Revolution," 17-20.

15. Saladino, "The Economic Revolution," 1-5; Decker, "The Rise and Decline of a Port," 253-256.

16. Saladino, "The Economic Revolution," 17.

17. Osterweis, *New Haven*, 75-76; Caulkins, *Norwich*, 309; Saladino, "The Economic Revolution," 4-17; Henretta, *The Evolution of Society*, 41; and Decker, "The Rise and Decline of a Port," 37-38.

18. For the details of this paragraph see William Deloss Love, *The Colonial History of Hartford* (originally published Hartford, 1914, Pequot Press edition, 1974), 232-250; Caulkins, *Norwich*, 311-335; Decker, "The Rise and Decline of a Port, 55-56; Bridenbaugh, *Cities in Revolt*, 41, 156, 163-164, 279; and William Weeden, *The Economic and Social History of New England, 1620-1789*, 2 vols. (originally published New York, 1890; Hillory House edition, 1963), I, 249.

19. Main, *Social Structure*, 37; and Henretta, "Economic Development and Social Structure in Colonial Boston," *WMQ*, 3d Ser., XXXII (1965), 75-92, 85-105.

20. Henretta, *The Evolution of Society*, chap. III; and Allan Kulikoff, "The Progress of Inequality in Revolutionary Boston," *WMQ*, 3d Ser., XXVIII (1971), 375-412, 384.

21. Caulkins, *Norwich*, 328.

22. Main, *Social Structure*, 35, 73, 116-123; and Bridenbaugh, *Cities in Revolt*, 361.

23. Carl Abbott, "The Neighborhoods of New York, 1760-1775," *New York History*, LXI (1974), 35-54, 35-52; Kulikoff, "The Progress of Inequality," 398-409; and Henretta, *The Evolution of Society*, 86.

24. Henretta, *The Evolution of Society*, 98; and Bridenbaugh, *Cities in Revolt*, 211.

25. Richard Bushman, *From Puritan to Yankee: Character and the Social Order in Connecticut, 1690-1765* (Cambridge, Mass., 1967), 183-221; Oscar Zeichner, *Connecticut's Years of Controversy, 1750-1776*, (Chapel Hill, N.C., 1949) chap. 2; James Walsh, "The Great Awakening in the First Congregational Church of Woodbury, Connecticut," *WMQ*, 3d Ser., XXVIII (1971), 543-562, *passim*; and Henretta, *The Evolution of Society*, 129-130.

26. C. C. Goen, *Revivalism and Separatism in New England, 1740-1800* (New Haven, 1962), 68-90, 115, 302-309.

27. Bruce E. Steiner, "Anglican Officeholding in Pre-Revolutionary Connecticut: The Parameters of New England Community," *WMQ*, 3d Ser., XXXI (1974), 269-406, 375, 377.

28. Osterweis, *New Haven*, 90, 111; and Decker, "The Rise and Decline of a Port," 40.

29. See Chapter 4 of the present volume.

30. For the Connecticut cities see Daniels, "Large-Town Officeholding in Eighteenth-Century Connecticut: The Growth of Oligarchy," *The Journal of American Studies*, IX (1975); and Daniels, "Family Dynasties in Connecticut's Largest Towns," *Canadian Journal of History*, VII (1973), 99-111, *passim*. For substantiation of this in other cities see Kulikoff, "The Progress of Inequality,"

390; Henretta, *The Evolution of Society*, 90-111; Murrin, "Anglicizing An American Colony," 264-265; and Michael Zuckerman, *Peaceable Kingdoms: New England Towns in the Eighteenth-Century* (New York, 1970), Appendix VIII.

31. Daniels, "Family Dynasties," and Murrin, "Anglicizing an American Colony," 264. Carl Bridenbaugh feels that the colonial aristocracy peaked in social prestige in the 1760s and 1770s. See Bridenbaugh, *Cities in Revolt*, 332.

32. Henretta, *The Evolution of Society*, 14, discusses the changing demographic characteristics of the cities. An example of demographic changes from unique American norms to English norms in a nonurban area can be found in Philip Greven Jr., *Four Generations: Population, Land and Family in Colonial Andover, Massachusetts* (Ithaca, New York, 1970). Lockridge, "Land Population," 467, makes the "overcrowded argument" and expands on it in "Social Change," 403-439. For the seventeenth-century communalism and unity of villages see Lockridge, *A New England Town: The First Hundred Years* (New York, 1970), 167-170, and Sumner Chilton Powell, *Puritan Village* (Middletown, Conn., 1963), 178-186.

33. Murrin, "Anglicizing an American Colony," 20. Murrin's thesis is the first major explicit treatment of Anglicization though Bridenbaugh in *Cities in Revolt* had implicitly dealt with the same theme, chaps., V, VI, and IX.

34. Henretta, *The Evolution of Society*, 42; and Bridenbaugh, *Cities in Revolt*, 341, 365.

35. Murrin, "Anglicizing an American Colony," 20-38. Edward E. Atwater (ed.), *History of the City of New Haven by an Association of Writers* (New York, 1887), describes some of these changes in New Haven in "The Bench and the Bar," and "Changes in Medicine and Surgery," chaps. XIII and XIV.

36. Murrin, "Anglicizing an American Colony," 28-38.

37. Sidney Kobre, *The Development of the Colonial Newspaper* (Gloucester, Mass., 1960), 97, 174, 177.

38. Weeden, *Economic and Social History*, 546, 763; Osterweis, *New Haven*, 102, 158; Love, *Colonial Hartford*, 230; Caulkins, *Norwich*, 299; Louis Leonard Tucker, *Connecticut's Seminary of Sedition: Yale College*, Connecticut Bicentennial Series VIII (Chester, Conn., 1974), 124.

39. Atwater, *New Haven*, 194.

40. Bridenbaugh, *Cities in Revolt*, 118-132.

41. Bushman, *From Puritan to Yankee*, 54-72, shows that often conflicts in Connecticut towns were between the rich inhabitants of town centers interested in commerce and the middle-class farmers in outlying areas. Walsh, "The Great Awakening," 559, shows ideological and religious splits often pitted the town center against the outlying farmers. Griffith, *American City Government*, 262-263, demonstrates that the same split between business district merchants and outlying farmers characterized most cities. Bridenbaugh, *Cities in Revolt*, 10, 11; and Murrin, "Anglicizing an American Colony," 267, also agree that urban-rural splits were crucial factors.

42. Christopher Collier, *Roger Sherman's Connecticut: Yankee Politics and The American Revolution* (Middletown, Conn., 1971), 197, 198, discusses the fights in New Haven. Love, *Colonial Hartford*, 348, discusses them in Hartford. Weeden, *Economic and Social History*, 735, discusses the anomaly of Hartford, containing a clear urban center, also producing vast amounts of wheat as late as the 1760s.

43. Love, *Colonial Hartford*, 343; and Osterweis, *New Haven*, 112.

44. Love, *Colonial Hartford*, 348, 349; Atwater, *New Haven*, 80, 81; and Osterweis, *New Haven*, 165, discuss the anxieties of the urban areas. David Roth, *Connecticut's War Governor: Jonathan Trumbull*, Connecticut Bicentennial Series, IX (Chester, Conn., 1974), 74; Collier, *Roger Sherman's Connecticut*, 198; and Love, *Colonial Hartford*, 348, show the heightened tension. For the acts of incorporation see *State Records*, V (January, 1784), 257-277, and V (May, 1784), 343-373. The similarities between the new cities and the English model can easily be seen by comparing the five corporations to English ones described in Sidney and Beatrice Webb, *English Local Government* IV, *Statutory Authorities for Specific Purposes* (originally published London, 1922, London, 1963), 353-373.

45. Love, *Colonial Hartford*, 343, 354-355; and Osterweis, *New Haven*, 157, 165.

46. For the increase in officeholding oligarchy see Daniels, "Large Town Officeholding," 1-12.

47. Jackson Turner Main, "Trends in Wealth Concentration Before 1860," *Journal of Economic History*, XXXI (1971), 445-447; and Kulikoff, "The Progress of Inequality," 376.

48. Chester Destler, *Connecticut: The Provisions State*, Connecticut Bicentennial Series, V (Chester, Conn., 1973), *passim*; Saladino, "The Economic Revolution," 43; and Henretta, *The Evolution of Society*, 167.

49. This discussion of the spread of urban values is based on Richard D. Brown, "The Emergence of Urban Society in Rural Massachusetts, 1760-1820," *Journal of American History*, LXI (1974), 29-51.

50. Boorstin, *The National Experience*, part three.

CHAPTER 9

1. See Stephen G. Kurtz and James H. Hutson (eds.), *Essays on the American Revolution* (Chapel Hill, N.C., 1973) for a collection of essays that represent a variety of mature consensus views of the Revolution. See Alfred F. Young (ed.), *The American Revolution: Explorations in the History of American Radicalism* (DeKalb, Ill., 1976) for a similar collection that represents the conflict view.

2. For other important statements see Pauline Maier, *From Resistance to Revolution: Colonial Radicals and the Development of American Opposition to Britain, 1765-1776* (London, 1973; Edmund S. Morgan, "The American Revolu-

tion Considered as an Intellectual Movement," in Morgan, *The Challenge of the American Revolution* (New York, 1976) 60-87; and *The Development of a Revolutionary Mentality: Papers Presented at the First Library of Congress Symposium on the American Revolution* (Wash., D.C., 1972).

3. See also Catherine Albanese, *Sons of the Fathers: The Civil Religion of the American Revolution* (Philadelphia, 1976); Sacvan Bercovitch, *The Puritan Origins of the American Self* (New Haven, Conn., 1975); Rhys Isaac, *The Transformation of Virginia, 1740-1790* (Chapel Hill, N.C., 1982); William McLoughlin, "The Role of Religion in the Revolution: Liberty of Conscience and Cultural Cohesion in the New Nation," in Kurtz and Hutson (eds.), *The American Revolution*, 197-255; and Harry S. Stout, "Religion, Communication, and the Ideological Origins of the American Revolution," *William and Mary Quarterly*, 3d Ser., XXXIV (1977), 519-541.

4. For a representative sample of the eighteenth-century community studies outside of Massachusetts see Richard R. Beeman, *The Evolution of the Southern Backcountry: A Case Study of Lunenburg County, Virginia, 1746-1832* (Philadelphia, 1984); Daniels, *The Connecticut Town: Growth and Development, 1635-1790* (Middletown, Conn., 1979); Jessica Kross, *The Evolution of an American Town: Newtown, New York, 1642-1775* (Philadelphia, 1983); James Lemon, *The Best Poor Man's Country: A Geographical Study of Early Southeastern Pennsylvania* (Baltimore, 1972); and Stephanie Grauman Wolf, *Urban Village: Population, Community, and Family Structure in Germantown Pennsylvania, 1683-1880* (Princeton, N.J., 1976).

5. Jesse Lemisch, "The American Revolution Seen from the Bottom Up," in Barton Bernstein (ed.), *Towards a New Past: Dissenting Essays in American History* (New York, 1968), 29. See especially the following essays in Young (ed.), *The American Revolution*: Edward Countryman, "Out of the Bounds of Law: Northern Land Rioters in the Eighteenth Century," 37-70; Marvin L. Michael Kay, "The North Carolina Regulation, 1766-1776: A Class Conflict," 71-124; and Ronald Hoffman, "The Disaffected in the Revolutionary South," 273-318.

6. For examples of the process in individual colonies, see Richard L. Bushman, *From Puritan to Yankee: Character and the Social Order in Connecticut, 1690-1765* (Cambridge, Mass., 1965); and A. Roger Ekirch, *"Poor Carolina": Politics and Society in Colonial North Carolina, 1729-1776* (Chapel Hill, N.C., 1981).

7. See, for example, Wallace Brown, *The King's Friends: The Composition and Motives of the American Loyalist Claimants* (Providence, R.I., 1965); Robert McCluer Calhoon, *The Loyalists in Revolutionary America, 1760-1781* (New York, 1973); Linda K. Kerber, *Women of the Republic: Intellect and Ideology in Revolutionary America* (Chapel Hill, N.C., 1980); Mary Beth Norton, *The British Americans: The Loyalist Exiles in England, 1774-1789* (Boston, 1973); and Norton, *Liberty's Daughters: The Revolutionary Experience of American Women, 1750-1800* (Boston, 1980).

8. Canfield, *Sam Adams's Revolution, 1765-1776* (New York, 1976), dust-jacket.

9. John C. Miller, *Samuel Adams: Pioneer in Propaganda* (Stanford, Cal., 1936); Clifford Shipton, "Samuel Adams," *Sibley's Harvard Graduates* (Boston, 1958), 420-465.

10. Pauline Maier, "Coming to Terms with Samuel Adams," *American Historical Review*, LXXXI (1976), 12-37; Richard D. Brown, *Revolutionary Politics in Massachusetts: The Boston Committee of Correspondence and the Towns, 1772-1775* (Cambridge, Mass., 1970); and Charles Akers, "Sam Adams—and Much More," *New England Quarterly*, XLVII (1974), 120-131.

11. Page Smith, *John Adams*, 2 vols. (New York, 1962), VII, 10.

12. John R. Howe, Jr., *The Changing Political Thought of John Adams* (Princeton, N.J., 1966).

13. Peter Shaw, *The Character of John Adams* (Chapel Hill, N.C., 1976), 10-12.

14. Withey, *Dearest Friend: A Life of Abigail Adams* (New York, 1981). See too Charles W. Akers, *Abigail Adams: An American Woman* (Boston, 1980), which also emphasizes the force and quality of Adams's (Abigail) mind.

15. Bailyn, *The Ordeal of Thomas Hutchinson* (Cambridge, Mass., 1974); and Pencak, *America's Burke: The Mind of Thomas Hutchinson* (Wash., 1982).

16. See Janice Potter, *The Liberty We Seek: Loyalist Ideology in Colonial New York and Massachusetts* (Cambridge, Mass., 1983) whose examinations of loyalists in New York and Massachusetts includes Hutchinson, Sewall, Peter Oliver, and Daniel Leonard.

17. Herbert Allan, *John Hancock: Patriot in Purple* (New York, 1953), 1-3; W. T. Baxter, *The House of Hancock: Business in Boston, 1724-1775* (Cambridge, Mass., 1945), 4-6; and Lorenzo Sears, *John Hancock: The Picturesque Patriot* (Boston, 1912), 12-15.

18. Two other studies that show the role of important clergymen in the Revolution are: Charles H. Lippy, *Seasonable Revolutionary: The Mind of Charles Chauncey* (Chicago, 1982); and Robert J. Wilson, III, *The Benevolent Diety: Ebenezer Gay and the Rise of Rational Religion in New England, 1696-1787* (Philadelphia, 1984).

19. Billias, *Elbridge, Deity Gerry: Founding Father and Republican Statesman* (New York, 1976). John Cary, *Joseph Warren: Physician, Politician, Patriot* (Urbana, Ill., 1961), tries similarly to elevate Joseph Warren to the first rank of Revolutionary patriots. Cary is unsuccessful in this, but the book is a valuable addition to Massachusetts biography.

20. Charles Royster, "Review of *American Patriots and the Rituals of Revolution*," *WMQ*, 3d Ser., XXXIX (July, 1982), 552.

21. Henretta, "Economic Development and Social Structure in Colonial Boston, *WMQ*, 3d Ser., XXII (Jan., 1965), 93-105.

22. Alice Hanson Jones, "Wealth Estimates for the New England Colonies About 1770," *Journal of Economic History*, XXXII (1972), 98-127; and Douglas L. Jones, "The Strolling Poor: Transiency in Eighteenth-Century Massachusetts," *Journal of Social History*, VII (1975), 28-54.

23. Hoerder, *Crowd Action*, 372. Pauline R. Maier, "Popular Uprisings and Civil Authority in Eighteenth-Century America," *WMQ*, 3d Ser., XXVII (1970), 3-35.

24. Wroth, "Review of *Crowd Action in Revolutionary Massachusetts, 1765-1780, WMQ*, 3d Ser., XXXVII (1980), 323-324.

25. Nash, *Urban Crucible*, 296.

26. Young, "George Robert Twelve Hewes (1742-1840): A Boston Shoemaker and the Memory of the American Revolution," *WMQ*, 3d Ser., XXXVIII (1981), 561-623.

27. Patterson, *Political Parties*, chap. I.

28. Pencak, *War, Politics, and Revolution*, XI, XIII, 228.

29. *Ibid.*, 3, 191, 197, 200.

30. Taylor's work was revisionist when it appeared. See Lee N. Newcomer's study of the West, *The Embattled Farmers: A Massachusetts Countryside in the American Revolution* (New York, 1953), published just one year earlier.

BIBLIOGRAPHICAL NOTE:
AN AGENDA FOR SOCIAL HISTORIANS
OF NEW ENGLAND

Thousands of books, articles, dissertations and theses have been written on colonial and Revolutionary New England. I have used a goodly number of them and anyone who wishes can easily assemble a list of these from the endnotes to each chapter. With so much written it seems pedantic—perhaps even silly—to ask for more. But, in spite of the abundance of historical studies, pockets of scholarly poverty exist amidst the riches. I would like to identify what I consider to be three unfortunate lacunae in the secondary literature.

First, the literature on New England as a region or on parts of New England as subregions is very thin. Most books with New England in the title discuss Massachusetts—often just eastern Massachusetts—or some other geographical fragment. Puritan historians at one time left Boston only for brief forays into the wilds of Suffolk County or to make a quick trip to Providence for a contrasting view. A cadre of young scholars in the 1960s and 1970s discovered Connecticut but proved themselves to be nearly as xenophobic as their chauvinistic Massachusetts predecessors. And, a few brave souls have recently sailed along Narragansett Bay or begun to climb the White Mountains. Social historians who examine localities have further atomized the whole process. We need to examine New England as a region or series of regions and we need to rediscover and recreate it as it was discovered and created by the colonists who celebrates their common identity even in the most divisive of times. No serious social history of New England has been published since William B. Weeden's *Economic and Social History of New England, 1620–1689* (New York, 1890).

Closely related to the need to uncover the common New England experience is the need to relate this to the other colonial regions and to England and Europe. The paucity of interregional or transatlantic colonial studies in social history is appalling. Those few books that do make wider comparisons show how productive such work can be. Multiauthored collections of essays and symposia furnish a partial remedy but they are a poor substitute for individual scholars collecting data that allow them to make comparative analyses between or among regions.

The third gap in the secondary literature is a methodological one. Colonial and Revolutionary historians of New England have become very skilled in their use of statistics. To this degree they have been on the front lines of history as social science. But, in general, New England scholars have not adopted as satisfactorily the theoretical parts of social science methodology. Predictive models that sketch out and test hypotheses are used too little. Hypotheses that are offered are usually tested only in graduate seminar debates instead of historical experiments. Central place theory is now in vogue among some of New England's social historians but other than that the region retains its curiously nonphysical history. Little emphasis is placed on the relationship between the material and nonmaterial worlds and even less is geographical theory used to analyze the relationship. Almost none of New England's recent economic history relies on conceptual models or explicitly applies theories of economic development.

I believe that the problems in the study of New England history stem from the fact that it was the first area of the colonies to be examined by the new social historians. With passion and energy they collected data, processed it, rendered obsolete many of the existing interpretations, and then, feeling that the historical mine had been overworked, left for better prospects. At the time, other regions did not have the work completed that allowed for meaningful comparisons and the use of theory was not sufficiently developed by historians to the extent that it could be readily applied to New England's past. Both the comparative data and sophisticated theory are now in place and await a new generation of historians. Many scholars have labored in New England throughout their careers, but there is no doubt that, for most social historians of the past decade, other regions have proven more attractive. New England now offers exciting new opportunities for historians once again to make the region the center of colonial social history.

INDEX

ABOUT THE AUTHOR

BRUCE C. DANIELS is Professor of History at the University of Winnipeg. His previous books include *Dissent and Conformity on Narragansett Bay: The Colonial Rhode Island Town*, *Connecticut's First Family: William Pitkin and His Connections*, and *The Connecticut Town: Growth and Development, 1635–1790*.